Excel

Get the Results You Want!

# SmartStudy 8

# English

Ally Chumley

PASCAL PRESS

ISBN 978 1 74125 603 1

Pascal Press
PO Box 250
Glebe NSW 2037
(02) 9198 1748
www.pascalpress.com.au

Publisher: Vivienne Joannou
Project editors: Mark Dixon and Rosemary Peers
Edited by Michael Wyatt
Answers checked by Cassandra Freeman
Proofread by Barbara Bessant
Cover and typesetting by Kim Webber
Printed by Vivar Printing/Green Giant Press



**Students**

All care has been taken in compiling this book, but please check with your teacher about the exact requirements of the course as these can change from year to year.

# TABLE OF CONTENTS

# TABLE OF CONTENTS

# STUDY STEPS TO SUCCESS!

## Step 1 Reading Work

- In each chapter, read the main text.
- Read the annotations on the text. These notes identify key features of the text and will be useful as you complete the questions and activities in each section.
- The main texts have been categorised as either informative, narrative or persuasive. However, some texts have features of more than one category and so the categorisation in this book depends upon the specific elements of style they contain. These, in turn, depend on each particular writer's purpose for creating that text. For example, someone writing a biographical text may have been more interested in telling a good story than merely providing factual information about the subject's life. They may have given the text all the hallmarks of a narrative.

## Step 2 Comprehension Work

- Read and answer the questions, using the hints to help you.
- Check each multiple-choice answer to ensure that it is the best response to the question.
- Re-read your longer answers to ensure that they make sense.

## Step 3 Spelling Work

- Read all of the information, rules and hints provided about spelling.
- For most questions, use the List Words provided to complete your answers.
- For open or creative questions, avoid writing basic or obvious responses.

## Step 4 Vocabulary Work

- Read all of the information and hints provided about improving your vocabulary.
- Check that you have the skills and knowledge you need to successfully complete the topic.
- Complete the questions and activities to test your knowledge and skills.

## Step 5 Grammar Work

- Read all of the information, rules and hints provided about grammar.
- Check that you have the skills and knowledge you need to successfully complete the topic.
- Complete the questions and activities to test your knowledge and skills.

## Step 6 Punctuation Work

- Read all of the information, rules and hints provided about punctuation.
- Check that you have the skills and knowledge you need to successfully complete the topic.
- Complete the questions and activities to test your knowledge and skills.

## Step 7 Writing Work

- Read the information about language forms and structures.
- Refer back to the main text to understand these forms and structures in context.
- Answer the questions to test your knowledge and understanding.

## Step 8 Writing Sample

- Study the writing sample carefully, reading all of the explanatory notes.
- Compare this text with the main text studied throughout the chapter so far, to reinforce your learning.

## Step 9 Writing Your Own Sample

- Check that you understand the terms and techniques relevant to this task.
- Using the sample text and the explanatory notes as a guide, compose a similar text inside the scaffold. You may wish to do this on separate paper or electronically, in order to give yourself more room.

## Step 10 Check Your Answers

- Check all of your answers at the back of the book.
- Whether or not you got the answers right, read through the whole answer section. Sample answers are provided along with explanations of why multiple-choice options are right or wrong.
- If you cannot understand a particular answer, revise the chapter notes and text annotations or ask your teacher for help.
- You should always attempt a question, even if you aren't confident in your answer, because in English you may still get some marks for a good attempt. Reading sample answers will help you write better answers next time.

## Step 11 Tips for the Sample Tests

- These useful tips appear on page 122. Read them before you attempt one of the Sample Tests.

## Step 12 Sample Tests

- Two Sample Tests are provided at the end of the book.
- Before attempting the Sample Tests, make sure that you have completed all of the work in the book and have worked through the answers to all questions that you answered incorrectly.
- Set aside the time allowed for the paper and complete it under test conditions—no sneaking a look at your notes!
- Work through the answers (at the end of the book) to any questions that you were unsure about. Write down your total marks for each section in the Your Score boxes at the end of each part of the paper, then add them up to get a total percentage for the test.

# HOW TO USE THIS BOOK TO STUDY FOR A CLASS TEST, HALF-YEARLY OR END-OF-YEAR EXAM

Depending on your teacher or school, you will be given a variety of tests and exams each year. There may be a single-topic test, a test that covers a number of topics, a semester test or exam, or even a half-yearly or yearly exam.

**Step 1**

## **Find out** which topics will be covered in the class test.

- To do this, look at your class workbook/textbook, laptop/tablet or online study program, and ask your teacher.
- For example, your class test may be on grammar.

**Step 2**

## **Match** the topics that your test is on to the topics in this book.

- For example, each unit has questions on grammar.

**Step 3**

## **Use** this book to study the topics being tested.

- Pages 6, 16, 26, 36, 46, 56, 66, 76, 86, 96, 106 and 116 all cover grammar. You can do the questions on these pages to study for your class test on grammar.

**Note:**

- When you are using this book to study for a **half-yearly** test, follow the same steps as above—the only difference being that you will have more topics to revise, of course.
- When you are using this book to study for an **end-of-year** test, you will more than likely need to study the whole book.

# READING
## *Types of Questions*

### Literal questions—the answer is right in front of you

This is the simplest type of reading task question that asks you to find a 'literal' answer.

**To answer these questions** you just have to locate specific facts and details to find the meaning.

For some literal questions you might have to:

* find facts, details and other forms of information from the text
* consider certain features of the text, including spelling, punctuation or common language techniques
* recount (or retell) details, sometimes in your own words
* consider the order in which facts are presented in a text
* recognise synonyms that are used for particular details and search for slightly different words from those in the question
* use your vocabulary
* use your comprehension
* identify who, what, where, when and how.

### Interpretive questions—the answer requires a synthesis of textual details

This type of question asks you to interpret the meaning of words, phrases and sentences.

**To answer these questions** you will have to combine facts and details to synthesise the meaning.

For some interpretive questions you might have to:

* synthesise meaning by putting various facts together to reach a conclusion—we synthesise meaning from texts all the time without even realising it
* consider multiple aspects of the text at once
* use logic to find additional meaning beyond the words
* interpret the meaning of facts and details as the meaning of some parts of the text may not be obvious from just a straightforward reading
* do simple calculations to find an answer
* look at language-related matters, such as meanings conveyed by certain words, phrases or symbols
* think about the connotations of words—meanings that extend beyond the words on the page
* describe, recount, explain, compare, summarise or give reasons
* make small but important distinctions between ideas. The words *bad*, *evil*, *naughty* and *diabolical* all mean a similar thing—but they have quite distinct shades of meaning. We might call a disobedient puppy naughty but not evil. Likewise, we wouldn't call a murderer naughty.

## Applied questions—the answer is conceptual and is not present in the text

These questions require you to understand a text's implications—the logical extension of facts and connotations. A composer can imply meaning, rather than simply state it. This allows us to extract meanings that go beyond the literal denotation (straightforward meaning) of the words a writer uses.

**To answer these questions** you have to apply multiple skills to infer the meaning.
Students sometimes confuse the terms 'imply' and 'infer'. Put simply, the composer implies meaning in a text and the responder infers meaning from the text.

For some applied questions you might have to:

- explain, prove, judge, evaluate, predict, solve, discuss or critique aspects of the text
- make an informed judgement or evaluation based on evidence from the text
- apply 'assumed knowledge'—information or understanding that the writer assumes you possess already
- interpret facts using additional knowledge from outside the text, such as allusions
- consider facts or details in specific combinations to arrive at a logical conclusion
- consider what you already know about textual features and their effects on meaning
- consider the usual rules of genre, form or type of text
- 'read between the lines' to infer meaning from the text
- 'read beyond the lines' to understand implications
- engage your senses
- apply thinking skills to develop insights and personal opinions
- consider what information may be missing from the text.

UNIT 1

# INFORMATIVE TEXT

## News article

**READING WORK**

## Animals in the news

*There's certainly no shortage of weirdos and wackos who make the news headlines. And then there are the animals.*

### Poodle used as a weapon

Police officer Bob Richards was attacked with an unusual weapon while on duty in 2004. He was pursuing a dangerous driver who suddenly pulled over, pretending that he wanted to give himself up. But when the officer approached the car to make the arrest, the driver thrust a tiny black poodle into his face. 'I've seen people ram cars. I've seen people fight. I've had a guy pull a pistol on me,' the shocked officer said. 'But to take a poodle on a leash and make it a weapon—that's a new extreme in bizarre behaviour.' The poodle-wielding driver was charged with a number of offences, including assault with a dangerous weapon. The dog was unharmed (and unarmed), and has since been adopted by a nice, law-abiding family.

### Paws for applause

Twinkle Toes, a short-haired ginger cat, has an unusual place in the *Guinness Book of Records*. Three year-old Twinkle has twenty-five toes, compared to the usual eighteen. Her mother has twenty-one toes, which is also more than usual. The scientific adjective for this condition is 'polydactyl' (multi-toed), which is not to be confused with 'pterodactyl'—that's a whole other problem!

*Cats and dogs often enjoy the media spotlight. But there are other species of publicity-hungry critters out there ...*

### Mary had a little lawsuit

An Australian preschool teacher was sued for bringing a pet lamb to work to show her young students. A snooping passer-by reported the lamb to the authorities, claiming that the teacher had violated a law against housing animals other than traditional pets. The teacher had often brought baby farm animals to the preschool and kept them in a fully fenced yard so the children could pet them. But the prosecutor in the case told the media, 'This lady is out of control. She might next decide to bring in a fifteen-foot killer python, poisonous bugs or killer bees.' Sadly, everyone loses: despite beating the charge, the case cost the teacher more than $6200 in legal fees and the lamb will not be returning to school.

### Snake killer could serve time

A brave man in the USA is in trouble with the law after doing a 'good deed'. He killed a venomous snake to protect a group of children. Instead of a bravery award, the unfortunate hero was presented with handcuffs and charged with 'killing a protected reptile without a permit'. He faces a possible jail sentence and a certain fine.

- This is a **contraction** that makes the language informal and suits the colloquial tone of the text.
- **Alliteration** and **slang** are combined here to create a startling effect.
- The **specific date** of the incident is provided to add authenticity.
- This is a play on words created using **rhyme**. It makes the text more entertaining for the reader.
- This is a **complex sentence** with a dependent clause ('a short-haired ginger cat'). It is used to make the expression more economical.
- The **technical term** is used to emphasise the authority of the writer as a commentator, while still retaining the humorous tone.
- This is a **metaphor** commonly used in conversational language.
- This **hyphenated adjective** allows the writer to express the idea economically.
- This is an American **idiom** for 'creatures' (a corruption based on accent).
- This is an **allusion** to the well-known nursery rhyme 'Mary had a little lamb', which adds interest and unexpected humour (irony) to the title.
- The **formal language** here matches the jargon-filled tone in which the legal details are explained.
- This is an example of **hyperbole**—deliberate exaggeration designed to emphasise the prosecutor's point.
- The use of a **colon** (:) signals that an explanation will follow.
- This amusing **inversion** sounds like a reference to a human child.
- This is an **idiom** for 'go to prison'. It could also be described as a **euphemism**, a polite, softer term for an unpleasant reality.
- **Contrast** is used to create irony to both shock and amuse the reader.
- This is an example of a sentence that includes an **integrated quote**. It has the effect of making the language flow smoothly, rather than being interrupted by a standalone quotation.

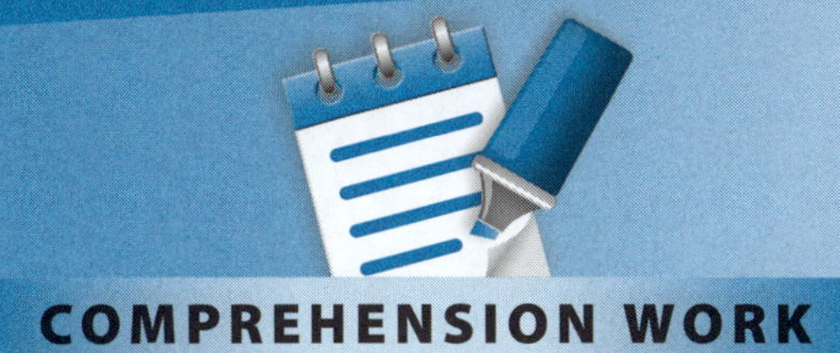

# INFORMATIVE TEXT

## News article

COMPREHENSION WORK

### Literal questions

*Hint: Read the text carefully to locate specific facts and details.*

**1** With which specific offence was the poodle owner charged?

**2** What type of law had the teacher violated by bringing a lamb to school?

**3** What is the minimum penalty the snake-killing man faces for his actions?

### Interpretive questions

*Hint: These questions require you to combine facts and details to synthesise the meaning.*

**4** 'A brave man in the USA is in trouble with the law after doing a "good deed".' What is the purpose of this line from the snake killer story?

**5** How do we know that the driver planned to use the poodle as a weapon?

**6** How would the *Guinness Book of Records* have found out about Twinkle Toes?

*Hint: Only one answer option is correct. Use the process of elimination to work through the options.*

**7** In the lamb story, how realistic are the prosecutor's fears that 'She might next decide to bring in a fifteen-foot killer python, poisonous bugs or killer bees'?

**a** very realistic **b** somewhat realistic **c** somewhat unrealistic **d** completely unrealistic

**8** It appears that the poodle's owner was forced to hand over the dog to authorities. We know this because

**a** the driver went to prison. **b** the dog has been adopted by another family.

**c** the policeman led the dog away on a leash.

**9** What does the inclusion of the detail about the 'fully fenced yard' tell us about the preschool teacher?

**a** She was acting responsibly. **b** She was acting irresponsibly. **c** She was a farmer.

**10** Which of these news items does not feature the animal as the main focus of the story?

**a** Snake killer could serve time **b** Paws for applause **c** Poodle used as a weapon

### Applied questions

*Hint: This question requires you to understand a text's implications to infer meaning from the text.*

**11** How many more toes than her mother does Twinkle Toes have?

**a** twenty-one **b** eighteen **c** four

**12** Of the three stories, which human mentioned has committed the worst crime?

**a** the snake killer **b** the preschool teacher **c** the dog owner

# INFORMATIVE TEXT

*News article*

## SPELLING WORK

### List Words

All of the words in the box below appear in the text 'Animals in the news'.

| | | | | |
|---|---|---|---|---|
| shortage | pursuing | apparently | bizarre | wielding |
| assault | eighteen | pterodactyl | lawsuit | violated |
| venomous | loses | legal | trouble | unfortunate |

### Tongue Twisters

The spelling of some words can be different to how they sound. Look at the use of *a* in the list words below.

**1** Rewrite these list words with their endings spelt correctly.

| Pronunciation | Correct spelling |
|---|---|
| short-IDGE | ______ |
| le-GOOL | ______ |
| unfortun-ERT | ______ |

**2** One **incorrectly spelt** word from the list appears in each of these sentences. Find the word and write it correctly on the line provided.

**a** The average cat has eightheen toes. ______

**b** Don't touch that snake: it's venomess! ______

**c** Playing with animals is fine until someone looses a finger. ______

**d** Keeping a poodle is legall, but using it as a weapon is not. ______

**3** Unscramble the letters to form words from the list.

**a** ubletro ______ **b** ageortsh ______

**c** errabiz ______ **d** ultassa ______

**4** Use slashes ( / ) to separate the list words in these letter chains. Spare letters have been added to both ends of each chain to trick you; cross these out. There are three list words hidden inside each chain.

**a** LILEGALEIGHTEENLOSESET **b** RASHORTAGETROUBLEBIZARRERE

**c** PTPTERODACTYLASSAULTVIOLATEDRS

**d** QUAPPARENTLYWIELDINGVENOMOUSKS

**5** Fill in the missing vowels to complete words from the list.

**a** p _ rs _ _ ng **b** l _ ws _ _ t **c** w _ _ ld _ ng **d** _ nf _ rt _ n _ t _

**6** Below, group together pairs of word fragments to form four list words that relate to the law.

| | | | |
|---|---|---|---|
| danger | law | ous | prose |
| suit | author | cutor | ities |

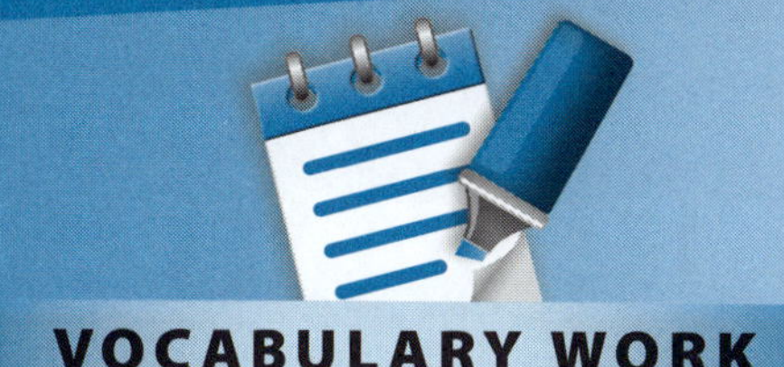

# INFORMATIVE TEXT

## News article

**VOCABULARY WORK**

**1** Complete these sentences by using a list word from the previous page. The meaning of each word is provided in parentheses.

**a** The dangerous driver was ______________________ an unusual weapon. (waving around)

**b** The police officer was ______________________ the dangerous driver in his car. (chasing)

**c** Using a poodle instead of a gun is ______________________. (very strange)

**d** The ______________________ on the police officer involved a poodle in the face. (attack)

**e** The man who killed a snake ______________ a law designed to protect endangered species. (broke)

**f** Twinkle Toes and her mother have ______________ been gifted with lots of extra toes. (seemingly)

**2** Are these word meanings correct? Write *true* or *false* next to each meaning given below.
*Hint: Look back at how the words are used in the article for clues.*

| Word | Meaning | True or False? | Word | Meaning | True or False? |
|---|---|---|---|---|---|
| **a** shortage | a lack of something | __________ | **b** legal | dangerous | __________ |
| **c** venomous | sparkly | __________ | **d** lawsuit | a court case | __________ |

**3** Use the words below to complete the definitions of the list words.
*Hint: Look back at how the words are used in the article for clues.*

minus appearances dangerous broke

| Word | Meaning |
|---|---|
| **a** apparently | based on ______________________ |
| **b** trouble | a difficult or ______________________ situation |
| **c** eighteen | twenty-five ______________________ seven |
| **d** violated | ______________________ a rule or law |

### Idioms

An idiom is an expression used by speakers from a particular place, group or time period. Here are some idioms and their meanings from the news article.

| Idiom | Meaning |
|---|---|
| wacko | strange, scary or unpredictable person |
| media spotlight | attention or fame in the media |
| pull a pistol | point a gun |
| serve time | go to prison |

**4** Use these idioms from the article to complete new sentences.
*Hint: The idioms are defined above.*

wacko media spotlight pull a pistol serve time

**a** I would never want someone to ______________________ on me.

**b** The car thief has been found guilty and will now ______________________.

**c** The celebrity enjoyed the ______________________.

**d** My neighbour becomes a ______________________ every New Year's Eve.

# INFORMATIVE TEXT

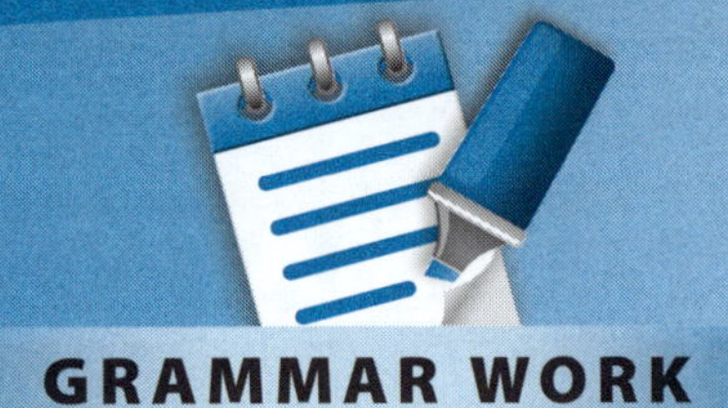

GRAMMAR WORK

## Nouns

**Nouns** are words that name people, places, events, things, ideas and emotions. Two categories of nouns are common and proper.

### Common nouns

- Name everyday things.
- Do not begin with capital letters, unless positioned at the start of a sentence.
- Include words like *truck*, *pineapple* and *mountain*.

### Proper nouns

- Refer to specific names.
- Name particular people, places, events or things.
- Begin with capital letters.
- Include words like *Finland*, *Valentine's Day* and *Superman*.

In multi-word proper nouns, each noun usually begins with a capital letter. Look at these examples: *New South Wales*, *the Russian Revolution*, *the Great Wall of China*.

Answer these questions about nouns.

**1** Are these nouns common nouns or proper nouns?

cat python lamb poodle

**2** Which three words in the sentence are common nouns?

The teacher had brought various animals to the preschool.

**3** Which word is a proper noun?

Assaulting someone with a poodle sounds more like something from a Hollywood movie than real life.

**4** Sort these nouns into common or proper by writing them in the correct columns.

| | | | |
|---|---|---|---|
| USA | pistol | Bob Richards | toes |
| animals | Australia | handcuffs | Thursday |

| Common nouns | Proper nouns |
|---|---|
| | |
| | |
| | |
| | |

**5** Capitalise the proper nouns in this sentence. *Hint: Only actual names require initial capital letters.*

The driver of a jeep grand cherokee was pulled over by a police officer in brisbane.

**6** Underline all of the common nouns in this sentence.

Many people choose to keep unusual pets in their houses.

**7** Underline the two proper nouns found in this sentence.

A cat named Twinkle Toes has been featured in the *Guinness Book of Records*.

**8** Underline the plural nouns in this passage.

There's certainly no shortage of weirdos and wackos who make the news headlines. And then there are the animals.

# INFORMATIVE TEXT

## News article

**PUNCTUATION WORK**

### Apostrophes

An **apostrophe** can be used to show ownership of something. The apostrophe always comes after the owner or owners. Look at this example: *The police officer's car was his best protection.* This tells us that one police officer owns the car. If more than one police officer owns the car, the apostrophe comes after *officers*; another *s* is not needed. It would be written like this: *The police officers' car was their best protection.*

So the two ownership rules are: one owner + apostrophe + *s* two or more owners + apostrophe

**1** In each sentence below, each apostrophe shows ownership. Write the owner or owners on the lines.

- **a** The snake's venom was a threat to the children. ____________________
- **b** The children's playtime was interrupted by the snake. ____________________
- **c** The teacher's lamb came to school. ____________________
- **d** The animals' yard was fenced. ____________________
- **e** The cat's mother has twenty-one toes. ____________________

**2** Add an apostrophe to the highlighted word to show ownership in each sentence below.

- **a** The **drivers** poodle was thrust at the officer.
- **b** During the **preschoolers** lunchtime, they would be allowed to pet farm animals.
- **c** **Twinkle Toess** feet have landed her a world record.
- **d** The **mans** good deed got him arrested.

Now see if you can do these ones without the highlighting.

- **e** The *Guinness Book of Records* lists the number of a famous cats toes.
- **f** The drivers use of a dog to threaten a police officer was a serious offence.

**3** There are two punctuation mistakes in each of these sentences. Circle the mistakes.
*Hint: Apostrophes are not used to make plurals (more than one of something).*

- **a** There's no shortage of weirdo's and wacko's who make the news headlines.
- **b** The Dog was (unharmed.
- **c** A snooping pass-erby reported, the lamb to the authorities.
- **d** the case cost the teacher more than $620,0 in legal fees.
- **e** 'Ive seen people ram cars.' I've had a guy pull a pistol on me,' the officer said.

**4** Each sentence below is missing two punctuation marks. Proofread the sentences and add the missing punctuation marks.

- **a** He was pursuing a dangerous driver, who suddenly pulled over pretending that he wanted to give himself up
- **b** The poodle-wielding driver was charged with 'assault with a dangerous weapon
- **c** Her mother has twenty one toes which is also more than usual.
- **d** The prosecutor in the case told the media This lady is out of control.'
- **e** instead of a bravery award the unfortunate hero was presented with handcuffs.

# INFORMATIVE TEXT

## News article

WRITING WORK 1

### News articles

**News articles** are informative texts that provide factual details about a topic. They exist in a wide variety of forms and are published in newspapers, magazines and digital media products. Graphic features like illustrations, photographs or diagrams help make news articles more effective.

**1** Describe two illustrations that would be suitable to use with the text 'Animals in the news'.

___

___

### Roundup news articles

The news article featured in this unit is composed of a number of short news pieces put together into a collection. This form of **news article** is known in print media publishing as a '**roundup**'. It is designed to provide an entertaining summary of news pieces connected by a particular theme; in this case, animals that have been involved in a newsworthy event.

**2** How is a roundup different from a regular news article? ___

___

**3** Think of two topics that would be suitable for the roundup form in a local newspaper.

___

**4** Why might people prefer to read a roundup than a series of full-length news articles?

___

**5** Which of the following statements best describes the writer's purpose for the text 'Animals in the news'? Tick one.

- ☐ The writer intends to inform readers about interesting news snippets in a lighthearted manner.
- ☐ The writer intends to inform readers about some dangerous practices of pet owners.
- ☐ The writer intends to inform readers of important news and to persuade them to adopt a particular opinion about the topic.

### Structural features of a roundup news article

To write a **roundup** successfully, a writer must:

- collect or create a number of related newsworthy stories
- create an overall heading that ties the stories together
- write a brief introductory statement that suitably presents the topic or theme
- use punchy subheadings that capture the reader's attention
- write sentences that capture the essential newsworthy element of each story
- present each story using engaging and economical language
- include facts supported by specific details, data, statistics, names or quotations
- employ language techniques to get the biggest impact from the fewest words
- use connective words and phrases to create a unified piece.

**6** To ensure a finished piece of high quality, each item presented in a roundup news article must earn its place. What do you think this sentence means?

___

# INFORMATIVE TEXT

## News article

**WRITING WORK 2**

**7** Complete this table by writing the missing content into the empty cells.
*Hint: Use the annotations on the original text to help you.*

| | Language feature | Example from the text | Effect in the text |
|---|---|---|---|
| **Elements of informal language** | colloquialisms | **a** | **Colloquialisms** help the writer achieve a lighthearted tone, which makes the article feel accessible to ordinary people. |
| | **b** | publicity-hungry critters | The word 'critters' is a popular American **idiom** for animals that are pests. Its use here creates an amusing image of familiar animals doing odd things so they can get into the news and receive attention. |
| | contractions | **c** | **Contractions** create an informal tone, making it seem more conversational and enjoyable to read. |
| **Elements of humour** | irony | **d** | **Irony** turns our expectations upside down. This unexpected outcome gives the article a stronger impact on the reader. The contrast between the actual outcome and the expected cause and effect sequence surprises the reader. |
| | rhyme | The dog was unharmed (and unarmed). | **e** |
| **Other language features** | metaphor | the media spotlight | **f** |
| | **g** | But to take a poodle on a leash and make it a weapon—that's a new extreme in bizarre behaviour. | **Direct speech** adds drama to the story when we hear the officer's shocked reaction in his own words. His words echo our thoughts as we react to the article. |
| | allusion | **h** | Because it is fitting for the preschool context, this subheading alludes to the children's nursery rhyme, 'Mary had a little lamb', drawing a parallel between the rhyme and this story about a lamb being denied entry to a school. The **humorous effect** is compounded by the substitution of the word 'lawsuit'. The alliterative phrase 'little lawsuit' is ironic, as lawsuits are known to be expensive. |
| | hyperbole | **i** | The **deliberate exaggeration** in the prosecutor's statement makes him look foolish, supporting the writer's message that this particular lawsuit is ridiculous. |
| | **j** | **k** | **Alliteration** is used in writing to add emphasis to key phrases by creating sound effects. |

# INFORMATIVE TEXT

News article

WRITING SAMPLE

Here is a sample text showing you how to structure and write a roundup news article.

## Pets behaving badly

✱ **Use a heading that captures attention.** The alliterative phrase 'behaving badly' is often used in titles of entertaining or funny roundup texts and video compilations featuring animals or people.

They may be guilty or they may just be misunderstood but all of them are busted! Here are some pets that make your dog look like an angel!

✱ **Write a brief introduction to the roundup topic.** Here, the second person storytelling mode is used to draw in the reader.

### Polly and the police

✱ **Use a subheading to introduce the first story.** This one contains alliteration and a slang term.

They say that just about anything can happen in South America but this story is still a 'what the?!'. A parrot in Argentina was accused of withholding information and interrogated by police for five days.

✱ **Begin with one or two sentences that reveal the most newsworthy aspect of the first story.** Here, slang and a combination of punctuation marks called an interrobang (?!) add to the drama.

Neighbours Jorge and Roberto both claimed to own Pepo the parrot. A judge sent the bird to prison and held it in custody until it admitted who its real owner was. Five days later, Pepo squawked 'Jorge!' and then sang the anthem of the San Lorenzo soccer club. An ecstatic Jorge said, 'I knew he wouldn't let me down! He's a true friend … and we support the same football team!'

✱ **Present the details of the first story in order.** Begin with a key point (in a topic sentence) and add specific details, facts, data, statistics, names and/or quotations. This story starts with a sentence about a fairly ordinary situation, then a surprising complication follows. Lots of specifics are given.

### KFC: Kill the Freaky Chook

✱ **Use a subheading to introduce the second story.** Establish a pattern so that your subheadings complement each other in their style. A well-known initialism relating to chickens (KFC) is used here, then given a surprising translation.

Pepo's story had a happy ending, but not all feathered felons escape the law as easily. At least there's the rule of innocent until proven guilty … or until it lays an egg.

✱ **Summarise the most newsworthy aspect of the second story.** This one uses a transitional sentence to link the first story to the second. Use connective phrases as links.

In the 1400s in Basel, Switzerland, a chicken laid an egg. WOW, right? Unfortunately, someone thought she was a rooster. The poor fowl was arrested, then sentenced to be burned at the stake for her 'heinous and unnatural crime'. Witches were thought to use 'rooster eggs' (no, they don't exist) in their spells, and this hen looked suspiciously rooster-like. It's not too tragic: she was probably destined for the barbecue anyway!

✱ **Present the details of the second story.** Use a variety of language features. Here, historical details, sarcasm, a direct quote, parentheses, varied punctuation and a lighthearted ending all help to make the story interesting.

### Cat the Ripper

✱ **Use a subheading to introduce the third story and follow the pattern established.** This one uses a pun on 'Jack the Ripper', which is an allusion to a famous killer who was never caught.

Did you know you might be living with a homicidal maniac? Just because she's soft and furry doesn't mean she isn't making plans involving your liver … or your appendix, in this case.

✱ **Present the most newsworthy aspect of the third story or show how it links to or varies from the other two.** This one contains a rhetorical question.

Kitka, a Himalayan cat and surgeon-in-the-making, picked open her owner Brad's appendectomy stitches in the middle of the night with her scalpel-sharp claws. Brad did not wake during the 'procedure' due to the heavy painkillers still in his system after his real surgery. Imagine Kitka's surprise when she opened him up only to find his appendix missing!

✱ **Provide the details of the third story.** It is a good strategy to present the odd one out or the strangest, most surprising story last. This one sustains the idea that a cat wants to be a surgeon. This technique is called anthropomorphism.

When choosing your next pet, don't settle for boring! Jailbird parrots, witchy chicks and killer kitties are a small sampling of the marvellous menagerie of pets on offer. Just keep some emergency funds ready for legal fees.

✱ **Provide a punchy ending to conclude.** This one uses three different devices: pun, assonance and alliteration. It also addresses the reader directly like the introduction, which it is designed to match.

# INFORMATIVE TEXT

## News article

## WRITING YOUR OWN SAMPLE

Plan your sample on the lines provided.

- **Use a heading that captures attention.** Use a literary technique (e.g. alliteration) to add interest.
- **Write a brief introduction to the roundup topic.** Tie the elements together. Use the second person storytelling mode to draw in the reader, with pronouns like *you* or *we*.
- **Use a subheading to introduce the first story.** Include a technique such as alliteration or slang.
- **Begin with one or two sentences that reveal the most newsworthy aspect of the first story.** Use an engaging technique like a rhetorical question, slang or specialised punctuation mark such as the interrobang.
- **Present the details of the first story in order.** For each paragraph, begin with a key point (in a topic sentence) and add specific details, facts, data, statistics, names or quotations. Remember: you must present information that is interesting to your readers. Keep the details in logical order so that the reader can easily follow the story.
- **Use a subheading to introduce the second story.** Establish a pattern so that your subheadings complement each other in their style. The model story achieves this by using an initialism. Why not try an acronym or a rhyming phrase?
- **Summarise the most newsworthy aspect of the second story.** This will help maximise reader interest in every statement. Use connective phrases as links.
- **Present the details of the second story.** Follow the same structure as in the first story so that a sense of order is created. This element of the article should be related to the first story by topic or theme. Use a variety of language features including short sentences and some varied punctuation such as parentheses.
- **Use a subheading to introduce the third story and follow the pattern established.**
- **Present the most newsworthy aspect of the third story, or show how it links to or varies from the other two.** Use interesting language that will compel your reader to stay engaged. For example, you could pose a rhetorical question to achieve this.
- **Provide the details of the third story.** Remember to save up any potential drama or humour for the end. For example, you could make this story the odd one out—the most surprising, ironic or strange of all the stories.
- **Provide a punchy ending to conclude.** This will ensure the reader reaches the end satisfied that the key details have been provided. They should feel that a fitting ending or concluding message has been presented.

# Indigenous Sydney

For thousands of years, Indigenous Australians have enjoyed a special connection to Country. This unique map of Sydney Harbour shows some sites that demonstrate the city's rich Indigenous heritage. Next time you visit Sydney, if you take the time to visit the places marked on the map, you'll be walking in the footprints of people who thrived here long before us.

## Indigenous heritage sites around Sydney Harbour

Sandstone rock overhangs, like the one at Balmoral Beach, were used as shelters by Indigenous people of the past. At living sites like this one, you'll see charcoal pits and smoke stains on the ceilings of caves from ancient cooking fires where families ate their meals. Fossilised bones from fish, wallabies, kangaroos and wombats reveal the diversity of diets of the people from each area. The depth and size of the compacted middens (mounds of discarded shells and food waste) show that some caves were in continual use for centuries.

**KEY**

1 **Arabanoo's Lookout,** Manly Cove
2 **Midden,** Reef Beach
3 **Lookout,** Dobroyd Head
4 **Engravings,** Grotto Point
5 **Cave shelter,** Balmoral Beach
6 **Living site,** Bennelong Point
7 **Barangaroo's land,** Barangaroo
8 **Bennelong's land,** Goat Island
9 **Whale engraving,** Balls Head
10 **Gadyan track**, Berry Island

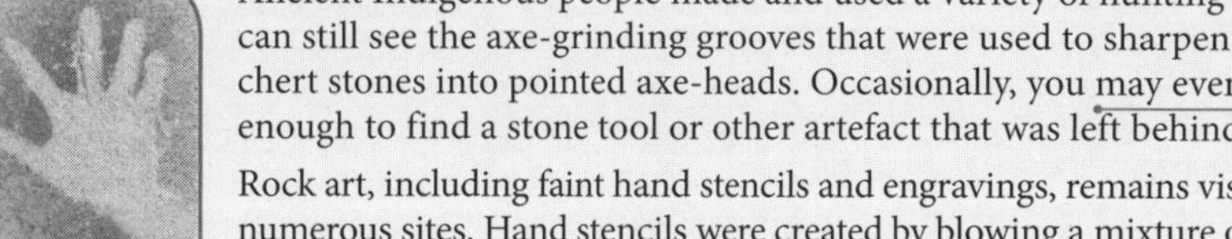

Ancient Indigenous people made and used a variety of hunting tools. You can still see the axe-grinding grooves that were used to sharpen silcrete and chert stones into pointed axe-heads. Occasionally, you may even be lucky enough to find a stone tool or other artefact that was left behind.

Rock art, including faint hand stencils and engravings, remains visible at numerous sites. Hand stencils were created by blowing a mixture of ochre and water over the hand to create an outline.

*Hand stencil rock art*

Engravings were made on smooth rock surfaces by drilling holes around the outline with a sharp tool, then joining them by etching lines into the sandstone. Sometimes white ochre was added to highlight the grooves. One of the best known is the whale engraving at Balls Head. It is best viewed at dawn or dusk when the sunlight is parallel to the rock surface.

Some sites are valuable because of their associations with specific individuals—including Arabanoo, Bennelong and Barangaroo—rather than their artefacts.

### Arabanoo

Arabanoo was a Cadigal man captured by the governor at Manly Cove. The abduction was a failed effort at facilitating communications with the local Indigenous people, and tragically resulted in Arabanoo's death from disease. The Arabanoo Lookout at Dobroyd's Head is named in his memory.

### Bennelong

Bennelong was a Wangal man after whom the Sydney Opera House site is named. He was the traditional owner of Goat Island, then known as 'Mamila'. He was captured in another forced abduction and was used by authorities to act as a mediator between the European and Indigenous people.

### Barangaroo

Barangaroo was a woman from the Cammeraygal clan and the second wife of Bennelong. The precinct on the southern shore of the Sydney Harbour Bridge is named after Barangaroo, whose people were the traditional owners of that area of Sydney Harbour.

---

- This is an attention-grabbing **heading** that juxtaposes Australia's Indigenous heritage with a modern city named after a European one.
- The word 'Country' is punctuated with a **capital letter** to reflect the way in which Indigenous Australians refer to their land and waters.
- These **adjectives** create a richer description.
- Here we see the topic being identified and a brief **introduction** given.
- These **personal pronouns** involve the reader more directly.
- Here we have a **definition** of an unfamiliar term.
- **Jargon** specific to geology is used to add interest.
- This positive **emotive language** provides a sense of personal involvement.
- A **caption** is added to explain the content of the image.
- One of the sites is described more specifically with **detailed factual information** provided.
- The feature text provides **more detailed information** about people rather than artefacts found at places. Traditional personal and group names are given to emphasise the **specific identification** of individuals from the past with places and with each other.

# INFORMATIVE TEXT

*Brochure*

**COMPREHENSION WORK**

## Literal questions

*Hint: Read the text carefully to locate specific facts and details.*

**1** What place in Sydney Harbour was once called 'Mamila'? ____________________

**2** What type of artwork depicts a whale at the Balls Head site? ____________________

**3** How do we know that the cave shelter at Balmoral Beach was used by families to eat their meals?

____________________

## Interpretive questions

*Hint: These questions require you to combine facts and details to synthesise the meaning.*

**4** '… you'll be walking in the footprints of people who thrived here long before us.'
Of which literary technique is this line an example?

**a** a metaphor **b** emotive language **c** a rhetorical question

**5** With whom does the writer of this text appear to lay the blame for Arabanoo's death?

____________________

**6** What do historical sources tell us about the diet of the people who lived around Sydney Harbour?

____________________

**7** Why are the hand stencils described as 'faint'?

____________________

*Hint: These questions require you to understand a text's implications to infer meaning from the text.*

**8** What artefacts might have been visible at Bennelong Point before the Sydney Opera House was built?

**a** a whale engraving **b** middens, fossilised bones and fire residue **c** a carving of Arabanoo's name

**9** What does the identification of the Cadigal, Wangal and Cammeraygal people groups by name add to our understanding of the text?

**a** It shows that people moved around a lot in the past.

**b** It shows that the three famous Indigenous Australians named in the text were all related.

**c** It reminds us that Indigenous Australians represent distinct people groups, not just a single culture.

**10** What is the main focus of the text?

**a** the beauty of rock art **b** the rich heritage of the Sydney Harbour area **c** the biography of Bennelong

## Applied questions

*Hint: This question requires you to understand a text's implications to infer meaning from the text.*

**11** Why are there no English place names marked on the map in this text?

**a** To show the region as Indigenous Australians knew it, before European contact.

**b** To emphasise the fact that Sydney Harbour is a very big place.

**c** To make it easier to follow driving directions to the sites.

*Hint: This question requires you to make an informed judgement based on the evidence.*

**12** Why are the Sydney Harbour Bridge and the Sydney Harbour Tunnel represented as a snake on the map?

**a** because they look exactly like a snake

**b** because the snake is a species unique to the Sydney Harbour region

**c** because it is a symbol associated with Indigenous Australian cultures

# INFORMATIVE TEXT

*Brochure*

## SPELLING WORK

### List Words

*All of the words in the box below appear in the text 'Indigenous Sydney'.*

| | | | | |
|---|---|---|---|---|
| harbour | occasionally | ochre | specific | southern |
| continuous | mediator | centuries | numerous | governor |
| valuable | fossilised | abduction | traditional | precinct |

The pronunciation of the letter *c* in some words can be soft instead of hard.

**1** Look at these list words and circle whether each *c* should be sounded as a hard 'k' sound or a soft 'ss' sound.

**a** continuous hard / soft  **b** ochre hard / soft

**c** centuries hard / soft  **d** abduction hard / soft

*Hint: Sometimes, in words with two cs, one is sounded hard and the other soft.*

**2** Which two of these words have both the soft and hard 'c' sound? Circle them.

specific  occasionally  precinct

**3** Which words in the sentences below are spelt incorrectly?

**a** Barangaroo was the traditional owner of land on the southen side of the Sydney Harbour Bridge.

**b** Some cave sites were in continous use by Indigenous Australians for many centuries.

**c** Bennelong's abduction was carried out on the orders of the goverer of New South Wales.

**d** Hand stencils were made using a mixture of ocher and water in specific quantities.

**e** Valuable historical discoveries have been made around Sydney Harbour, including fosillised bones.

**4** Which two list words end with the suffix *ous*?

____________________ ____________________

**5** Write a word beginning and ending for each of the following to form list words.

**a** ________ tinu ________  **b** ________ sil ________

**c** ________ tur ________  **d** ________ mer ________

**e** ________ cif ________  **f** ________ dit ________

**6** How many syllables are in each of these words?
*Hint: Syllables relate to units of sound that combinations of letters make. They usually contain a vowel. Treat the suffix* sion *or* tion *as a single syllable (pronounced 'shun').*

**a** harbour  **b** continuous  **c** occasionally  **d** traditional

**e** fossilised  **f** southern  **g** abduction  **h** ochre

**7** Here are two list words that contain the vowel blend *ou*. Next to each one, write a word that rhymes with the way the sound 'ou' is pronounced in that list word.

**a** harbour ____________________  **b** southern ____________________

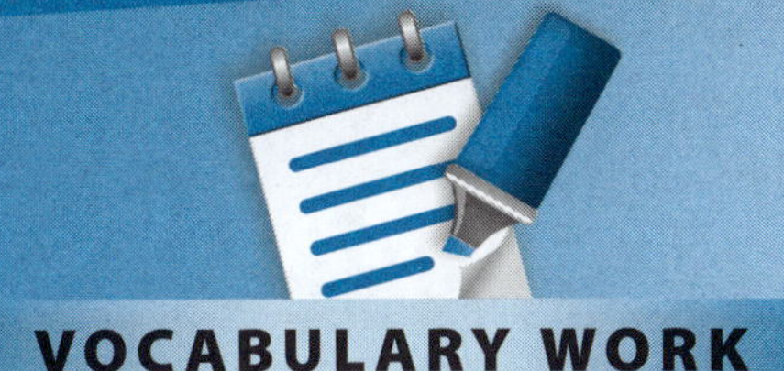

# INFORMATIVE TEXT
## *Brochure*

**VOCABULARY WORK**

Brochures contain many facts and details that must be presented in a concise, easy-to-read manner. Space is limited so it's important that we choose the best, most economical words to express the content.

**1** In each of these sentences, one word is missing. Compare each sentence to the original versions from the text then supply the missing word. Write definitions in your own words to complete the table.

**a** For thousands of years ____________________ Australians have enjoyed a connection to Country.

**b** Ancient Indigenous people made and used a ________________ of hunting tools.

**c** Engravings were made on smooth rock surfaces by drilling holes around the outline with a tool, then joining them by ________________ lines into the sandstone.

**d** Hand ________________ were created by blowing a mixture of ochre and water over the hand to create an outline.

| | Missing word | Definition |
|---|---|---|
| **a** | | |
| **b** | | |
| **c** | | |
| **d** | | |

**2** Separate these nonsense words into pairs of list words.

**a** southcenternuries ________________________ and ________________________

**b** valuspecifableic ________________________ and ________________________

**c** prefossilcinctised ________________________ and ________________________

**d** numoccasionerallyous ________________________ and ________________________

**e** abmedduciatortion ________________________ and ________________________

**3** Answer these questions by changing the form of the list word to fit into the definition.

**a** A counsellor is a person who m________________________ between people in a dispute.

**b** The singular of the word we use to describe a hundred years is c________________________________.

**c** A group of people who are in authority over a region or nation is called the g________________________.

**4** Indigenous Australians use all kinds of idioms, many of which are shared by all Australians. Some common idioms that are specific to Indigenous Australians appear below. Write the letters in the correct spaces to define them.

**a** aunty and uncle ____ refers to something that is pretend or false

**b** sorry business ____ means 'really awesome', 'wicked' or 'mad'

**c** deadly ____ means 'Ain't it?' or 'Isn't it?'

**d** gammon ____ terms of respect for people who may not be relatives

**e** unna ____ refers to mourning and funerals for the dead

# INFORMATIVE TEXT
## Brochure

### GRAMMAR WORK

**1** The names of places are proper nouns. They always begin with a capital letter. Many Australian places have names drawn from the languages of Indigenous Australians.

Look at this list of words from the text and decide whether each one is a common noun or proper noun. Circle *common noun* or *proper noun*. *Note: Capital letters have been omitted.*

| | | |
|---|---|---|
| **a** arabanoo | Common noun | Proper noun |
| **b** authorities | Common noun | Proper noun |
| **c** wife | Common noun | Proper noun |
| **d** cammeraygal | Common noun | Proper noun |
| **e** sydney opera house | Common noun | Proper noun |
| **f** bennelong | Common noun | Proper noun |
| **g** european | Common noun | Proper noun |

**2** From each of these trios of nouns, circle the one that is specific to Indigenous Australian languages. *Note: Capital letters have been omitted on purpose so you'll have to look at each word in its textual context.*

| | | | | | |
|---|---|---|---|---|---|
| **a** sydney | barangaroo | grotto | **b** balmoral | whale | gadyan |
| **c** cadigal | goat | cave | **d** island | fossils | wallaby |
| **e** smoke | mamila | opera | **f** manly | bridge | wangal |

**3** Complete the table by adapting these nouns from your list words to form other parts of speech.

| Noun | Adjective | Adverb |
|---|---|---|
| occasion | occasional | |
| south | | southerly |
| specification | | |
| | traditional | |

**4** Prepositions are words that show the relationships of nouns. Choose from the words in the box below to fill in the missing prepositions in these sentences.

| | | | | |
|---|---|---|---|---|
| above | with | at | since | into |
| through | across | to | toward | under |
| until | up | behind | on | |

**a** When you visit Sydney, try to explore some of the places marked __________ the map.

**b** There are many artefacts to see ____________ ancient living sites.

**c** Indigenous Australians of past times left many stone tools __________________.

**d** Whole families took shelter ______________ sandstone rock ledges.

**e** Carvings have been found that were made by etching lines ___________ the sandstone.

# INFORMATIVE TEXT
*Brochure*

**PUNCTUATION WORK**

## Capital letters

Capital letters are used to begin sentences and for proper nouns. In some names of people, places and events, all the words should be capitalised. For example, each word in the state name *New South Wales* begins with a capital letter. In some names, though, only the first word is capitalised. An example is *Australian red cedar*. This is because some of the words in the name are not proper nouns. *Red* is an adjective and *cedar* is a common noun.

**1** Decide whether or not the highlighted words in these phrases should take initial capital letters. Tick *capital letter* or *lower case* for each one.
*Hint: First check the context to see if they are adjectives, verbs or adverbs, in which case they will not require capital letters. If they are nouns, think about whether they are common or proper nouns.*

- **a** A common pigment used in cave painting is **white** ochre. Capital letter ☐ Lower case ☐
- **b** There's an engraving of a whale at a place called **balls** Head. Capital letter ☐ Lower case ☐
- **c** Sunset is a good time to see some **rock** engravings. Capital letter ☐ Lower case ☐
- **d** A popular lookout is named after **arabanoo**. Capital letter ☐ Lower case ☐
- **e** The harbour's southern shore belonged to a **cammeraygal** woman. Capital letter ☐ Lower case ☐
- **f** Shell **middens** are evidence of eating places from long ago. Capital letter ☐ Lower case ☐
- **g** The walking track on **berry** Island is an interesting historical site. Capital letter ☐ Lower case ☐

## Bullet point lists

When punctuating **bullet point lists**, also known as dot point lists, the sentence that introduces the list should begin with a capital letter as usual. This sentence is called the stem. There is no need to add punctuation at the end of bullet points that are not complete sentences—except for the last, which takes a full stop to show that the sequence is complete. Because each bullet point is designed to continue the stem, we do not capitalise the first letter of each bullet point unless it is a proper noun.

**2** Add the correct punctuation to this bullet point list.
*Hint: You'll need to add a colon, the bullet points and a full stop.*

We should preserve historical sites because

they have cultural significance to many people

we can learn a lot from the past

they can never be replaced

it is respectful to those who've gone before us

**3** Find an instance of each of these punctuation features in the text and write the line numbers where they appear.

- **a** the first word with a possessive apostrophe ____________ (line ____)
- **b** the first contraction ____________ (line ____)
- **c** a phrase in parentheses ____________ (line ____)
- **d** a proper noun in quotation marks ____________ (line ____)
- **e** two three-word proper nouns with initial capital letters ____________ (line ____)

# INFORMATIVE TEXT

## Brochure

**WRITING WORK 1**

### Brochures

**Brochures** may include visual elements that help organise and convey the content. When composing printed informative texts, using visuals is a good way of reducing the amount of written text so that the brochure looks interesting. Visuals also present summaries that help readers understand and retain what they've read.

### Structural features of a brochure

Brochures usually contain the following features:

- a main heading
- subheadings
- short blocks of information
- a logical sequence
- facts and details relevant to the topic
- supporting descriptions
- bullet point lists
- a variety of typefaces in multiple sizes
- visual features such as photographs, drawings, graphic organisers, diagrams, tables, charts and maps.

**1** Name two structural features of brochures that help summarise the content.

______________________ ______________________

**2** What are three types of visual features that may be found in a brochure?

______________________

______________________

______________________

**3** Think of the different types of brochures you've seen. Show that you understand some of the different purposes of brochures by completing these sentences using topics of your choice.

A brochure may educate people about ______________________.

A brochure may be promoting a particular brand of ______________________.

A brochure may be aimed at raising awareness about ______________________.

A brochure may present an introduction to ______________________.

A brochure may contain advertising material about ______________________.

A brochure may help people learn about ______________________.

**4** Look at the text 'Indigenous Sydney' and answer these questions.
List three visual features present in the text.

______________________

______________________

______________________

**5** In the brochure, what is the purpose of the key?

______________________

# INFORMATIVE TEXT

## Brochure

WRITING WORK 2

### Language features of a brochure

**Brochures** contain these **language features**:

- simple sentences (sometimes not written as complete sentences)
- short paragraphs
- concise language created through the use of short phrases and precise choices in wording
- precise and often specialised vocabulary
- adjectives to describe features or attributes of the topic or subject
- captions
- the presentation of information in a highly organised structure
- the presentation of facts and details using concrete language rather than figurative expressions.

**6** Look at the text 'Indigenous Sydney' and match each of these features with the example drawn from the text. Write the correct letters in the spaces.
*Hint: Use the process of elimination to help you.*

| | | |
|---|---|---|
| **a** heading | _____ | smooth rock surfaces |
| **b** subheading | _____ | hand stencil rock art |
| **c** specialised jargon related to the topic | _____ | Indigenous Sydney |
| **d** adjective that describes objects | _____ | Indigenous heritage sites around Sydney Harbour |
| **e** caption for an illustration or photograph | _____ | middens |

**7** Informative texts are written in language that is often very precise. Can you find examples of precise and specific vocabulary in the brochure? Write them in the spaces using the letter clues to help you.

**a** specific names of places

_ o _ _ o _ _ _ _ a d     _ a _ _ y _ _ v _

B _ l _ _ _ _ _ B _ _ _ _     B _ _ _ _ _ _ _ g _ _ _ _ t     G _ _ _ _ s _ _ _ _

**b** specific names of people and people groups

_ _ a _ a _ _ _     _ _ r _ n _ _ _ _ o     _ a d _ g _ _     _ _ m m _ _ _ _ _ _ l

**c** jargon (specialised words not in common use) associated with archaeology and geology

_ _ l c _ _ t _     c h _ _ _     _ c h _ _

**8** What other features of Indigenous Sydney mentioned in the brochure could be further described using illustrations rather than just text? Describe appropriate subject matter for five illustrations that would add to the informative power of the text.

______________________________________________

______________________________________________

______________________________________________

______________________________________________

**9** Describe the colour palette you would use if you were to produce a full-colour version of this publication, explaining your reasoning.

______________________________________________

______________________________________________

# INFORMATIVE TEXT

Brochure

WRITING SAMPLE

## Create an urban hobby farm

**✱ Create an attention-grabbing heading.** This heading presents a contrast by mentioning city living and farming side by side.

People living in urban areas may feel that their dream of operating a hobby farm is unachievable. Let us show you how to maximise the space around you, however tiny your backyard may be.

**✱ Present a brief introduction to the topic of the brochure.** The text should be concise and provide a clear introduction to the main purpose of the brochure: to convey information about the topic. Personal pronouns are used to involve the reader more directly.

Don't let city living make you give up on your farming dream. With a little imagination you can achieve a wonderful, sustainable lifestyle right in your own backyard.

**✱ Use adjectives and emotive terms appropriate to the topic.** Here they are used to create a richer description of the details. An idiom is also used to personalise the message ('right in your own backyard').

We've listed just a few of the many options for different types of urban yard spaces. As the size of the space increases, add more ideas to those in the previous one.

Find your space in the list and start planning.

**✱ Use subheadings to break up factual information into manageable sections.** The different types of backyards are listed in a hierarchy from smallest to largest. This helps reinforce the idea that all backyards have possibilities and that these possibilities increase as the size increases.

**A balcony**
As well as potted plants, you can use hanging baskets to grow herbs, strawberries, salad leaves, chilies and many other types of fresh produce. When space is very tight at home, consider gathering wild foods from open spaces such as by roads, railroad tracks and bicycle paths in the city.

**✱ Create a logical list order.** The order allows the reader to locate the information most relevant to their situation. This list works by having the first item provide a basis upon which each subsequent item builds.

**A front or back patio**
You can upcycle old boxes, containers and even furniture to create a multi-layered garden on a patio. If the area is always shaded, use a solar panel on the roof to capture energy that can power a small hothouse. Strategic planting of flowers will attract insects to help your crops pollinate (or reproduce).

**✱ Use bold text and bullet points.** This emphasises the structure of the list. The points also conform to a consistent pattern. In this case the word 'A' begins each one. A definition is provided to clarify the meaning of an unfamiliar term.

**A small paved courtyard**
If your courtyard has a wall or fence, maximise space by using a wooden trellis or other structure that enables you to hang planter boxes for flowers or climbing vines such as beans or grapes. If space permits, a small tank to collect rainwater would be a wonderful asset.

**✱ Ensure that each listed point is supported by more detailed information.** Details are provided to add interest using concise, direct expression.

**A little bit of lawn**
Why not keep a couple of **Isa Brown hens** in a timber **ark** that you can move around the grass? Then you can add chook **manure** to your thriving garden pots and plots. A **worm bin** can help transform manure and kitchen waste into **nitrogen-rich compost** and **mulch** for your mini-garden.

**✱ Employ jargon where necessary to add specificity.** Here jargon relevant to the topic area is included to aid precision and variety in conveying factual information.

**A standard backyard**
On a **quarter-acre** block, there's ample room to plant fruit trees and **in-ground veggie garden beds.** You could keep a pair of goats or sheep for milk and create a fishpond that cycles the water through a reed bed for natural filtration. You could also consider installing a greenhouse, recycling bin, bird bath and seating area. And if you're really adventurous, bring in a beehive to top it all off.

**✱ Use specific language in the active voice relevant to the purpose of the brochure.** Here the language gives people ideas for urban farming. The active voice is used to increase reader engagement and maintain a positive tone.

Plan your sample on the lines provided.

- **Create an attention-grabbing heading.** You could use contrast, alliteration or assonance, a pun or irony to capture attention.

- **Present a brief introduction to the topic of the brochure.** Your writing should be concise and provide a clear introduction to the main purpose of the brochure: to convey information about the topic. Use personal pronouns.

- **Use adjectives and emotive terms if appropriate to the topic.** Use them to create a richer description of the details. Consider using idioms to personalise the message.

- **Use subheadings to break up factual information into manageable sections.** Use a hierarchy with a clear organisational structure that makes logical sense.

- **Create a logical list order.** Use an order that allows the reader to locate the information most relevant to their situation.

- **Use bold text and bullet points.** The points should have a consistent pattern. Consider whether you need to provide any definitions to clarify the meaning of unfamiliar terms.

- **Ensure that each listed point is supported by more detailed information.** Details add interest but remember to use concise, direct expression.

- **Employ jargon where necessary to add specificity.** Use jargon relevant to the topic area to aid precision and variety in conveying factual information.

- **Use specific language in the active voice relevant to the purpose of the brochure.** Use the active voice to increase reader engagement and maintain a positive tone.

# INFORMATIVE TEXT

## Online news piece

**READING WORK**

### World War I sketch recovered after 32 years

**German soldier's artwork depicts the 1914 Christmas Day Truce**

*by Cal Renton*

A valuable piece of memorabilia from World War I has turned up in a garage sale in the Perth suburb of Lockridge. It's a sketch of soldiers having a kickabout with a tin can during an unofficial truce between German and Allied soldiers on the Western Front in 1914. The artwork was drawn in charcoal by an unnamed German soldier during the war on the Western Front.

The artwork was given to Private Jack Shelley, a British soldier with the Somerset Light Infantry, when he was defending the town of Frelinghien, France. The sketch is an important historical document, as it provides evidence that the tales of enemy soldiers socialising together are true. But for Private Shelley's descendants it has even greater value, since it was Jack's prized possession. Jessie Shelley, Jack's great-granddaughter, recalls fond memories of the old man sharing stories about his experiences in the war when he came to live permanently in Australia in 1930. The family lost track of the artwork after Jack's possessions were moved during the sale of his estate when he died in 1984.

'Pop had a tobacco tin with a dozen or so buttons from the uniforms of men from both sides. He told us all the details of every one of those buttons. To Pop they represented real people he'd known, some who hadn't come home from the war. He had at least two buttons from German uniforms that he told us were exchanged between the men involved in the Christmas Day Truce.'

During these unofficial truces, the most famous of which occurred on Christmas Day of 1914, the soldiers came out of their trenches into no-man's-land and shared food and drinks, cigarettes and some even exchanged small gifts. Remarkably, the men sang carols and even played football games together. Later, this spirit of cooperation continued in unofficial agreements between the sides to refrain from shooting at mealtimes, during stints of exercise and even at times when soldiers were working in the open.

This fascinating image of peace and humanity amid war has endured through the years. The sketch is a symbol of the potential for humanity, hope and kindness to prevail in even the harshest and most violent of circumstances.

The sketch and the tin of buttons are among the items currently on display at the Australian War Memorial's commemoration of the Christmas Day Truce in Canberra.

- A **main heading** is used to summarise the topic.
- The **subheading** adds a newsworthy detail to the topic.
- The **by-line** gives the journalist's name.
- In journalistic writing, the **first paragraph summarises** the story and the remaining paragraphs supply the details in short blocks of text.
- **Contextual information** is provided as a background to the story.
- A **contrast** is drawn between 'tales' and 'evidence' to stress the importance of the find as a historical source.
- **Details such as names and dates** are given to emphasise the reliability of the story.
- **Direct speech** is used to present a quote from the person interviewed, adding a sense of authenticity.
- The term 'no-man's-land' refers to the space between the two opposing trenches that was literally controlled by nobody. Being caught there meant certain death, as you would be exposed to enemy fire immediately.
- **Specific details** help readers see the story as believable and in line with historical facts already known.
- The journalist adds language that conveys his **personal reaction**.
- **Emotive language** is used to show the journalist's own view.
- The journalist **draws a meaning** out of the story that can be generalised from this specific incident to apply to war more broadly.
- This instance of **emotive language** encourages an emotional response from the reader.
- The journalist provides **currently relevant information** and it is here that discerning readers will realise that the point of the story has actually been to promote this exhibition.

# INFORMATIVE TEXT

Online news piece

COMPREHENSION WORK

## Literal questions

*Hint: Read the text carefully to locate specific facts and details.*

**1** What rank in the army was Jack Shelley in World War I?

**a** Captain **b** Major **c** Private

**2** What type of songs were sung by German and Allied soldiers in the unofficial truce?

______________________________

**3** Of what 'tales' did the discovery of the artwork provide historically significant evidence?

______________________________

**4** At which three regular times did enemy soldiers agree to withhold fire in a spirit of cooperation?

______________________________

## Interpretive questions

*Hint: These questions require you to combine facts and details to synthesise the meaning.*

**5** In what month and year did Jack Shelley acquire buttons from the uniforms of German soldiers?

______________________________

**6** What is the meaning of the term 'his estate' in line 19 of the text?

**a** his body **b** his possessions **c** his neighbourhood

**7** Why is the sketch relevant to the Australian War Memorial when it was owned by a British soldier, not an Australian? ______________________________

**8** What game or sport does the term 'kickabout' imply was being played in the image?

**a** basketball **b** tennis **c** soccer

**9** Which word from the text tells us that Jack attached great personal value to the sketch?

**a** socialising **b** prized **c** fond

**10** Why were the buttons in the tobacco tin valuable to Jack Shelley?

**a** because they were made of solid gold **b** because they represented people he'd known

**c** because they'd belonged to his grandfather

## Applied questions

*Hint: This question requires you to understand a text's implications to infer meaning from the text.*

**11** Why does the journalist view the sketch as a symbol of hope, humanity and kindness?

**a** because it was given in a spirit of friendship by an enemy soldier in a time of war

**b** because it saved Jack Shelley's life during the war

**c** because it proves who won the war

**12** What explanation is the most likely for the reason why the sketch was not valued and was found in a garage sale?

______________________________

______________________________

# INFORMATIVE TEXT

*Online news piece*

## SPELLING WORK

**List Words** All of the words in the box below appear in the text 'World War I sketch recovered after 32 years'.

| | | | | |
|---|---|---|---|---|
| soldier | memorabilia | defending | exchanged | occurred |
| uniforms | possession | socialising | circumstances | historical |
| infantry | descendants | violent | remarkably | agreements |

**1** Correct the spelling of these misspelt list words.

**a** solider ______________ **b** posession ______________

**c** exchaged ______________ **d** uninforms ______________

**e** remarkeably ______________ **f** ocurred ______________

**g** vilent ______________ **h** descendents ______________

**2** How many syllables are in the following list words?
*Hint: Say them out loud and count the syllables you hear.*

**a** infantry ________ **b** defending ________ **c** historical ________ **d** exchanged ________

**3** Write the base words of each of these list words.

**a** memorabilia ______________ **b** historical ______________

**c** agreements ______________ **d** defending ______________

**e** possession ______________ **f** socialising ______________

**g** occurred ______________ **h** descendants ______________

**4** Write the missing prefixes for each of these words from the text.
*Hint: use the clues in brackets to help you work out each word.*

**a** ________forms (prescribed clothing) **b** ________presented (stood for)

**c** ________operation (working together) **d** ________ern (opposite of eastern)

**e** ________work (for example, a sketch) **f** ________daughter (female child of one's son or daughter)

**g** ________named (not identified) **h** ________ball (equipment used in sport)

**5** Circle all the misspelt words in this passage.
*Hint: Read the words in their context to help trigger your memory of how they should be spelt.*

Soldeirs in World War I endured many hardships. They were placed on strict food rations and sometimes experienced hungar for weeks. They suffered from a condishon called 'trench foot' which was caused by having wet feet for extendid periods of time. There were many rats and parasites in the trenchs, which led to outbrakes of dissease among the men. Worst of all, these dificulties were nothing compared to the continul attacks from the enemy by gunfire, shells and gas. To survive the war at all under these sircumstances was an amazing feet.

# INFORMATIVE TEXT
*Online news piece*

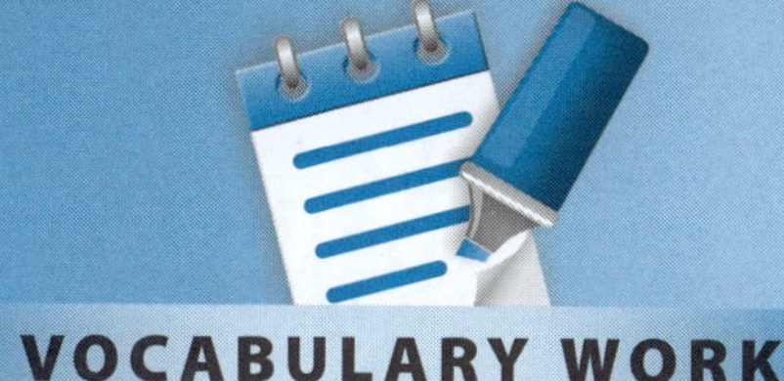

## VOCABULARY WORK

**1** Complete these sentences by inserting the correct word from this list of vocabulary terms.

| commemoration | refrain | prevail | stints | amid | dozen |
|---|---|---|---|---|---|

**a** Anzac Day is a time when a formal ____________ is held to honour people who died in wars.

**b** In times of truce, soldiers would ____________ from actively firing their weapons.

**c** We refer to a group of twelve as a ____________.

**d** To find ways to cooperate with hostile soldiers ____________ war is a rare achievement.

**e** Sometimes human decency will ____________ in even the most difficult circumstances.

**f** Many soldiers did ____________ of exercise in no man's land, which was very risky.

**2** Write antonyms for these words.

**a** unofficial ____________

**b** war ____________

**c** friend ____________

**d** elderly ____________

### Idioms

When we study **idioms**, it's important to remember that a true idiom must be **figurative**—that is, the words should not be taken literally. These two expressions from our focus text are **colloquialisms** but they are not idioms because they are both literal descriptions.

**3** Write definitions for these two colloquialisms from the text. Use the annotations to help you.

**a** no-man's-land ____________

**b** kickabout ____________

**4** Complete these descriptions of Australian idioms that were commonly heard in the speech of World War I soldiers in the past century.

**a** A person who is acting foolishly is said to be 'coming the r______ (uncooked) prawn'.

**b** Another word for a fool is a g__________ (a pink and grey native bird).

**c** A jumbuck is an old name shearers used for a s____________ (woolly animal).

**d** If you're talking about a remote place in the middle of nowhere, you might say it's out by the black s__________. (part of a tree)

**e** If you're talking about someone quite close by, or within hearing distance, they are said to be within c__________. (a call made in a cavernous space or to make an echo)

**f** A person who was highly skilled, such as a good shearer, was said to be a g__________ (firearm).

**g** A person with red hair was called B__________ (another primary colour).

**h** A short break was called a s__________ (referring to using tobacco).

**i** Soldiers who dug trenches in World War I were known as d____________ (workmen who make holes).

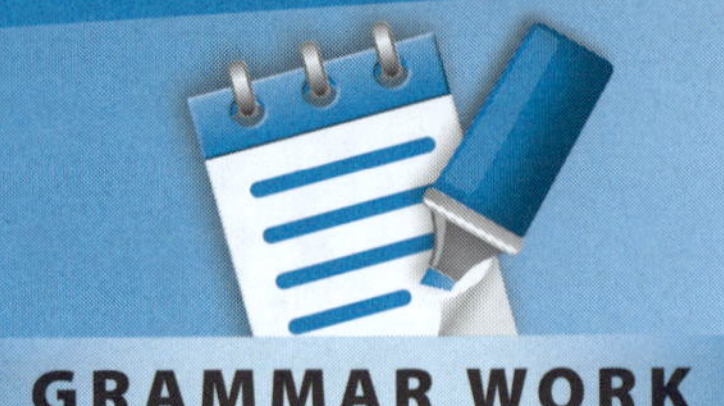

# INFORMATIVE TEXT

*Online news piece*

GRAMMAR WORK

## Pronouns

We use pronouns to take the place of nouns in a text. Usually, pronouns substitute for nouns to avoid text sounding too repetitive. For example, there's no need to use a person's name five times in a sentence when just the first mention is required.

Consider this sentence: *Finn told me he won an award for his short film, which he based on his experiences in Canada.*

Imagine if there were no pronouns used in the sentence. It would read like this: *Finn told me Finn won an award for Finn's short film, which Finn based on Finn's experiences in Canada.*

**1** How many words in this passage are pronouns? Write the number: ______________

Jessie Shelley, Jack's great-granddaughter, recalls fond memories of the old man sharing stories about his experiences in the war when he came to live permanently in Australia in 1930. The family lost track of the artwork after Jack's possessions were moved during the sale of his estate when he died in 1984.

**2** Whose name do the pronouns represent in the passage? ______________

**3** How many words in this passage are pronouns? Write them on the line provided.

'Pop had a tobacco tin with a dozen or so buttons from the uniforms of men from both sides. He told us all the details of every one of those buttons. To Pop they represented real people he'd known, some who hadn't come home from the war. He had at least two buttons from German uniforms that he told us were exchanged between the men involved in the Christmas Day Truce.'

______________

Personal pronouns refer to specific people and things. The words *I, we, he, she* and *they* are all personal pronouns. Their meanings change depending on who is speaking.

**4** Find all the personal pronouns in this sentence and write them on the line.

I was really pleased when the Australian War Memorial staff told me that they wanted to put my great-grandfather's items on display.

______________

**5** Using the same sentence, change all the personal pronouns in this sentence to represent more than one person. Rewrite the sentence. *Hint: You will need to change the word 'was' to 'were'.*

______________

______________

**6** What are the common nouns in this sentence? Write them on the line.

The soldiers came out of their trenches and shared food and drinks, cigarettes and small gifts.

______________

**7** What are the proper nouns in this sentence? Write them on the line.

The sketch and the tin of buttons are among the items currently on display at the Australian War Memorial's commemoration of the Christmas Day Truce in Canberra.

______________

# INFORMATIVE TEXT

## PUNCTUATION WORK

We use **quotation marks** in written text to indicate a speaker's actual words. These punctuation symbols are also called speech marks. Only the words that are actually spoken need quotation marks; not the text that tells us who said the words.

**1** Which of these sentences are presented as direct speech in the text 'World War I sketch recovered after 32 years'?

**a** To Pop they represented real people he'd known, some who hadn't come home from the war.

**b** The sketch is a symbol of the potential for humanity, hope and kindness to prevail.

**c** Remarkably, the men sang carols and even played football games together.

We use a **comma** to indicate the end of the spoken words in direct speech. The comma goes inside the closing quotation mark, right before the phrase that tells us who has spoken. For example, *'I have won three awards this year,' said Finn.*

**2** Correct the punctuation of the direct speech in these sentences.

**a** Private Shelley's items have attracted a lot of public interest said the spokesperson.

**b** We are laying a wreath at the commemoration service an army cadet told me.

**Indirect speech** is **reported speech**; that is, it doesn't present the speaker's actual words. Indirect speech doesn't require quotation marks.

**3** Fix the punctuation in these sentences. First decide whether they contain direct or indirect speech. Then rewrite the sentences on the lines, using or removing quotation marks as necessary.

**a** My great-grandfather told me 'not to read his personal letters'.

______________________________

**b** Our ancestor was a talented sketch artist, the German soldier's grand-nephew told me during our interview.

______________________________

**4** Which sentence has the correct punctuation?

| | Correct or Incorrect? |
|---|---|
| **a** The french town of Frelinghien was the location of the truce. | ______ |
| **b** I heard reports that the soldiers played with a tin can instead of a football. | ______ |
| **c** I remember being shot very clearly a young soldier said looking at me intently. | ______ |
| **d** 'We were stuck in those wretched trenches for many months,' the man said as he stared at the photographs. | ______ |
| **e** 'I saw captain Barrow had been wounded,' said the medic gravely, 'but we couldn't get to him until the firing ceased." | ______ |

**5** Rewrite this sentence, correcting the punctuation.

I wrote to mum telling her of the rumours that the war would soon be over but by the time the letter reached her I was already home private burke said.

______________________________

______________________________

# INFORMATIVE TEXT

## Online news piece

**WRITING WORK 1**

### Online news pieces

**Online news pieces** are informative texts that are designed to present the latest news. They are factual accounts of events that have happened recently. The content for online news stories may be local, national or global in its significance. In online news stories the lead paragraph gives the basic details. Next the main body of the story is presented, with details given that flesh out the material in the lead paragraph.

### Structural features of an online news piece

Online news pieces contain these features:

- a headline
- subheadings
- a by-line or by-lines
- a lead paragraph
- the main body broken into short, readable blocks of text
- a logical order of presentation of the facts and details
- background information that provides a proper context for the reader
- quotations presented as direct speech from witnesses or other commentators
- developments arising from the story
- a link to current or future events to reinforce its relevance to the reader
- hyperlinks to other relevant online content
- images that illustrate the topic.

**1** Name two structural features of online news pieces that help summarise the content and make the user click on the link.

______________________________________________

**2** What do we call the line of text that gives the name of the journalist who wrote the news piece?

______________________________________________

**3** Demonstrate your understanding of the informative purpose of online news pieces by completing these sentences. Unscramble the words in brackets and write them in the spaces provided.

**a** An online news piece presents the (afcts) ____________ about a recent event of interest to the target audience.

**b** An online news piece may contain (otquanosti) ____________ gathered by interviewing people who witnessed the event.

**c** An online news piece may be useful in raising public (waraness) ____________ about an important community issue.

**d** Following the lead paragraph that summarises the story, online news stories usually present facts and details in a (glialoc) ____________ order.

**e** (magies) ____________ captured at the scene of a breaking news event are often presented alongside online news stories.

# INFORMATIVE TEXT

**Online news** is written for the specific target audience that is known to access the specific news feed on which it is published. Like all news writing, the piece begins with a **headline**. Unlike headlines in printed newspapers, online headlines are often accompanied by a **subheading**, a line of explanatory text that helps to capture the interest of readers so that they will click on the link to the story. They are usually **illustrated** with an accompanying image, such as a photo, diagram or other graphic element.

**4** Describe an attention-grabbing image to accompany the online news piece 'World War I sketch recovered after 32 years'.

**5** The text 'World War I sketch recovered after 32 years' contains authoritative phrases that we commonly see in online news pieces. Can you separate authoritative statements from statements of opinion?

Complete the table by marking these extracts from the text as *authoritative* or *opinion only*. Use ticks to indicate your responses.

| Extract from the text | Authoritative | Opinion only |
|---|---|---|
| **a** The artwork was drawn in charcoal | | |
| **b** This fascinating image of peace and humanity amid war | | |
| **c** Remarkably, the men sang carols | | |
| **d** The sketch and the tin of buttons are among the items currently on display | | |

**6** Comment on the suitability of each of these alternative headlines for the news piece by following these steps for each headline.

- Write your opinion of whether or not the headline is suitable.
- Explain why you think it is or is not suitable.
- When you have responded to all four headlines, identify which of the options would be the most appropriate and explain why.

| Headline | My opinion | Why I think so |
|---|---|---|
| **a** Old sketch found | | |
| **b** Treasure found in Lockridge garage sale | | |
| **c** Private Shelley's artwork found | | |
| **d** Long-lost sketch proves WWI mateship between enemies | | |

# INFORMATIVE TEXT

## *Online news piece*

**WRITING SAMPLE**

Here is a sample text showing you how to structure and write an online news piece.

### Tree limbs spear through caravan

✱ **Create a main heading** that clearly summarises the topic.

*by Sarah Duck*

✱ **Write your name as the by-line,** giving the writer credit for the article.

Holiday-makers at Brookeside caravan park came within inches of losing their lives in the early hours of Wednesday morning. The force of high winds caused two large gum tree limbs to snap off, one of which came crashing through the roof of Hamish and Natasha Harrison's caravan. The other narrowly missed the van, slamming onto a concrete slab nearby.

✱ **Write a clear summary of the story in the first paragraph.** You will use the remaining paragraphs to supply more detailed information. It's also important to reinforce the content of the lead paragraph with visual images to support the text.

The larger of the limbs, almost a metre in diameter, fell in tandem with one that speared its branches through the roof in two places. One piece went through the ceiling of the kitchen area, while the second sheared through the bedroom, missing the bed where they were sleeping by inches.

✱ **Add contextual information to show how the event unfolded.** Use a logical order in which to present the content. Include vivid details to add to the reader's understanding of what happened.

'It mustn't have been our time to go,' Mrs Harrison concluded as she showed neighbours the damaged interior of the van. 'We'd only just returned from the amenities block when it happened. Had we not been back in bed, it could have been much worse.' The bed area was the only space in the van that was spared. The ceiling of the caravan was crushed inwards, leaving two massive holes in the roof letting in the rain and the daylight.

✱ **Insert a quotation from someone close to the event.** This adds credibility to the story and links it to real people, which encourages a sense of empathy in the reader.

Mr Harrison, from Wauchope, NSW, identified the tree as a swamp gum. 'It has a very brittle interior. When the wind hit it at that speed, instead of flexing it just snapped like a carrot. Natasha and I are lucky to escape with our lives, that's for sure.'

✱ **Use a technique to create imagery, such as a simile,** to add visual details and drama to the story.

The noise of Tuesday night's violent winds caused many Brookeside residents a sleepless night. Some have expressed concerns over Rosewood Street's tall trees, which have limbs dangerously overhanging many houses. Only last week, the electricity company sent a representative to the location to mark out branches for lopping.

✱ **Use a cause and effect statement to link paragraphs together.** Here we see the words 'caused', 'only last week', and 'already scheduled', which gives the piece forward momentum.

High above the ground in the offending tree, a koala was found clinging in the easing wind and rain, just below the point where the limbs broke off.

✱ **Use strong verbs and adverbs** to add interest and depth to the story. Some news stories may have only limited potential to be widely appealing.

Seth Josson from the local Koala Hospital came to assess the animal for any injuries, but it appeared unharmed and was later released. Mr Josson said that it's important that members of the public keep an eye out for wildlife that may have been injured in the storms. 'Our treatment service operates cost-free and is staffed entirely by volunteers. We'd like to encourage people to make reports so that we can rehabilitate the animals and birds that have been displaced.'

✱ **Give the story a secondary purpose.** For example, this article has been used to promote a community cause—a koala rehabilitation clinic. A statement from the representative of the clinic is given to link the topic of the article (the storm) to the work of the community service providers.

State Emergency Service crew member, Ian Towers, supervised the removal of the tree limbs from the caravan park, after attending a number of other scenes of tree damage to residential properties. Mr Towers reports that there has been an unprecedented number of houses and businesses damaged by the storm, including the local health-food store, which had its roof completely torn off. Repair work will continue for several months.

✱ **Include an indirect quote or report from an authority figure** to add weight and credibility to the story. Here, we see an SES worker being interviewed about the storm and its effects on residents. He also makes a prediction about future outcomes.

# INFORMATIVE TEXT

## Online news piece

## WRITING YOUR OWN SAMPLE

Plan your sample on the lines provided.

- **Create a main heading** that clearly summarises the topic.
- **Write your name as the by-line.**
- **Write a clear summary of the story in the first paragraph.** Use the remaining paragraphs to supply more detailed information. Select a visual image to support the content of the lead paragraph.
- **Add contextual information to show how the event unfolded.** Use a logical order to present the content. Include vivid details to add to the reader's understanding of what happened.
- **Insert a quotation from someone close to the event.**
- **Use a technique to create imagery, such as a simile,** to add visual details and drama to the story.
- **Use a cause and effect statement to link paragraphs together.**
- **Use strong verbs and adverbs** to add interest and depth to the story.
- **Give the story a secondary purpose.**
- **Include an indirect quote or report from an authority figure** to add weight and credibility to the story.

# INFORMATIVE TEXT

## *Web page*

READING WORK

# Bush tucker

Home | Qld | NT | WA | Vic. | Tas. | SA | NSW | Recipes | FAQs

For most of us, being stranded somewhere without any food or water is the stuff of nightmares. But it might surprise you to learn that the bush has everything you could possibly need.

| Plants | | Birds | Seafood | Fish |
|---|---|---|---|---|
| small-leaf tamarind | Kakadu plums | wild birds (and eggs) | oysters | barramundi |
| lemon myrtle | wild grapes | bush turkeys | yabbies | sharks |
| blue flax lily | wild passionfruit | herons | periwinkles | stingrays |
| lilly pilly | grevillea flowers | wild ducks | mudcrabs | catfish |
| bunya nuts | yam roots | | mussels | longtoms |
| macadamia nuts | pandanus seeds | | | bream |
| wild figs | boab leaves | **Reptiles** | **Animals** | |
| green plums | boab roots | lizards | kangaroos | |
| red bush apples | boab nuts | turtles (and eggs) | wallabies | |
| seaweed | waterlilies | crocodiles | echidnas | **Insect foods** |
| sea celery | | monitors | | witchetty grubs |
| | | goannas | | sugarbag (wild bees) |

Dark blue background: Sunshine Coast White background: Arnhem Land Light blue background: The Kimberley

### On the Sunshine Coast, Queensland

According to the Gubbi Gubbi folk, there are plenty of tasty bush foods to be found on the Sunshine Coast.

The **small-leaf tamarind** is a seasonal red fruit used to make tangy cordials and chutneys. It can be eaten as a fresh fruit straight from the tree.

**Lemon myrtle** leaves can be used to make tea and medicines. The flowers and seeds are used as a source of fragrant oil.

The **lilly pilly** plant has small, dark pink fruit with an apple-like crunch. Lilly pillies are packed with vitamin C, and are used to make delicious chutneys, sauces and jams.

### In north-east Arnhem Land, Northern Territory

Arnhem Land is bursting with bush treasures, wisdom the Yolngu people have faithfully passed down for millennia.

The **Kakadu plum** or gurumal is a tasty fruit that can be eaten straight off the tree. It is a rich source of vitamin C, and has been used for medicinal purposes for thousands of years.

**Waterlilies** are a good source of fibre and vitamins. Their flowers, seeds, stems and crunchy white roots can be eaten raw and used as salad vegetables.

All species of **mussels** are packed with protein and healthy omega oils. These salty shellfish are easily harvested by hand and steamed until their shells open.

### In the Kimberley, Western Australia

These foods in the Kimberley ranges make your survival in the wilderness a breeze, according to the incredibly knowledgeable and resourceful Wanjina–Wunggurr people.

The **bush turkey** (or Australian bustard) is found in the Kimberley region of Western Australia. Bush turkeys and other meat sources are still plentiful today, even in the desert.

The **boab** (or bottle tree) is a mighty useful find—the trunk, roots, nuts and leaves. Boab nuts have a sugary, citrus taste and a powdery, fizzy texture like sherbet. The trunks of these trees can hold up to 120 litres of fresh, clean drinking water. If you drill a hole into the trunk, you can tap into a water supply.

**Sugarbag** is a type of wild honey found in the bush. It is made by non-stinging wild bees. Some Indigenous people are experts at finding sugarbag. Here are their top tips for harvesting this sweet treat.

1 Find some bees and follow them to the tree that contains their hive.
2 Tap on the trunk to locate the sugarbag. It makes a hollow sound.
3 Remove the wax plug and drain the contents into a container.

**Click your state on the map to learn about bush tucker in your backyard.**

**Click for links to related websites.**

- The **page title** is presented in decorative typeface to attract the user's attention and clearly identify the topic.
- This is the **navigation bar** linking this web page to the whole site.
- The **background image** is directly related to the topic.
- To begin, we are presented with this **introductory text.**
- An **information table** (graphic organiser) is used as an efficient means of presenting detailed content.
- **The information table** organises the content by category.
- **Subheadings** are used to organise the text and aid navigation.
- The **body text** is presented in short blocks to enhance onscreen readability.
- **Subheadings** are organised in logical order.
- These features provide **supporting text for the images.**
- **Site links** are included for the user's convenience.
- The **feature icon** also has an explanatory caption.

# INFORMATIVE TEXT
## *Web page*

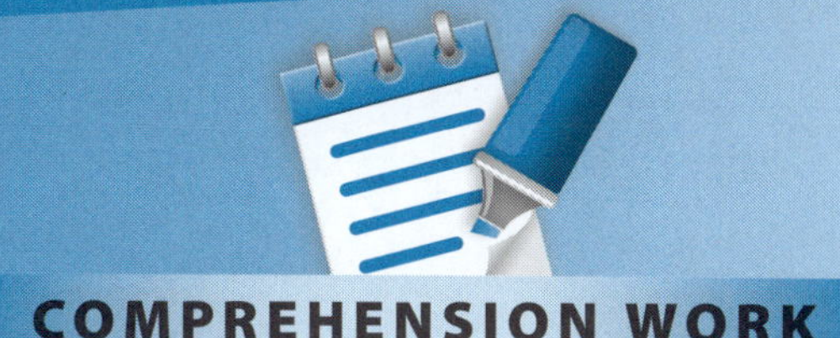

**COMPREHENSION WORK**

### Literal questions

*Hint: These questions require you to read the text carefully to locate specific facts and details.*

1 How many Australian states are mentioned in the text? ____________________

2 The eggs of which two creatures are part of the array of bush tucker available in north-east Arnhem Land?

____________________

3 What are the edible parts of the waterlily plant? ____________________

4 How many plant foods in total are listed as bush tucker sources of north-east Arnhem Land?

**a** six **b** two **c** nine

5 What do the local Indigenous people call the Kakadu plum of Arnhem Land?

**a** witchetty grub **b** gurumal **c** longtom

### Interpretive questions

*Hint: These questions require you to combine facts and details to synthesise the meaning.*

6 What is the composer's attitude toward Indigenous Australians and their traditional bush tucker?

____________________

7 Who might be the target audience for this text? Explain your answer.

____________________

*Hint: Only one answer option is correct. Use the process of elimination to work through the options.*

8 The bush turkey's alternative name is the Australian bustard. Who would use this name?

**a** Indigenous Australians **b** the scientific community **c** professional chefs in Australia

9 Could the steps outlined for finding sugarbag be placed in a different order? Justify your response.

____________________

10 What does the information about the boab tree reveal about the Indigenous people of the area?

**a** that they valued the resources around them and worked hard to find multiple uses for things in order to avoid wastage

**b** that they had little idea of the usefulness of the boab tree

**c** that they had no need for the resources offered by the boab tree

### Applied questions

*Hint: This question requires you to understand a text's implications to infer meaning from the text.*

11 Which of these is the most logical conclusion to reach about why the writer has not presented information about bush tucker in Tasmania?

**a** There is no bush tucker to be found in Tasmania.

**b** All of the bush tucker mentioned can be found in every area of Australia, including Tasmania.

**c** The writer's purpose was to present just a sample of the bush tucker available in certain areas of Australia.

12 What can we reasonably assume about the historical age of the name 'sugarbag' for a wild bees' nest?

**a** that it is an ancient Indigenous name

**b** that it is a name randomly invented

**c** that it is a name first used after 1780

# INFORMATIVE TEXT

## Web page

## SPELLING WORK

### List Words

All of the words in the box below appear in the text 'Bush tucker'.

| | | | |
|---|---|---|---|
| wallabies | plentiful | species | wilderness |
| oysters | millennia | bream | echidnas |
| seasonal | medicinal | indigenous | knowledgeable |

**1** These sentences contain spelling mistakes that have been highlighted. Write the correct spelling for each word. *Hint: Refer to the list words to help you.*

**a** The Gubbi Gubbi people are experts at hunting **ecidnas**. ______________

**b** The Kakadu plum is a rich source of Vitamin C that grows in the **wildness** of Arnhem Land. ______________

**c** The Kimberley Ranges are home to many **speshies** of wild birds. ______________

**d** Aboriginal people have inhabited the Australian continent for **millenia**. ______________

**2** These sentences contain spelling mistakes that have not been highlighted. Write the correct spelling for each misspelt word.

**a** Kangaroos and walabies are both species of macropods. ______________

**b** Certain plant and animal products can be used for medicinel purposes. ______________

**c** Shellfish such as osyters and mussels can be eaten raw or cooked. ______________

**d** There are numerous species of brim, but all of these fish have a similar body shape. ______________

Spelling can be easier when we recognise base words. For example, the base word of both *fishing* and *fisherman* is *fish*. The base word of *natural* and *naturalist* is *nature*.

**3** What is the simplest base word identifiable in each of these words?

**a** wilderness ______________ **b** medicinal ______________ **c** plentiful ______________

A prefix is placed at the beginning of a word. Some common prefixes are *de, in* and *pro*. A suffix is placed at the end of a word. Common suffixes are *ness, ful* and *able*.

**4** Some of your list words are made up of prefixes or suffixes attached to base words. Add the correct prefix or suffix to these base words. You will need to choose whether to use the space before or after the base word.

**a** ______knowledge______ **b** ______credibly______ **c** ______plenti______ **d** ______medic______

**5** Which word correctly completes the sentence? For each one, unscramble the letters and write the word on the lines provided.

**a** Spiny anteaters are also known as ______________________. (chdns iae)

**b** Many sweet fruits are ______________________ to Australia. (ndgns iieou)

# INFORMATIVE TEXT

## Web page

## VOCABULARY WORK

**1** Re-read the text carefully then circle *true* or *false* to answer each of these questions.

| | | | |
|---|---|---|---|
| **a** The tamarind is a fruit. | True | False | |
| **b** The lemon myrtle is a reptile. | True | False | |
| **c** The flax lily is green in colour. | True | False | |
| **d** The lilly pilly is a sweet fruit. | True | False | |
| **e** Bunyas and yabbies are nuts. | True | False | |
| **f** Jam can be made from seaweed. | True | False | |
| **g** The yam is a plant. | True | False | |
| **h** Sharks are eaten in Arnhem Land. | True | False | |
| **i** Wild passionfruit is poisonous. | True | False | |
| **j** A pandanus is a type of stingray. | True | False | |

**2** By looking at the context, what type of living things are each of these? Tick your response.

| | | | |
|---|---|---|---|
| **a** periwinkle | ☐ plant | ☐ bird | ☐ shellfish |
| **b** witchetty grub | ☐ reptile | ☐ fish | ☐ insect |
| **c** gurumal | ☐ plant | ☐ bird | ☐ insect |
| **d** heron | ☐ plant | ☐ bird | ☐ reptile |
| **e** longtom | ☐ reptile | ☐ fish | ☐ insect |
| **f** monitor | ☐ reptile | ☐ fish | ☐ insect |
| **g** sea celery | ☐ plant | ☐ shellfish | ☐ insect |
| **h** barramundi | ☐ fish | ☐ shellfish | ☐ insect |

**3** Which word correctly completes the sentence? Circle your choice from the answer options.

**a** The word *citrus* describes a _______________ like oranges and lemons.

texture | taste | sound | feeling

**b** The word *harvesting* means _______________ a food from its source.

gathering | adding | reaching | keeping

**c** The term *flight path* means the route taken by _______________ insects.

walking | creeping | crawling | flying

**d** The term *nectar* refers to a substance found in _______________.

mammals | reptiles | plants | water

**4** Classify these sets of words by matching them with their key topic. Write the letters in the correct spaces.

| | |
|---|---|
| **a** wax, honey, hollow, nectar, trunk, hive | _____ boab trees |
| **b** fizzy, tap, litres, nuts, powdery, roots | _____ mussels |
| **c** oil, seeds, medicines, team, fragrant | _____ lilly pilly |
| **d** omega oils, steamed, shells, protein, harvested | _____ lemon myrtle |
| **e** Vitamin C, jams, sauces, pink, crunch | _____ tamarind |
| **f** seasonal, cordial, fresh, leaf, chutneys | _____ wild bees |

**5** Write your own definitions to explain the meaning of these idioms from the text.

**a** 'being stranded' ________________________________________________

**b** 'the stuff of nightmares' ________________________________________________

# INFORMATIVE TEXT
## *Web page*

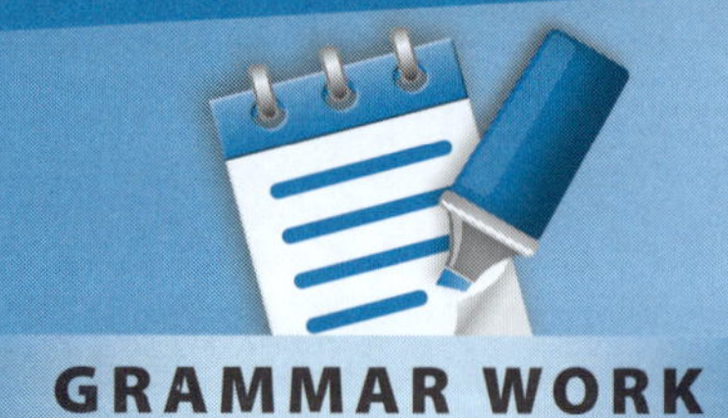

**GRAMMAR WORK**

### Adjectives

**Adjectives** describe nouns and pronouns. They can be used to:

- describe people, objects, places, feelings and ideas
- give us a picture of how something looks, sounds, smells, tastes and feels
- specify colours, shapes and sizes.

For example, *yellow, turquoise* and *black* are all adjectives, as are *large, tiny, massive, puffy, sticky, round* and *angular*.

**1** Which of the list words are adjectives? Circle them. *Hint: Don't mistake adverbs (often ending in* ly*) for adjectives.*

| | | | |
|---|---|---|---|
| wallabies | plentiful | species | wilderness |
| Indigenous | knowledgeable | oysters | millennia |
| bream | echidnas | seasonal | medicinal |

**2** What nouns do these colour adjectives describe in the text? Write them in the spaces.

| Adjective | Item described | Adjective | Item described |
|---|---|---|---|
| **a** blue | ______ | **b** dark pink | ______ |
| **c** white | ______ | **d** green | ______ |

**3** Think of adjectives that describe the way these items look. Write two for each noun listed. An example has been done for you.

| Noun | Adjective 1 | Adjective 2 | Noun | Adjective 1 | Adjective 2 |
|---|---|---|---|---|---|
| catfish | scaly | whiskered | | | |
| **a** kangaroo | ______ | ______ | **b** mudcrab | ______ | ______ |
| **c** yam root | ______ | ______ | **d** wild birds | ______ | ______ |
| **e** turtle | ______ | ______ | **f** wild grapes | ______ | ______ |
| **g** yabbies | ______ | ______ | **h** bunya nuts | ______ | ______ |
| **i** echidna | ______ | ______ | **j** bream | ______ | ______ |

**4** Find the nouns in the text that are described with adjectives related to the sense of taste. Write the foods they describe in the spaces.

| Taste adjective | Food described | Taste adjective | Food described |
|---|---|---|---|
| **a** sweet | ______ | **b** salty | ______ |
| **c** tangy | ______ | **d** sugary | ______ |

**5** Complete this table of adjectives made from nouns, following the pattern shown in the example. The first one has been done for you. *Hint: Adjectives describe nouns.*

| Noun | Adjective | Noun | Adjective |
|---|---|---|---|
| taste | tasty | **a** ______ | medicinal |
| water | **b** ______ | cleanliness | **c** ______ |
| freshness | **d** ______ | **e** ______ | healthy |
| nut | **f** ______ | **g** ______ | plentiful |
| region | **h** ______ | use | **i** ______ |

# INFORMATIVE TEXT

## Web page

**PUNCTUATION WORK**

### Capital letters

**Capital letters** are used:

- to begin sentences
- for proper nouns, including names of people, places, things, events, and names of days and months
- for proper nouns, including titles of works of art or literature such as books, poems, songs, films and plays
- for brand names, and organisation and business names
- for acronyms (made from the initial letters in a multi-word name, such as *ANZAC*)
- to punctuate the personal pronoun *I*.

In most proper nouns all the main words should be capitalised (for example, *New South Wales*) but not the minor words, like *in* or *the*, such as in *Lost in the Desert*. But when a proper noun forms only part of the name, only that word is capitalised (for example, *Australian bustard*).

**1** Are these sentences showing the correct or incorrect use of capital letters? Circle *correct* or *incorrect*.

**a** I saw a mob of kangaroos grazing around a billabong in the scrub. Correct Incorrect

**b** The bunya nut is a product harvested in the glasshouse mountains. Correct Incorrect

**c** The gubbi gubbi people have passed traditional knowledge down. Correct Incorrect

**d** Magenta Gold is a commercial brand of lilly pilly jam. Correct Incorrect

**e** The leaves of the lemon myrtle tree can be made into an aromatic Tea. Correct Incorrect

**f** We became stranded in the kimberley ranges after our plane crashed in the desert. Correct Incorrect

**g** Les Hiddins was known as the Bush Tucker Man and had his own television show. Correct Incorrect

**2** Three of these words should include one or more capital letters. Rewrite them correctly in the spaces.

today wallabies queensland yellow kakadu plums citrus vitamin c

__________ __________ __________

**3** Three of these phrases should include capital letters. Rewrite them correctly in the spaces.

arnhem land turtle the northern territory wild bees australian bush 120 litres

__________ __________ __________

**4** Correctly punctuate the following with all the missing capitals letters.

**a** i enjoy aussie bush tucker when i am camping. __________

**b** It seems i'll need to light a fire very soon. __________

**c** i've had a really interesting outback adventure. __________

**d** Why couldn't i find my way back to my ford ranger?

__________

**5** Here are some invented book titles about the following bush food sources. Rewrite them on the lines correctly.

**a** secrets of the amazing boab tree __________

**b** how to find sugarbag and other bush tucker sweets

__________

**c** i survived in the australian desert __________

**d** camping and cooking in the Kimberley __________

# INFORMATIVE TEXT
## *Web page*

**WRITING WORK 1**

### Informative web pages

An **informative web page** is designed to communicate information in a precise and authoritative manner. It is presented in a format that maximises the potential for variety that the online environment provides, from simple text and graphics to animation, video and sound grabs, links, live feeds and numerous navigation options.

### Capturing the user's attention

People browsing online typically spend only a few minutes on any given web page. This means that composers have only a short time in which to **capture** and hold **the user's attention**.

### Principles for presenting text online

Composers need to strike a good balance between providing relevant and complete information without bombarding the user with too much text at once. To achieve this, designers **present information** using multiple formats that appeal to the user visually, rather than just including lots of text. Long passages of text need to be organised into smaller blocks, which may be introduced using subheadings.

**1** Answer *true* or *false* to these questions by ticking the correct answer box for each one.

a Informative web pages aim to convey an impression of authority so that people feel they can trust the information being presented is accurate. ☐ True ☐ False

b Using precise language usually makes online content less authoritative. ☐ True ☐ False

c The online environment has a lot of potential for variety in interactive functions. ☐ True ☐ False

d Animations are one format suitable for use in presenting information online. ☐ True ☐ False

e When creating online texts, capturing the user's attention is not an important consideration. ☐ True ☐ False

f People browsing online usually spend only a few minutes on any given web page. ☐ True ☐ False

g When composing texts for the online environment the usual rule is the more text on the page, the better. ☐ True ☐ False

h Designers present information using multiple formats that appeal to the user visually, rather than just including lots of text. ☐ True ☐ False

i Subheadings can be used to break up long passages of text into smaller blocks. ☐ True ☐ False

### Features of an informative web page

To compose a useful **informative text** for the online environment, we must include some basic **features** that are common to most web pages:

- page title
- background or feature image
- navigation bar
- introductory text
- short blocks of body text
- headings
- subheadings
- graphic organisers
- images
- captions for images
- supporting text for images
- hyperlinked keywords
- feature icons
- feature icon captions
- supporting text for feature icons
- metadata
- site links.

# INFORMATIVE TEXT

## *Web page*

As we consider these features, we also need to identify certain **elements of design** common to many visual texts. These include the colour scheme, typeface design and size, positioning of features, page borders, background wallpaper, shapes and lines.

**2** Why is it important to break online text into smaller chunks?

______________________________

Answer these questions by circling one answer from each pair of options.

**3** Which of the following features would be most appropriately presented in a large-sized typeface?

short blocks of body text headings

**4** Which of these features might use a decorative typeface?

metadata page title

**5** Which of these features might make use of different coloured text?

hyperlinked keywords introductory text

Write short answers to these questions.

**6** Think of a web page that you visit regularly. Estimate how many words of text appears on the home page.

Write your estimate here: ______________ words.

In your opinion is this too much, too little or just the right amount of textual content?

______________________________

**7** What effect might increasing space between lines have on onscreen text?

______________________________

**8** How do graphic organisers help composers design useful web pages?

______________________________

**9** Fill in the missing words in this passage.

| speed | organise |
| --- | --- |
| fast | locate |

The online environment is perceived as a ______________ way to access information. Blocks of text ______________ up the process of locating specific details. Subheadings help ______________ these blocks of text, allowing users to quickly ______________ the details they are seeking.

**Font or typeface?**
Here's a fun fact. A **font** is the program you use to create a **typeface**. Font specifications control the size, slant and special attributes of the typeface, but the actual appearance of the letters is not a font. These days, most people say **font** when they really mean the **style** of their lettering, such as Times New Roman or Arial, but these are actually called **typefaces**.

# INFORMATIVE TEXT

## Web page

WRITING SAMPLE

Here is a sample text showing you how to structure and write a web page.

## Dromedairy—a camel milking enterprise

✱ **Use a page title that directly relates to the topic.** The title includes a pun on the word dromedary, a type of camel, by adding an *i* to make it read *dairy*.

✱ **Add a background or feature image.** The image of the camel in the dairy helps set the mood of the page and ties the elements together with colour, form and shape.

**About us | Our farm | Camel milk | Getting started | Store**
**The Dromedairy Brand | Map | Photo gallery | Links | FAQs**

✱ **Create a navigation bar.** This is the menu that allows users to navigate to the other pages in the site.

Camel milk is taking the world by storm. Welcome to Dromedairy—your one-stop site with everything you need to know about camel milk.

✱ **Write the introductory text to present the topic.** Choose keywords that search engines can use to determine the site's ranking.

**Why milk camels?**
Camel milk is highly nutritious and is great to drink. It has a slightly salty taste compared to cow's milk but is easier to digest and is packed full of beneficial enzymes and vitamins. It is also believed to benefit people with autism, asthma, eczema and food intolerances.

**How difficult is camel farming?**
Camels are docile creatures that can be trained to accept milking routines. They live for decades and yield up to 10 litres in a milking session. Camels are intelligent, hardy animals that can graze on unimproved pasture, making them a great option for farmers on poor-quality land. They cope well with drought and have no natural predators.

**How profitable is camel farming?**
Camel farmers in Australia report earnings of between $1000 and $1400 per week per camel. In comparison, an average dairy cow earns the farmer about $200 each week. Lower numbers of animals mean lower costs of production, including feed, water facilities and veterinary fees.

✱ **Organise the body text with subheadings.** Here we see a series of questions that the user might be asking. There's a logical order and each subheading is short, with blocks of text containing information relevant to the topic. The language is clear and concise, with every word earning its place. Web users easily become impatient with unbroken passages of text. Organise text into readable chunks, using subheadings as signposts to guide the reader through the material and motivate them to keep reading.

✱ **Select an image to help illustrate the content.**

*Heli-mustering feral camels in the Northern Territory*

✱ **Add an explanatory caption to the image.**

✱ **Add a feature icon that is hyperlinked to supporting text containing extra details about one aspect of the topic.**

There are more than ten thousand wild camels in Australia. At a cost of around $1500 per camel, prospective farmers can obtain a milking herd delivered to their property. Camels live for 20 years, on average, making them a solid investment.

✱ **Add supporting text for the feature icon.** This feature icon links to a list of dot points. In other web pages, this feature could be a bullet point list, map, instructions, recipe or diagram.

camels, camel milk, dromedary, Dromedairy, camel farming, dairy industry, milk products, dairy products, camel soap, camel products

✱ **Create a list of metadata.** Web pages are indexed by robots that feed keywords to search engines. This metadata includes keywords that help users find the page.

The Australian Farmers' Association
Camelot Camel Dairy
Dromedary Breeders Australia

✱ **Add site links to related websites.** This enables the user to further explore the topic.

Plan your sample on the lines provided.

- **Use a page title that directly relates to the topic.** This is the main name of the web page and should be in a large-sized typeface.
- **Add a background or feature image.** It should relate to the topic and tie the elements of the page together with colour, form and shape, setting the mood of the page.
- **Create a navigation bar.** Provide a menu that allows users to navigate from this page to the others on the website.
- **Write the introductory text** to present the topic. It should provide a clear introduction to the topic. It must contain keywords that search engines will use to determine the site's ranking.
- **Organise the body text with subheadings.** You should use a logical order to present the information. Keep each subheading short, using one for each block of text. Each block should contain information specifically relevant to the topic.
- **Select an image to help illustrate the content.**
- **Add an explanatory caption to the image.**
- **Add a feature icon that is hyperlinked to supporting text with extra details about one aspect of the topic.**
- **Add supporting text for the feature icon.** There are many possibilities for this feature. It could be a bullet point list, as in the sample text, or a map, instructions, recipe or diagram.
- **Create a list of metadata.** Create a list of keywords and specific search terms that will allow users to search for and find the page by topic and content.
- **Add site links to related websites.** Include some useful hyperlinks to related websites that enable the user to explore the topic further.

# UNIT 5 NARRATIVE TEXT

## Recount

## READING WORK

### Meat and greet

I'll never forget the first and only time I shook hands with a Vice Admiral. It was a cold winter and I was undergoing training in the New Entry Officer's course and already I'd been in trouble. Within the first ten minutes on the parade ground, I'd been sent marching back to my room to fix my hair into a neat bun with a hairnet. After breakfast I'd disgraced myself by leaning on a wall while being addressed by my Division Officer. At lunch, I'd walked with my hands in my pockets, another naval no-no. And to top off the day, I'd failed to salute the grass before crossing the field known as the 'quarterdeck'. I didn't know that was a thing. In the navy, everything on land is named and treated as its counterpart on board a ship. Each floor of a building is a 'deck' and our rooms are 'cabins'. The quarterdeck is the area on a ship where it's customary to salute the commanding officer before officially coming aboard.

After my afternoon room inspection, I'd also been reprimanded for daring to make my freezing cold bunk up with an electric blanket I'd brought with me. I'd fixed the bed, making sure that the thin, standard-issue blanket was laid 'blue anchors up'. Then I'd changed out of my grey overalls and into the white dress uniform that had looked so appealing when I was still a civilian. It felt stiff and uncomfortable.

On my way to dinner, I actually remembered to respectfully salute the grass and remove my hat before entering the mess hall. Things were looking up. Now here I was, all buttoned up and seated with a hundred or so other new arrivals and about to be privileged with a visit from some top brass.

Somewhat overawed by the occasion, I meekly took my food tray along to the servery window, where I chose the roasted chicken. After retrieving a highly mobile and insubordinate bread roll that I'd managed to drop from my tray, I trotted off to the nearest table and sat down. Everyone began eating. The chicken was good but a little on the tough side.

Absorbed in enjoying my dinner, I hadn't noticed that the person directly opposite me at the table was the guest of honour, the Vice Admiral himself. He'd humbled himself considerably by taking a seat among the newest recruits. I was having a tricky time cutting up my food. The chicken stubbornly resisted my blunt knife and, to my annoyance, suddenly sent a piece flying off my plate and into oblivion. I glanced around quickly but it was nowhere to be seen. Sneaking a look under the table, I was puzzled as to where it had gone. But no one else had noticed so I let out a grateful little sigh and returned my attention to my plate.

Presently, an order came from the front of the mess hall to introduce ourselves to the dignitaries present. Chairs scraped as we stood up to shake hands. I saw that the Vice Admiral was holding out his hand to me in a gesture of military solidarity. For a moment I stood mesmerised by the gold embroidery on his coat sleeve. I gazed smiling into his steely blue eyes, extended my own hand and instantly discovered that lost piece of chicken. It had shot straight up my stiffly starched uniform sleeve and with impeccable timing had now made its way right into my sweating palm. The Vice Admiral and I shook hands solemnly. He never said a word but he didn't need to. His left eyebrow said it all.

- This is an **attention-grabbing heading** (also a pun on the phrase *meet and greet*).
- The tale is presented in **first person narrative** mode to make its personal nature sound more authentic.
- This identifies an officer of the third-highest rank in the navy.
- The **orientation** is brief and pointed.
- The **context and situation** is established early in the text.
- **The past tense** is used to add some backstory for context.
- This is a **tongue-in-cheek expression,** revealing that the supposed misdemeanour was not taken seriously by the writer.
- This is **naval jargon**, originally referring to part of a ship.
- This **colloquial expression** reflects everyday language.
- The **chronological order of events** provides a simple structure, where each incident is presented in a single paragraph.
- Here we see a **tongue-in-cheek** detail that builds the writer's tone to mock the strict rules and procedures of the military.
- This expression is **naval jargon** for a bed.
- These are **adjectives** used to add detail to factual descriptions.
- This is a **personal comment** expressing the writer's feelings about the situation.
- Here we see a **telescoping device** being used to move the recount forward in time to the main incident being described.
- **Informal language** conveys a general idea rather than an exact number.
- This is a **colloquialism** for high-ranking military officers.
- This is a direct **description of the writer's feelings.**
- This **humorous image** includes a military cliché that makes the bread roll seem at fault rather than the writer.
- This is a **description of physical actions** that can be visualised.
- We are presented with the writer's **personal opinion.**
- This is a **cause and effect connective structure.**
- This is a **personal comment** expressing the writer's feelings.
- This is an example of **hyperbole**, used for humorous effect.
- Humorous and descriptive **visual image** is used to create a visual image that is amusing, given the circumstances.
- This is an expression indicating the **passage of time.**
- This is **military jargon** for the communal eating space.
- This **action verb** provides a precise detail.
- This is a **description of physical details** as well as the author's psychological impressions.
- Another **action verb** is used to convey the scene.
- This **action verb** carries emotional implications.
- This is the **climax** of the anecdote that ends the recount.

# NARRATIVE TEXT

## Recount

**COMPREHENSION WORK**

### Literal questions

*Hint: Read the text carefully to locate specific facts and details.*

**1** What was the first rule relating to personal appearance that was broken by the writer?

- **a** Her hair wasn't properly tied into a bun with a hairnet.
- **b** She was wearing civilian clothes instead of her uniform.
- **c** She was wearing the wrong shoes.

**2** What clothing had the writer been wearing before she changed for the evening meal?

**a** white dress uniform **b** grey overalls **c** jeans and a T-shirt

**3** Summarise the main incident in this recount in one sentence.

______________________________________________

### Interpretive questions

*Hint: These questions require you to combine facts and details to synthesise the meaning.*

**4** What pattern was featured on the standard-issue blanket? ______________________

**5** What idea does this language convey in the text? 'privileged', 'top brass' and 'humbled himself'

______________________________________________

**6** Why did the Vice Admiral raise his eyebrow?

______________________________________________

*Hint: Only one answer option is correct. Use the process of elimination to work through the options.*

**7** What does the phrase 'I chose the roasted chicken' imply?

- **a** that it was tender and perfectly cooked
- **b** that there were other meal choices available
- **c** that the writer had chicken instead of a bread roll

**8** Paragraph five (lines 30–38) is mostly describing which activity?

**a** eating **b** laughing and joking **c** shaking hands

**9** In mentioning the rules about hairstyles, leaning on walls, walking with hands in pockets and failing to salute grass, what is the writer trying to convey about life in the navy?

______________________________________________

**10** How has the writer organised the recount of specific rules she'd broken?

**a** in alphabetical order **b** in reverse order **c** in chronological order

### Applied questions

*Hint: These questions require you to understand a text's implications to infer meaning from the text.*

**11** What does the incident about the electric blanket tell us about regulations in the navy?

- **a** Personal luxuries are not the highest priority in the navy.
- **b** The navy prefers recruits to be cold.
- **c** The navy's regulations are far too relaxed.

**12** Why are various areas and structures on land named after places on board a ship?

______________________________________________

# NARRATIVE TEXT

## SPELLING WORK

### List Words

All of the words in the box below appear in the text 'Meat and greet'.

| | | | | |
|---|---|---|---|---|
| admiral | officially | considerably | grateful | mesmerised |
| parade | respectfully | resisted | dignitaries | impeccable |
| customary | privileged | annoyance | solidarity | solemnly |

### Working with base words

We can use **base words** to help us spell more complex words correctly. Longer, more difficult words can usually be separated into their base word and a prefix or a suffix (sometimes both). A base word is the simplest form of a word within a particular word family. For example, the word *strong* is the base word of the words *stronger*, *strongest* and *strongly*. Try out this strategy in this activity.

**1** Write the base word of these list words.

**a** customary ______________ **b** officially ______________

**c** respectfully ______________ **d** privileged ______________

**e** resisted ______________ **f** annoyance ______________

**g** dignitaries ______________ **h** considerably ______________

**2** Write the missing suffixes for each of the base words in question 1 to make them back into their list word form.

**a** ______ **b** ______ **c** ______ **d** ______ **e** ______ **f** ______ **g** ______ **h** ______

**3** Write two other words from the same family as each of these base words.

**a** consider ______________ ______________

**b** respect ______________ ______________

**4** Correct the spelling of these misspelt list words.

**a** admirel ______________ **b** parrade ______________

**c** greatful ______________ **d** solidarety ______________

**e** priviledged ______________ **f** mezmerized ______________

**g** impeckable ______________ **h** solemly ______________

**5** Below, group together pairs of word fragments to form four list words.

| impecc | offic | par | digni | ially | tarries | able | ade |
|---|---|---|---|---|---|---|---|

**a** ______________ **b** ______________ **c** ______________ **d** ______________

**6** Write these list words out on the lines in alphabetical order.

| parade | officially | respectfully | resisted | privileged | solidarity | solemnly |
|---|---|---|---|---|---|---|

______________________________________________

______________________________________________

# NARRATIVE TEXT

## Recount

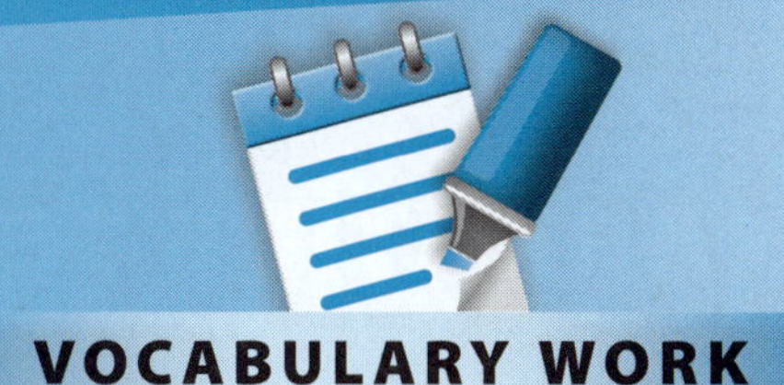

**VOCABULARY WORK**

### Jargon

Some of the vocabulary used in the text 'Meat and greet' refers specifically to military life, which puts it into the category of language we call **jargon**. Jargon is language understood by a particular group of people who do the same job, share the same interests or belong to the same subculture. Jargon includes technical terms that other people outside the specialised group would not understand. The jargon found in this text is related specifically to life in the navy. Some jargon words have become so familiar to us through movies and other media texts that we have learned what they mean without belonging to the specific group from which they originated.

**1** Write definitions for each of the following terms by 'reading around' them in the text. *Hint: The sentence in which a term appears gives you important contextual clues that can help you decipher its meaning.*

a parade ground ______________________

______________________

b Division Officer ______________________

c dress uniform ______________________

______________________

d civilian ______________________

e insubordinate ______________________

f military solidarity ______________________

______________________

An **idiom** is an expression that does not have a literal meaning. Idioms are used by speakers from a particular place, group or time period.

**2** Here are some naval idioms and their meanings. Match them correctly by writing the letters in the appropriate spaces.

| | |
|---|---|
| a a brew | ______ items forbidden on the naval base or ship |
| b bunk | ______ the signal sounded to awaken new recruits |
| c cabin | ______ a cup of tea or coffee |
| d wakey wakey | ______ an inspection of your uniform and personal belongings |
| e the head | ______ a helicopter |
| f squared away | ______ your room |
| g kit muster | ______ neat and tidy |
| h contraband | ______ a medic |
| i helo | ______ a shipboard toilet |
| j scab lifter | ______ a bed |

**3** Write one synonym and one antonym for each of these words from the first paragraph of the text. Look at the context of the words to help you select synonyms that properly reflect the meaning.

| | | | | |
|---|---|---|---|---|
| a first | synonym | ______________ | antonym | ______________ |
| b cold | synonym | ______________ | antonym | ______________ |
| c neat | synonym | ______________ | antonym | ______________ |

**1** Work out which of these words are plural nouns. Write *plural noun* next to your choices.
*Hint: First check that they are actually nouns. Then decide whether or not they are plural.*

**a** admirals ______ **b** customs ______ **c** parading ______
**d** impeccably ______ **e** considers ______ **f** respect ______
**g** resistance ______ **h** gratefully ______ **i** officials ______
**j** privileges ______ **k** annoying ______ **l** indignities ______

**2** Each of these words is grammatically related to a list word. Write the correct list words in the spaces provided.

**a** gratitude ______ **b** disrespect ______
**c** solemnity ______ **d** dignified ______
**e** unofficial ______ **f** admiralty ______

A **collective noun** is a naming word that refers to a group of things rather than a single item. For example, the collective noun for a group of kittens is a *litter* and the collective noun for a group of kangaroos is a *mob.*

**3** This list is in the form of an acrostic. It's formed from the letters of the alphabet in order from A to Z. Use the list of words in the box below to write the correct collective noun in each space to complete the list. The alphabetical sequence of the list will help you. Use the process of elimination to help you with the tricky ones.

| | | | | | | |
|---|---|---|---|---|---|---|
| poems | mosquitoes | aces | jets | zombies | galaxies | quail |
| boats | uniforms | rabbits | knights | trees | cards | lions |
| infants | witches | hay | stormclouds | fish | disease | yarn |
| elephants | voters | owls | x-rays | names | | |

**a** a pair of *aces* **b** a flotilla of ______
**c** a deck of ______ **d** an epidemic of ______
**e** a herd of ______ **f** a school of ______
**g** a cluster of ______ **h** a bale of ______
**i** a crèche of ______ **j** a squadron of ______
**k** an order of ______ **l** a pride of ______
**m** a swarm of ______ **n** a list of ______
**o** parliament of ______ **p** an anthology of ______
**q** a flock of ______ **r** a warren of ______
**s** a bank of ______ **t** a stand of ______
**u** a rack of ______ **v** an electorate of ______
**w** a coven of ______ **x** a file of ______
**y** a skein of ______ **z** a horde of ______

# NARRATIVE TEXT
## Recount

**PUNCTUATION WORK**

### Contractions

**Contractions** are two words that have been joined together to make one word. In contractions, apostrophes show that one or more letters have been left out. For example, *didn't* is the contraction of *did* and *not*. Using contractions makes our writing more informal. It reflects how we pronounce words in conversational language or everyday speech. We can make formal language take on a conversational tone simply by changing the proper forms of words into their contracted forms.

**1** For each of the following, write out the two words that have been contracted.

a wouldn't ______________________ b could've ______________________

c hadn't ______________________ d she'll ______________________

e we'd ______________________ f they're ______________________

g haven't ______________________ h we're ______________________

**2** Answer these multiple-choice questions about contractions. Shade the box to select your answer.

a Which two words form the contraction *they'll*?

☐ she will ☐ he will ☐ they are ☐ they will

b Which two words form the contraction *aren't*?

☐ a not ☐ are not ☐ aren't not ☐ has not

c Which two words form the contraction *I'll*?

☐ I well ☐ I have ☐ I would ☐ I will

d Which contraction is punctuated correctly?

☐ wouldn't ☐ willn't ☐ would'f ☐ woud'nt

e Which contraction is punctuated correctly?

☐ hav'nt ☐ had'nt ☐ hadnt ☐ haven't

**3** Rewrite these sentences using contractions.
*Hint: In some there may be more than one contraction present.*

a We are going to have dinner with the dignitaries who have come to the naval base tonight.

______________________________________________

b There is always a punishment for attending an official event when you are out of uniform.

______________________________________________

c Those recruits are upset because they are not allowed off the base until they have graduated.

______________________________________________

d I have never forgotten that incident with the piece of chicken and I am sure the Vice Admiral has not either.

______________________________________________

# NARRATIVE TEXT

## Recount

**WRITING WORK 1**

### Recounts

A **recount** is a narrative text that retells an incident that happened to the writer in real life. This type of personal recount is also called an **anecdote**. Factual details are important but the purpose of a recount is primarily storytelling, rather than informing. Writers of recounts often make an effort to build a picture of the circumstances in which the main incident occurred. In doing this, they are helping their readers to engage with the topic.

In a recount, the writer's tone is very important. The tone of a text can be summarised as the writer's attitude toward the topic, as revealed by the language they use. Recounts are written for diverse purposes, from conveying entertaining personal anecdotes to publishing serious news stories. Because the recount form is short, the trick to writing good ones is to know what to leave out.

### Structural features of a recount

To write a **good recount**, a writer must:

- write an orientation at the beginning
- organise paragraphs in chronological order (the order of the events in real time)
- ensure that each paragraph details one specific event or aspect of the incident
- create links between paragraphs
- express the resolution within a cause and effect structure
- provide a punchy ending to conclude.

### Language features of recounts

**Language features** commonly used in writing **recounts** include:

- first person past tense mode
- statements describing the writer's personal feelings or impressions
- connective phrases used as links between paragraphs
- emotive language used to build the desired tone
- expressions relating to timing to give the recount forward momentum
- action verbs.

1 What is the main purpose of a recount?

2 In what order should the events be presented?

3 What is one effect created when a writer uses emotive language?

4 How can paragraphs be linked to those before and after them in a recount?

5 Why do you think the writer of the text 'Meat and greet' wrote about other troubles she'd had before the chicken incident?

The text 'Meat and greet' contains a number of specific language features common to recounts that help create a particular tone.

**6** Complete this table by writing the missing content into the white cells.
*Hint: Use the annotations on the original text to help you.*

| Language feature | Example from the text | Contribution to the tone of the text |
|---|---|---|
| pun | Meat and greet | a |
| first person mode | I'll never forget … | b |
| contraction | c | Contractions create an informal tone, making it seem more conversational and enjoyable to read. |
| jargon (specific to the navy) | d | The selective use of naval jargon adds a sense of authenticity to the text, while remaining comprehensive. |
| colloquial language | e | Colloquial language helps the writer achieve a lighthearted tone, which makes the article feel accessible. |
| action verb | sweating | f |
| adjectives | tricky, grateful, impeccable | g |

**7** Descriptive language has an important function: to convey clearly and descriptively a sense of the setting of the text. Look at the text 'Meat and greet' and underline all the adjectives from the second paragraph. List the words you underlined here.

**8** The third paragraph of the text (lines 21–24) has fewer adjectives than the others. Rewrite the third paragraph using more adjectives. Can you see how they add descriptive details to the scene?

# NARRATIVE TEXT

## Recount

**WRITING SAMPLE**

Here is a sample text showing you how to structure and write a recount.

### My freakiest toy

* **Use a heading that captures attention.**

My freakiest toy was a doll I owned when I was four. Even today when I close my eyes I can still see the unnerving, frozen smile on its plastic face and its malevolent, icy stare.

* **Write an orientation to the topic,** including the people, time and things involved in the incident. This one tells us that the recount is about the time when the writer was a small child.

I hated that doll. On the day I'd received it from an elderly aunt, I buried it deep inside my toy box. But its presence still haunted me and I became too frightened to touch anything else in the box in case I accidentally uncovered one of the doll's foul, gleaming blue eyes.

* **Organise each paragraph in chronological order.** The first detail presented here is about the writer receiving the toy. This should logically be the first thing that is explained.

I confided in my elder sister who comforted me. I sobbed hysterically, struggling for breath as I sobbed, 'The eyes. It's the eyes!' She quietly took charge of the situation, removing the ghastly thing from my toy box and hiding it safely away in the toolshed which I rarely ventured to enter. All I had to do was stay clear of the shed.

* **Ensure that each paragraph details one specific event or aspect of the incident.** In this paragraph we read that the writer's sister took action as a result of the events that had happened earlier. This shows a cause and effect relationship that helps link the ideas together.

For a few weeks things improved and I began to relax, although I still thought about the vile doll frequently. But one fine day the evil toy reappeared. I was searching for my bounciest superball under the bed and there, lying face up, piercing eyes glinting at me cruelly, was the horror doll.

* **Present the details of a key aspect of the recount, using first person past tense mode.** The incident described here is significant because the writer thought the doll had been taken away. It implies that the doll has some kind of power of its own, building suspense.

Shrieking until I thought I'd burst my lungs, I fled the room. I was utterly convinced that the doll was out to kill me, or worse, drive me insane. I slept in my parents' room for a week afterwards and resumed sucking my thumb like a baby.

* **Add statements describing your personal feelings or impressions.** Here we read that the writer was terrified. Adjectives add detail and drama to the description.

I was eventually coerced to move back into my own bed after Dad swore on his *Encyclopedia of World War II Aircraft* that he'd destroy the doll the very next morning.

* **Use connective phrases as links between paragraphs.** This paragraph begins with 'I was eventually', linking it to the previous one, and ends with a foreshadowing statement about what was to happen the next morning.

I relented and went cautiously to my room. But just as I went to switch off the lamp, I caught sight of the wretched thing on top of my wardrobe, with its horrid, stubby legs dangling over like two hanged men. I ran screaming from the room and forced my father to take it out to the shed.

* **Employ emotive language to build the desired tone.** The words 'cautiously', 'wretched' and 'horrid' sustain the tone—the writer's attitude toward the topic. The tone here is a combination of genuinely remembered fright and a subtle acknowledgement that children over-dramatise their fears.

The next afternoon, while in the car with my mother, I glanced at the house and there it was. Its beastly, pale face was grinning at me from my bedroom window. When we came home, I locked myself in the bathroom.

* **Use expressions relating to timing so that the recount has forward momentum that keeps the reader engaged.** In this text, we skip to 'the next afternoon' and by the end, weeks have passed.

The next time I saw the nefarious doll, I nearly lost my mind with terror. You see, its eyes were missing. In their place were two revolting and utterly terrifying black holes that had done nothing at all to alter its expression or its evil will toward me. Now it appeared to gaze into my very soul. My sister had well-meaningly poked its eyes out in an effort to make it less terrifying. It had the opposite effect. Now they were rattling around inside its revolting, discoloured head.

* **Use emotive verbs to dramatise the action.** Here we read that the doll's eyes were 'missing' and 'terrifying', and that they gazed into the writer's soul. Details emerge about the doll having its eyes poked out and the eyes rattling around inside its head—all distasteful images that add to the scary effect that such a thing would have on a small child. The negative language used each time the doll is mentioned ('evil', 'revolting') adds humour to lighten the mood.

The horror doll saga finally came to an end when my long-suffering parents decided to burn the thing in the outdoor incinerator. Determined to see it put to death, I stood by the big drum as Dad lit the fire. He threw the doll into the flames and perversely, I risked one last glimpse.

* **Express the outcome of the incident within a cause and effect structure if possible.** Here we see the outcome of the promised destruction of the scary doll and the resolution appears to have been reached.

Too late, I realised it was a mistake. The plastic face had contorted into a monstrous, grinning form, melting in a grotesque parody of a human child. And the hideous black eyeholes were no longer empty. Now they were spewing out flames. The image haunts me to this day.

* **Provide a punchy ending to conclude.** It reveals that the writer will never be completely free of the doll because of childhood memories.

# NARRATIVE TEXT

*Novel*

## COMPREHENSION WORK

### Literal questions

*Hint: Read the text carefully to locate specific facts and details.*

1 What type of seagoing transport did Crusoe have on the island? ____________________

2 What are seven potential food sources found by Crusoe?

____________________

*Hint: Only one answer option is correct. Use the process of elimination to work through the options.*

3 How did Crusoe feel about his discoveries at the brook and meadows?

a confused and disappointed b frightened and homesick c surprised and glad

### Interpretive questions

*Hint: These questions require you to combine facts and details to synthesise the meaning.*

4 Why did Crusoe dry the grapes in the sun?

a because he didn't like grapes b so he could make raisin cakes c so they would keep for a long time

5 What does the word 'opening' mean in the context of line 21?

a unwrapping b a gap between hills c a doorway

6 Which two foods do we know for sure that Crusoe actually tasted or ate in the valley?

a grapes and limes b oranges and apples c lemons and cocoa

*Hint: Only one answer option is correct. Use the process of elimination to work through the options.*

7 What is the setting of the story?

a an island in the year 2057 b an island in the 1700s c an island in the last ice age

8 How do we know that Crusoe has been on the island for some time already?

____________________

____________________

9 What does Crusoe mean by the phrase 'at least not then' in line 32 of the passage?

____________________

10 Why was the valley so green and garden-like?

____________________

### Applied questions

*Hint: This question requires you to understand a text's implications to infer meaning from the text.*

11 On what date does Crusoe discover a valley where lime trees are growing?

a 15th July b 4th July c 16th July

12 Does Crusoe believe he will be rescued soon? Explain your answer.

____________________

____________________

# NARRATIVE TEXT

## SPELLING WORK

### List Words

All of the words in the box below appear in the text 'Crusoe discovers a pleasant vale inland'.

| | | | | |
|---|---|---|---|---|
| cultivation | abundance | island | pleasant | approaching |
| flourishing | surveying | inheritance | delicious | proceeded |
| refreshing | descended | afterwards | wholesome | excellent |

**1** These sentences contain spelling mistakes that have been circled. Write the correct spelling for each word. *Hint: Refer to the list words to help you.*

a Crusoe found orange and lemon trees that were in need of proper **cultevation**. ______________

b The grape vines Crusoe found in the valley were healthy and **fluorishing**. ______________

c The grapes were made into raisins, which were sweet and **delishous**. ______________

d When he had **desended** into the valley, Crusoe stopped to rest. ______________

e Crusoe felt as if he owned the valley as he stood **survaying** it. ______________

f Lime juice can be made into a **reffreshing** drink. ______________

g Crusoe stored up food supplies for the **aproaching** wet season. ______________

**2** Which list words come from these base words?

a cultivate ______________ b fresh ______________

c proceed ______________ d please ______________

e approach ______________ f abound ______________

g flourish ______________ h excel ______________

**3** Write these list words so that the vertical lines ( | ) break them into their syllables. For example, the word *pleasant* has two syllables, *pleas|ant*. *Hint: Every syllable must have a vowel. Prefixes and suffixes should remain intact. Double consonants should be split.*

a cultivation _____ | _____ | _____ | _____ b surveying _____ | _____ | _____

c island _____ | _____ d wholesome _______ | _______

e excellent _____ | _____ | _____ f inheritance _____ | _____ | _____ | _____

**4** Which list word contains a silent *s*? ______________

**5** Which list word contains a silent *w*? ______________

**6** Which two list words contain the vowel blend *ou*? ______________ and ______________

**7** Rewrite this sentence from the text using contractions to make the language sound more modern.

After I had eaten, I went up where I had first brought my rafts on shore.

______________________________________________

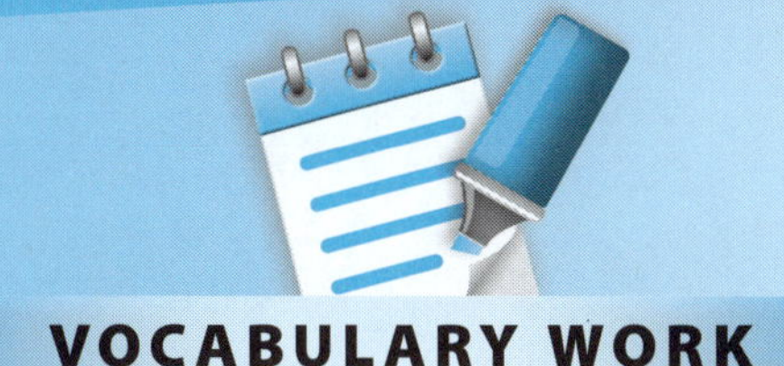

# NARRATIVE TEXT

## Novel

## VOCABULARY WORK

The vocabulary used by Daniel Defoe in his novel *Robinson Crusoe* contains many expressions that appear old-fashioned to us. But we can work out their meaning by the context in which they appear in the text.

**1** Rewrite these expressions so that they are in plain English that modern readers would understand. *Hint: Go back and read each sentence in the context of the passage to determine the meaning.*

**a** One day Crusoe discovered a pleasant vale inland.

______________________________

**b** I began to take a more particular survey of the landscape.

______________________________

**c** I went exploring and happened upon a little brook.

______________________________

**d** I saw several sugar canes, but wild and, for want of cultivation, imperfect.

______________________________

**e** I found melons upon the ground in great abundance.

______________________________

**f** There were many limes and I was exceeding glad of them.

______________________________

**g** I slept not at my habitation that night. ______________________________

**h** This was the first night I had lain from home.

______________________________

**i** Green plants abounded, with everything being in a constant flourish of spring.

______________________________

**j** I resolved to lay up a store of food. ______________________________

### Idioms

An **idiom** is an expression made of a group of words that don't have a literal meaning or have a double meaning. Here are some idioms and their meanings that have been drawn from *Robinson Crusoe*. In the novel, Crusoe finds an indigenous man on the island who voluntarily becomes his helper. Because of the day on which they meet, Crusoe calls him 'Friday'.

**2** To complete each definition, unscramble the letters to form each missing word and write them in the spaces.

| Idiom | Meaning |
|---|---|
| **a** You're not Robinson Crusoe. | You're not ______________. (o n e l a) |
| **b** Only Robinson Crusoe had everything done by Friday. | I can't get my __________ finished on time. (k w o r) |
| **c** … if the worst comes to the worst | … if the worst possibility ______________. (s h a n p e p) |

# NARRATIVE TEXT

## *Novel*

**GRAMMAR WORK**

### Verbs

**Verbs** are words that describe actions. We use verbs in sentences to show what nouns are doing. Simple actions like running, jumping or swimming spring to mind when we think of verbs. But verbs also tell us about more complex activities, like having or being.

**1** Which words in each sentence are verbs, including auxiliary (helper) verbs? Underline them.

a Mary had stepped close to the robin, and suddenly the gust of wind swung aside some loose ivy trails.

b It was because it had been shut up so long that she wanted to see it.

c She put her hands under the leaves and began to pull and push them aside.

d She put her hand in her pocket, drew out the key and found it fitted the keyhole.

e She took a long breath and looked behind her up the long walk to see if anyone was coming.

f No one ever did come, it seemed, and she took another long breath, because she could not help it.

g Then she slipped through it and shut it behind her.

### Auxiliary verbs

Verbs can be modified (have their meaning changed or clarified) by auxiliaries, or helper verbs such as *do*, *is* and *have*. In this way **auxiliary verbs** enable verbs to be used in different tenses—past, present and future. Many past tense verbs end in *ed*.

**2** Write the antonyms of these auxiliary verbs. Then write them in their contracted forms.
*Hint: One has been done to show you what to do.*

| | Antonyms | Contracted forms |
|---|---|---|
| a will | will not | won't |
| b should | ______ | ______ |
| c are | ______ | ______ |
| d have | ______ | ______ |
| e is | ______ | ______ |
| f were | ______ | ______ |
| g did | ______ | ______ |
| h does | ______ | ______ |
| i might | ______ | ______ |
| j can | ______ | ______ |

**3** Choose the correct spaces for these words.

| Past tense | Present tense |
|---|---|
| a was | ______ |
| c ______ | does |
| e did | is ______ |

| Past tense | Present tense |
|---|---|
| b were | ______ |
| d had | ______ |

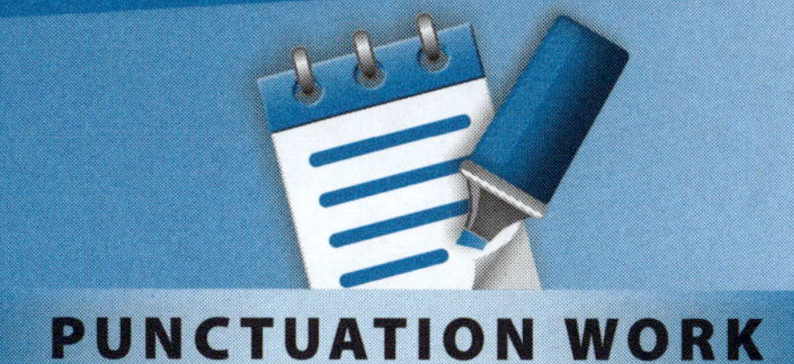

# NARRATIVE TEXT

## Novel

## PUNCTUATION WORK

The **contraction** *it's* means 'it is'. This is different to the possessive pronoun *its*. If you aren't sure which one to use, try reading the sentence and replacing the word *its* with *it is*. If it makes sense, then add the apostrophe.

**1** Circle the correct word in the brackets to complete these sentences. *Hint: Possessive pronouns (*his, hers, yours, its*) do not need apostrophes.*

- **a** *Robinson Crusoe* shows us that living as a castaway has (it's / its) advantages and disadvantages.
- **b** The popularity of the novel is because of (it's / its) exploration of the human will to survive against all odds.
- **c** (It's / Its) a strange but true fact that the novel is actually based on a true story involving Alexander Selkirk.
- **d** (It's / Its) believed that Selkirk spent four years living as a castaway in the Juan Fernández Islands off Chile.
- **e** He had fears for the safety of the ship due to (it's / its) many leaks and asked to be left behind on an island.
- **f** Selkirk's fears were justified, as the ship sank in later months, drowning many of (it's / its) crew.
- **g** The story lent some of (it's / its) details about Selkirk's survival techniques to the novel *Robinson Crusoe.*

**Plurals** do not need apostrophes unless they are showing ownership.

*Hint: When showing possession with an apostrophe, check to see how many things are involved.*

**2** Decide whether the bold words are plurals (with no apostrophe needed) or possessives. Circle *plural* or *possessive* for each one. *Hint: Use the context to help you.*

| | | | |
|---|---|---|---|
| **a** | The door to the secret garden was covered by **vines**. | Plural | Possessive |
| **b** | The key had been hidden for many **years**. | Plural | Possessive |
| **c** | A decade of neglect had made the garden overgrown with **weeds**. | Plural | Possessive |
| **d** | Nothing could ruin the **childrens** delight at finding the garden. | Plural | Possessive |
| **e** | **Marys** discovery of the door left her breathless with excitement. | Plural | Possessive |
| **f** | The door would've remained undiscovered without the **robins** help. | Plural | Possessive |

**3** Complete these plurals, applying the rules about apostrophes to decide whether the *s* is added before or after the last letter of the base word. Indicate where the *s* is added by circling *before the last letter* or *after the last letter.*

| | | | |
|---|---|---|---|
| **a** | the joy of the two girls discovery (two girls) | Before the last letter | After the last letter |
| **b** | the little birds nest (one bird) | Before the last letter | After the last letter |
| **c** | the boys name (one boy) | Before the last letter | After the last letter |
| **d** | the fruit trees leaves (three fruit trees) | Before the last letter | After the last letter |

Answer these multiple-choice questions by ticking the correct box.

**4** In the text 'Crusoe finds a pleasant vale inland' the words *Robinson Crusoe* are in italics because

☐ they have a special pronunciation. ☐ they are from another language. ☐ they are a title.

**5** In the text, the publication date of the book is written

☐ in italics. ☐ in parentheses. ☐ in capital letters.

**6** In the text the names of the fruits Crusoe finds do not begin with capital letters because

☐ they are proper nouns. ☐ they are not proper nouns. ☐ they are verbs.

# NARRATIVE TEXT
## *Novel*

**WRITING WORK 1**

### Novels

A common form of narrative text is the **novel**. Novels are works of fiction written to present the author's ideas, feelings and attitudes about particular topics. Authors write novels with the aim of provoking us to think about particular themes and become emotionally involved with the story.

### Structural features of a novel

Novels are written according to certain conventions. They contain the following structural features:

- a title
- chapters that separate the story into sections, which may have their own titles
- a plot: the main storyline composed of events that happen to the character (including an introduction, conflict, complication, climax and resolution)
- a setting: the place and time where the events happen
- characters: the main character and other major and minor characters
- a theme: the key aim, message, moral or point the author delivers through the novel.

Novelists tell stories about fictitious (made-up) events that happen to one or more characters. A character is any figure in the novel that has a distinct personality, aims, hopes and the ability to think and reason. Characters are not always humans—they can be animals, fantasy creatures or even objects.

The main character of a novel is called the protagonist. Sometimes the protagonist has an enemy that has opposing aims and motives; this figure is usually called the antagonist. Characters can interact with one another in novels through dialogue (written conversation).

1 What does the term *plot* mean? ______________________________

______________________________

2 What two elements make up the setting of a novel? ______________________________

3 Write a definition of the word *theme*. ______________________________

______________________________

4 What do we call the sections into which most novels are separated? ______________________________

### Language features of a novel

We can analyse an author's style of creating **language features** in a **novel**. Some language features found in novels are:

- a sequence of events that happen to the main character
- the telescoping of time
- foreshadowing or flashbacks
- often, a narrator who tells the story using first person mode
- descriptive language
- imagery, often used to describe the physical setting
- emotive language
- a particular mood, often determined by the setting
- details about the characters
- direct speech and dialogue through which characters communicate
- symbolism
- figurative language
- tone—the writer's attitude toward the subject of the novel that helps convey the theme.

# NARRATIVE TEXT

## *Novel*

**WRITING WORK 2**

The text 'Crusoe discovers a pleasant vale inland' contains a number of specific language features that are commonly found in novels.

**5** Complete this table by writing the missing content in the blank cells. *Hint: Use the annotations on the original text to help you.*

| Language feature | Example from the text |
|---|---|
| **a** emotive language | |
| **b** precise date | |
| **c** visual description of the vines | |
| **d** chapter title | |
| **e** foreshadowing statement | |

**6** Re-read the text 'Crusoe discovers a pleasant vale inland' and write a descriptive summary of these three structural features in the text.

**a** The plot: ______________________________

______________________________

**b** The setting: ______________________________

______________________________

**c** The protagonist: ______________________________

______________________________

**7** Organise these features of the text in the correct columns in the table below.

| | | | | | |
|---|---|---|---|---|---|
| aim | introduction | place | minor | antagonist | climax |
| mood | message | time | conclusion | tone | conflict |
| moral | protagonist | imagery | dialogue | | |

| Plot features | Setting features | Character features | Theme features |
|---|---|---|---|
| | | | |
| | | | |
| | | | |
| | | | |

# NARRATIVE TEXT

## *Novel*

### WRITING SAMPLE

Here is a sample text showing you the structure of an extract from a novel. This extract comes from *The Secret Garden* by Frances Hodgson Burnett. The protagonist, not named until late in this extract, is Mary.

She looked at the key quite a long time. She turned it over and over, and thought about it.

* **Present the main conflict.** In this text the writer has used a symbol to do so. The key symbolises Mary's chance to experience freedom from the confines of her restricted life.

It was because it had been shut up so long that she wanted to see it. It seemed as if it must be different from other places and that something strange must have happened to it during ten years.

* **Use repetition to add emphasis.** Here we see the word 'it' used to refer to the secret garden. The repetition of the word indicates that the garden fills Mary's thoughts.

Besides that, if she liked it she could go into it every day and shut the door behind her

* **Use connectives to link paragraphs together.** The connective phrase 'besides that' links the two paragraphs.

and she could make up some play of her own and play it quite alone, because nobody would ever know where she was, but would think the door was still locked and the key buried in the earth. The thought of that pleased her very much.

* **Use varied language in creating repetition.** The idea of Mary's desire to be alone is repeated, using a variety of words and phrases, including 'her own', 'quite alone' and 'nobody would ever know'.

One of the nice little gusts of wind rushed down the walk, and it was a stronger one than the rest. It was strong enough to wave the branches of the trees, and it was more than strong enough to sway the trailing sprays of untrimmed ivy hanging from the wall.

* **Provide sensory descriptions** to describe the gust of wind and the movement of the trees and vines, creating visual and tactile images. This adds details that help us imagine the setting.

Mary had stepped close to the robin, and suddenly the gust of wind swung aside some loose ivy trails, and more suddenly still she jumped toward it and caught it in her hand. This she did because she had seen something under it—a round knob which had been covered by the leaves hanging over it. It was the knob of a door.

* **Develop suspense.** Here suspense is created by the use of complex sentences at the start of the paragraph, followed by a simple sentence that contrasts markedly with what has come before it. The pace abruptly shifts from fast to a sudden halt when Mary discovers the door knob.

She put her hands under the leaves and began to pull and push them aside. Thick as the ivy hung, it nearly all was a loose and swinging curtain, though some had crept over wood and iron.

* **Enrich details with verbs and adjectives.** There are contrasts between the thickness but looseness of the ivy, and the textures of the leaves against wood and iron. Try to engage multiple senses as you create descriptions.

What was this under her hands which was square and made of iron and which her fingers found a hole in?

* **Use indirect description to add variety.** Here the character's unspoken thoughts are used as a form of indirect description of the object she is discovering.

It was the lock of the door which had been closed ten years and she put her hand in her pocket, drew out the key and found it fitted the keyhole. She put the key in and turned it. It took two hands to do it, but it did turn.

* **Refer back to an earlier plot detail.** Here the detail is in relation to the mention of a time 'ten years' earlier in the passage, signalling a resolution to the conflict about the lost garden that Mary desperately wants to enter.

And then she took a long breath and looked behind her up the long walk to see if anyone was coming. No one was coming. No one ever did come, it seemed, and she took another long breath, because she could not help it, and she held back the swinging curtain of ivy and pushed back the door which opened slowly—slowly.

* **Create smooth transitions between paragraphs.** This paragraph is connected with the previous one using the conjunction 'and', giving the impression that these actions taken by the character are continuous and hurried. The repetition in the phrases 'anyone was coming', 'no one was coming', and 'no one ever did come' tells us the character's thoughts. This builds suspense, which is brought to a climax by the last line, again featuring repetition, this time the word 'slowly', contrasting with the rapid pace established earlier.

Then she slipped through it, and shut it behind her, and stood with her back against it, looking about her and breathing quite fast with excitement, and wonder and delight.

* **Employ emotive language to elicit a response from the reader.** Here, the emotive words 'excitement', 'wonder' and 'delight' reveal the reaction of the character to the events.

She was standing inside the secret garden.

* **Present a resolution to the central conflict.** In this text, the final line solves the problem of being unable to find the garden and learn its secrets. Because it is not at the end of the novel, it isn't completely satisfactory, as the reader must wait for the final resolution of the various conflicts.

# NARRATIVE TEXT

*Novel*

## WRITING YOUR OWN SAMPLE

Plan your sample on the lines provided.

- **Present the main conflict.** You could introduce it using a symbol—a specific item that represents something more complex.
- **Use repetition to add emphasis.** Repetition can be created among words, phrases, ideas and events. You can also use repetition to convey the thoughts and feelings of characters.
- **Use connectives to link paragraphs together.** Connective words and phrases help create a sense of unity and coherence across the text.
- **Use varied language in creating repetition.** Rather than simply repeating words, consider using a variety of words and phrases to achieve this effect.
- **Provide sensory descriptions.** This allows you to add details that help the reader imagine the setting.
- **Develop suspense.** You can do this through sentence structure as well as your choice of words. Using complex sentences at the start of the paragraph followed by a simple sentence can create suspense effectively.
- **Enrich details with verbs and adjectives.** Try to engage multiple senses as you create descriptions.
- **Use indirect description to add variety.**
- **Refer back to an earlier plot detail.**
- **Create smooth transitions between paragraphs.** This can produce a range of effects, including suspense.
- **Employ emotive language to elicit a response from the reader.**
- **Present a resolution to the central conflict.** Remember: because this text is not a complete novel you will only be able to present a partial resolution of the conflict presented in this sample passage.

UNIT 7

# NARRATIVE TEXT

## Ballad

**READING WORK**

This famous poem by Henry Lawson is a ballad—a storytelling poem with a regular structure and rhythm that allows it to be spoken or sung.

### Andy's Gone with Cattle

Our Andy's gone with cattle now—
Our hearts are out of order—
With drought he's gone to battle now
Across the Queensland border.

He's left us in dejection now,
Our thoughts with him are roving;
It's dull on this selection now,
Since Andy went a-droving.

Who now shall wear the cheerful face
In times when things are slackest?
And who shall whistle round the place
When Fortune frowns her blackest?

Oh, who shall cheek the squatter* now
When he comes round us snarling?
His tongue is getting hotter now
Since Andy crossed the Darling.

Oh, may the showers in torrents fall
And all the tanks run over;
And may the grass grow green and tall
In pathways of the drover;

And may good angels send the rain
On desert stretches sandy;
And when the summer comes again
God grant 'twill bring us Andy.

*Henry Lawson*

- The **repetition** of the pronoun 'our' emphasises Andy's belonging within the community united in their concern for him.
- The **repetition** of 'now' at the end of some lines establishes the ballad's structure. The rhyme scheme is ABAB.
- **Symbolism** is used to establish the conflict.
- A place name establishes the **setting**.
- A **colloquialism** is used to reflect the speech of the people of the time.
- This term, used in the colonial period to describe a landholding, helps establish the era.
- A **colloquialism** is used to reflect the speech of the people of the time.
- This is the first of a series of **rhetorical questions** designed to describe Andy's personality and his contribution to life on the selection.
- Here we see an **emotive term** ('cheerful') describing Andy's personality, his appearance and the sound of his whistling and cheek toward the squatter.
- Fortune is **personified** as an angry and volatile woman.
- This is an appeal to **assumed knowledge** about the role of squatters in Australia's colonial past that intensifies the potential for conflict.
- This is a **zoomorphism**—the squatter is characterised as a wild dog.
- A **metaphor** is used to describe the squatter's angry tirades, extending the idea of heat and drought established earlier in the poem.
- This mention of the Darling river is another geographical reference to indicate **setting**.
- This is a prayer of blessing that expresses the typical wishes of people living on the land.
- The showers and grass are **natural images** that emphasise the significance of the weather in the outback.
- The **alliteration** of the 's' sound emphasises the dryness of the sand.
- Here we see a **contrast** between the rain and the dry, sandy desert.
- This is a **poetic contraction** of the phrase 'it will'.
- The poem **ends** with a wish that links Andy's safe return with the change of seasons.

*squatter—In this context, a livestock grazier who operated on a large scale and controlled the activities of smaller farmers. Squatters were often involved in disputes over land with 'selectors', such as Andy's family in this poem.

# NARRATIVE TEXT
## *Ballad*

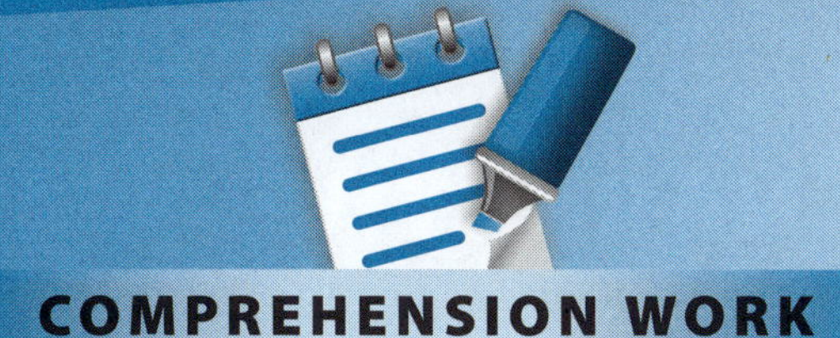

COMPREHENSION WORK

### Literal questions

*Hint: Read the text carefully to locate specific facts and details.*

**1** What is the occupation of Andy, the person who is the focus of the poem?

**a** a squatter  **b** a jockey  **c** a drover

**2** What weather-related disaster is mentioned in the poem?

**a** a bushfire  **b** a draft  **c** a drought

**3** What is a 'squatter'?

______________________________

### Interpretive questions

*Hint: These questions require you to combine facts and details to synthesise the meaning.*

**4** Which word in line 23 of the poem suggests that the name 'Andy' will be mentioned in the last line?

______________________________

**5** What is the setting (the place and time period) of the poem?

______________________________

**6** Based on the content of the poem, how might Andy be described physically?

______________________________

*Hint: Only one answer option is correct. Use the process of elimination to work through the options.*

**7** What is the mood dominating the first half (lines 2–13) of the poem?

**a** dejection  **b** joy  **c** surprise

______________________________

**8** What is Henry Lawson implying about how people living on the land viewed drovers, using Andy as a character that represents them?

______________________________

**9** Which of these people is the poem's speaker most likely to be?

**a** a relative of Andy's  **b** an angel  **c** Andy

**10** The poem is presented in two distinct phases. At which line does the focus move from sorrows to hopes?

**a** line 5  **b** line 18  **c** line 25

### Applied questions

*Hint: This question requires you to understand a text's implications to infer meaning from the text.*

**11** Which group of needs appears to have been most important to drovers and their families?

**a** water and feed for livestock  **b** jokes and dealing with the squatter  **c** money and holidays

*Hint: These questions require you to read between the lines to infer meaning from the text.*

**12** What is the impression of livestock farming in Australia conveyed by this poem?

______________________________

# NARRATIVE TEXT
## *Ballad*

SPELLING WORK

### List Words

All of the words in the box below relate to poetry.

| | | | | |
|---|---|---|---|---|
| ballad | stanza | structure | rhetorical | repetition |
| poetry | rhythm | colloquial | personification | alliteration |
| imagery | rhyme | emotive | metaphor | symbolism |

**1** Which word correctly completes the sentence? For each one, unscramble the letters in parentheses and write the word in the space provided.

**a** Poets who write ________________ are known as balladeers. (ladbals)

**b** Poems can be written with a particular pattern of stressed syllables, which forms its ________________. (myhrht)

**c** Words at the ends of lines with the same vowel sound and consonant patterns ________________. (emryh)

**d** The word ________________ is used to describe techniques that help us form pictures in our minds. (magiery)

**e** Words that express feelings in poetry are said to be ________________. (motivee)

**f** A slang or informal term associated with a particular place is called ________________ language. (quoollical)

**2** Transform these list words into other forms and write them in the table.

| List word | Singular base word | Plural base word |
|---|---|---|
| poetry | poem | **e** |
| rhythm | rhythm | **f** |
| imagery | **c** | images |
| repetition | **d** | repeats |
| **a** | symbol | symbols |
| **b** | emotion | **g** |

**3** Fill in the missing vowels to complete words ending in *al* related to the list words.

**a** meta_ _oric_ _ **b** rhythm_ _ _ _ **c** struct_ _ _ _ **d** emotion_ _ _

**4** Use these word fragments to make six list words.

| | | | | | | |
|---|---|---|---|---|---|---|
| ery | bal | rep | rhetor | stan | ry | |
| za | ical | tion | poet | eti | imag | ad |

________________________ ________________________

________________________ ________________________

________________________ ________________________

# NARRATIVE TEXT

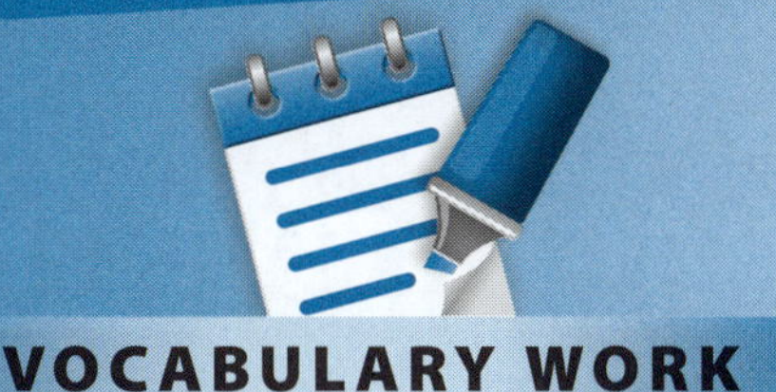

## VOCABULARY WORK

**1** Write the meanings of these words from the text 'Andy's gone with cattle'.

**a** cattle ____________________

**b** drought ____________________

**c** roving ____________________

**d** cheerful ____________________

**e** torrents ____________________

**f** squatter ____________________

**2** Choose the correct spelling of the word. Tick one box in each set to make your selections.

| | | | | | |
|---|---|---|---|---|---|
| **a** | drout ☐ | drought ☐ | **b** | wistle ☐ | whistle ☐ |
| **c** | slackest ☐ | slackist ☐ | **d** | frowns ☐ | frouns ☐ |
| **e** | angels ☐ | angles ☐ | **f** | roving ☐ | roveing ☐ |
| **g** | cheerful ☐ | cheerful ☐ | **h** | snaling ☐ | snarling ☐ |
| **I** | degection ☐ | dejection ☐ | **j** | battle ☐ | battel ☐ |

**3** Which of these words appears in the poem 'Andy's gone with cattle'? *Hint: Both are real words but only one in each set appears in the poem.*

| | | | | | |
|---|---|---|---|---|---|
| **a** | hearts ☐ | harts ☐ | **b** | reign ☐ | rain ☐ |
| **c** | boarder ☐ | border ☐ | **d** | dessert ☐ | desert ☐ |
| **e** | shall ☐ | shell ☐ | **f** | now ☐ | know ☐ |

An **idiom** is an expression that people from particular groups or areas use among themselves. Idioms cannot be interpreted literally. They make use of figurative language. Australians are well known for their odd idioms, many of which came from the activities of Europeans in the 1800s.

**4** Match these idioms with their definitions by writing in the correct letters.

**a** waltzing matilda ________ very thirsty

**b** stone the crows ________ a substitute

**c** a ring-in ________ trekking through bushland with a swag (roll of bedding) on your back

**d** in the mulga ________ honest; genuine

**e** fair dinkum ________ in rough country (actually a type of tree)

**f** dry as a drover's dog' ________ an exclamation of astonishment

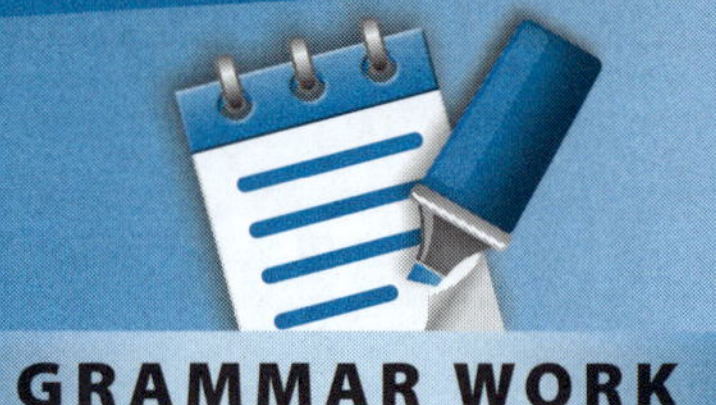

# NARRATIVE TEXT
## *Ballad*

**GRAMMAR WORK**

**Adverbs** add further meaning to verbs, telling how, when, where and why things are happening. They often end with the suffix *ly*.

**1** Change these base words to adverbs by adding *ly*.

**a** cheerful ____________ **b** thoughtful ____________

**c** bright ____________ **d** quiet ____________

**e** wild ____________ **f** mild ____________

**g** apparent ____________ **h** stubborn ____________

**i** proper ____________ **j** hopeless ____________

**k** real ____________ **l** clear ____________

**m** excited ____________ **n** obviously ____________

Some base words ending in *e* must keep the letter *e* when the suffix *ly* is added.

**2** Change these words into adverbs using the suffix *ly* and keeping the letter *e* of the base word.

**a** fierce ____________ **b** definite ____________

**c** nice ____________ **d** brave ____________

**e** large ____________ **f** precise ____________

**3** Double the last consonant of these words to make them into adverbs ending with *ly*.

**a** brutal ____________ **b** dismal ____________

**c** gradual ____________ **d** occasional ____________

**e** eventual ____________ **f** hopeful ____________

We use **conjunctions** to join parts of sentences. They link one idea with another to provide a logical flow to a sentence. Some conjunctions force one part of a sentence to depend on another part. These may be words or phrases and are called **connectives**.

**4** Underline the connectives in these sentences.

**a** Although there's been very little rain, we'll still get a reasonable harvest this season.

**b** My cows, unlike my neighbour's, are very fit and healthy.

**c** Our water tanks are full this summer but last summer they were bone dry for months on end.

**d** Despite the struggles involved in making a living from the land, we're making it work somehow.

**e** Beef cattle farmers raise livestock for meat, whereas dairy farmers raise them for milk.

# NARRATIVE TEXT

## *Ballad*

**PUNCTUATION WORK**

### Sentences

A **sentence** is a group of words that expresses a complete idea, feeling or thought. Sentences usually have a subject, a verb and an object. A sentence begins with a capital letter and has one of three possible ending marks: a full stop, a question mark or an exclamation mark.

**1** Correct the punctuation of these sentences by rewriting them.

**a** in past times, drovers took herds of Cattle, on long journeys to find better grass for Grazing?

______________________________

**b** Why do australian farmers stay working the Land when there is so little rainfall!

______________________________

**c** henry Lawson was a bush poet and Journalist who wrote a number of poems about drovers

______________________________

**d** We never heard whether or not andy came home safely from his travels

______________________________

**e** the darling is the river mentioned in the poem andy's gone with cattle.

______________________________

**2** What style of text do we use to present the title of a poem? ______________________________

**3** List all the proper nouns that have their first letter capitalised in the text 'Andy's gone with cattle'.

______________________________

**4** Work through the poem and look at the punctuation marks you find after each of these words. Complete the table by marking the symbols and names of each mark.

| Place in the text | Symbol of punctuation mark | Name of punctuation mark |
|---|---|---|
| **a** after the first occurrence of the word 'now' | | |
| **b** after the first occurrence of the word 'border' | | |
| **c** after the second occurrence of the word 'now' | | |
| **d** after the first occurrence of the word 'roving' | | |
| **e** after the word 'slackest' | | |
| **f** after the word 'squatter' | | |
| **g** at the first letter of the word 'Darling' | | |
| **h** before the word ''twill' | | |

# NARRATIVE TEXT
## *Ballad*

**WRITING WORK 1**

**Poetry** is classified in three major categories: lyrical, dramatic and narrative. Ballads fall into the category of narrative poetry.

### Structural features of narrative poetry

**Narrative poems** have specific characteristics that set them apart from other forms of poetry. They include:

- a narrator (or 'speaker')
- a setting (place and time)
- a basic plot (a description of an incident)
- one or two characters.

### General features of a ballad

The **ballad** form of narrative poetry has its own unique features, including:

- organisation into stanzas (verses) of even length
- a metered verse structure (with a regular pattern of rhythm and a clear rhyme scheme)
- presentation in the third person mode
- a dramatic climax or ending
- a sense of the passage of time.

### Language features in ballads

**Balladeers** employ a range of **poetic techniques** to create meaning in their works, including:

- similes and metaphors
- alliteration and assonance
- personification and zoomorphism
- rhythm and rhyme
- emotive language
- colloquial language
- jargon
- symbolism
- contrast.

Considering these features of narrative poetry and of ballads specifically, answer these questions.

**1** What three features do ballads have in common with regular stories?

______________________________________________

**2** What effect does the simple rhyming pattern have on the poem as a whole?

______________________________________________

______________________________________________

**3** Which of the following statements best describes the poet's purpose for the text 'Andy's Gone with Cattle'? Tick one.

- ☐ The poet intends to tell a story through poetry.
- ☐ The writer intends to inform readers about the lives of modern drovers.
- ☐ The writer intends to persuade readers to protest about the difficult lives lead by rural workers.

**4** Which of the following statements best describes the theme of 'Andy's Gone with Cattle'? Tick one.

- ☐ the hardships of life on the land
- ☐ the fact that drovers are really nice people
- ☐ the tragedy of a drover's death

# NARRATIVE TEXT

## *Ballad*

WRITING WORK 2

The text 'Andy's gone with cattle' contains a number of poetic language features that create specific effects.

**5** Complete this table by writing examples from the poem in the cells in the 'Example' column.
*Hint: Use the annotations on the original text to help you.*

| | Language feature | Definition | Example |
|---|---|---|---|
| Imagery | alliteration | repetition of consonant sounds that are identical or similar in sequences of words positioned closely together | **a** |
| | zoomorphism | attributing animal qualities to humans for poetic effect | **b** |
| | personification | attributing human qualities to non-human things for poetic effect | **c** |
| Structure | rhyme scheme | the pattern formed by the rhyming words in a poem (usually at the ends of lines) | **d** |
| Other poetic language features | emotive language | words that are associated with feelings and evoke strongly felt responses | **e** |
| | jargon | specialised language that pertains to a particular field | **f** |
| | colloquialism | informal language used in everyday speech, like slang | **g** |
| | contrast | presentation of two opposite ideas to emphasise the differences between them | **h** |

**6** Ballads are narrative poems designed to be spoken aloud as a way of storytelling. Write a short diary entry in which you narrate the story of Andy's return from droving. Imagine the events that unfold upon his return home. Then read your diary entry out loud to an audience.

# NARRATIVE TEXT

## Ballad

**WRITING SAMPLE**

Here is a sample text showing you how to structure and write a ballad.

### The *Alice Jean*

✱ **Use the title to specify the topic of the poem.** The subject matter of Robert Graves's poem is mysterious.

One moonlit night a ship drove in,
  A ghost ship from the west,
Drifting with bare mast and lone tiller;
  Like a mermaid drest
In long green weed and barnacles
  She beached and came to rest.

✱ **Write an even number of stanzas.** This is a structure common to the ballad form. This ballad is composed of six stanzas of even length. A simile refers to a mythical figure (a mermaid) creating a vivid mental image that deepens the sense of mystery about the fate of those lost at sea. Assonance is present in the form of long vowel sounds ('oh', 'ah', 'oo' and 'er'), representing eerie sounds. The emotionally evocative image of a 'ghost ship' makes us wonder if the ship is haunted.

All the watchers of the coast
  Flocked to see the sight;
Men and women streaming down
  Through the summer night,
Found her standing tall and ragged
  Beached in the moonlight.

✱ **Create a regular rhyme scheme.** The rhyme scheme here is ABCBDB, which creates a lulling rhythm that mimics the sound of the ocean waves. Sea imagery is used to describe the movements of the people to see the ship ('watchers of the coast', 'flocked', 'streaming down'), establishing a consistent mood.

Then one old woman looked and wept:
  'The *Alice Jean*? But no!
The ship that took my Dick from me
  Sixty years ago
Drifted back from the utmost west
  With the ocean's flow?

✱ **Use direct speech to provide the backstory.** The words of the old woman are presented in this and the next stanza to add a sense of drama and immediacy while revealing the backstory: her husband and his crew were lost at sea sixty years earlier. Direct speech is indicated by single quotation marks. In the next stanza, another opening quotation mark is used to show that she is still speaking.

'Caught and caged in the weedy pool
  Beyond the western brink,
Where crewless vessels lie and rot
  In waters black as ink,
Torn out again by a sudden storm—
  Is it the Jean, you think?'

✱ **Add details that contribute clues to the meaning.** In this stanza, the woman offers a possible explanation for what caused the ship to return, but the mystery remains about what happened to the crew. An allusion refers to fabled ships' graveyards in the most remote and unexplored parts of the ocean. Allusions allow you to communicate meaning using few words. Sensory imagery such as a simile creates strong visual impressions. Here we have a vivid picture of the sea.

A hundred women stared agape,
  The menfolk nudged and laughed,
But none could find a likelier story
  For the strange craft
With fear and death and desolation
  Rigged fore and aft.

✱ **Create personification to add drama.** Here the personifying of the ship's rigging with 'fear and death and desolation' implies that the sea will never yield all of its secrets to humans. Jargon is drawn from the nautical world—'fore and aft' implying that from beginning to end, the story will remain a mystery. Emotive language—the words 'strange', 'fear' and 'desolation'—contrasts with the laughter of the menfolk, telling us that the speaker feels the woman might be right.

The blind ship came forgotten home
  To all but one of these,
Of whom none dared to climb aboard her:
  And by and by the breeze
Sprang to a storm and the *Alice Jean*
  Foundered in frothy seas.

✱ **Pay close attention to diction.** The choice of words is critical in ballads, where the structure is tight and you need to be economical with words. The use of the phrase 'blind ship' suggests that the *Alice Jean* is under the control of mysterious forces. In a gripping conclusion to end the ballad the speaker resolves the mystery by naming the ship as the *Alice Jean* when it finally sinks in a storm.

*Robert Graves*

✱ **The poet's name**

# NARRATIVE TEXT

## Ballad

**WRITING YOUR OWN SAMPLE**

Plan your sample on the lines provided.

- **Use the title to specify the topic of the poem.**
- **Write an even number of stanzas.** This will ensure that your poem is clearly set out in the structure of a ballad. Create a simile to create a strong sensory image that enables the reader to develop a vivid impression in their mind or you could use another sound device. Use a visual image to create an emotive effect.
- **Create a regular rhyme scheme.** This can help you to illustrate the topic. Use a specific type of imagery appropriate to the topic. This helps to establish a consistent mood in the poem.
- **Use direct speech to provide the backstory.** This adds a sense of immediacy and provides background context in an economical manner.
- **Add details that contribute clues to the meaning.** Where the meaning is unclear, help the reader grasp it by offering clues or direct explanation where appropriate. Use an allusion to communicate meaning using few words. Use sensory imagery such as a simile to create strong visual impressions.
- **Create personification to add drama.** Employ specialised language such as jargon. Use emotive language. Create effects such as contrast, while eliciting emotional responses.
- **Pay close attention to diction.** The choice of words is critical in ballads, where the structure is tight and you need to be economical with words. Create a gripping conclusion to end the ballad; the conflict should be resolved at the end.
- **The poet's name:** write your name and take credit for your hard work.

UNIT 8

# NARRATIVE TEXT

## *Biography and autobiography*

**READING WORK**

### Bad Swedish

My father's first posting for the Union of Geological Sciences was to Sweden. It was a two-year contract, so we—his family of two boys, myself and our mother—leased our home, put most of our belongings into storage and went with him. We knew Dad would be travelling on his lecture tours and may not be with us all the time but we had never been out of our own country before and we were excited about the adventures to come.

Dad's first lecture was booked for the second morning of our arrival in the city of Uppsala. He'd asked us to attend and give him a critique on his performance. He told us he was nervous and needed a bit of moral support, which surprised Mum as he'd spoken in front of large audiences many times at home. Mum and I had our hair done nicely for the occasion and by eleven we'd taken our seats several rows back in the packed auditorium. Mum had convinced my brothers to come with the promise of a good feed afterwards.

As Dad took to the stage, I was feeling rather proud of him. He looked very composed and dignified. I was confident that he knew his subject very well. Little did I know that my optimism was unwarranted. Dad began his lecture by saying a few words of greeting in Swedish. We were quite impressed but I remember thinking that his pronunciation must've been slightly lacking because his words brought loud laughter and a few boos from the listeners. Some people could still be heard tittering as the lecture went on. When Dad sat down I saw the host lean over and whisper something to him. Until that day I'd never seen my father blush so deeply.

We met up with Dad at one of the cafés on campus later that day. I asked him why the audience had laughed at his introductory comments in Swedish. He sheepishly told us that he was trying to impress the audience with his language skills and thought he'd start by saying 'Good morning, ladies and gentlemen' in Swedish. He'd heard the phrase 'God morgon' before, so on the way to the lecture, he'd simply memorised the words from the signs on the restroom doors to complete his prepared greeting.

'When I stood up and gave that greeting,' he told us, 'what I actually said, as the host told me later, was "Good morning, toilets and urinals".' Thankfully my father's lecture tours went very well after he'd picked up a bit more of the language and today he's remembered as an expert in his field.

- The **orientation** establishes the context for the passage: an extended stay in Sweden, a country that we later learn is unfamiliar to the family.
- The sequence of events is presented in **chronological order** to make it easier for the reader to follow what is happening.
- **Precise facts and details** are given about the subject's thoughts, feelings and motivations to set the scene more effectively for what is to follow.
- The words 'nervous' and 'surprised' are examples of **emotive language**, which is aimed at evoking an emotional response from the reader.
- The **connective phrase** 'Little did I know' is used as a means of foreshadowing an unexpected outcome yet to be revealed.
- **Descriptive language** ('loud laughter' and 'boos') is used to recreate the sounds and sights associated with the scene.
- The specific word 'campus' provides an important detail about the **setting**—namely, that it is an academic institution.
- **Indirect speech** is used to present what the author's father told him and the **emotive word** 'sheepishly' signals the tone in which he did so.
- Here we see a reference to a detail drawn from the Swedish **social and cultural context**, using speech marks to mark out the specific phrase.
- **Direct quotes** are used to relay the writer's father's exact words.
- The **final point** establishes the relevance of the writer's father to society today, as a fitting means of concluding the anecdote.

# NARRATIVE TEXT

## Biography and autobiography

COMPREHENSION WORK

### Literal questions

*Hint: Read the text carefully to locate specific facts and details.*

**1** To which city was the author's father posted? ____________________

**2** What type of scientist was the author's father? ____________________

**3** How many children did the author's father have? ____________________

**4** Which line tells us that the author's father was expecting a large audience at his lecture? ____________

### Interpretive questions

*Hint: These questions require you to combine facts and details to synthesise the meaning.*

**5** What is the latest time that the lecture mentioned in the text could've started? ____________

**6** How do we know the author of this text is female?

____________________________________________

*Hint: Only one answer option is correct. Use the process of elimination to work through the options.*

**7** What does the title of the extract suggest about this incident?

- **a** that the Swedish are bad people
- **b** that the author's father made a mistake in the Swedish language
- **c** that the author's father was a bad man from Sweden

**8** What does the Swedish phrase 'God morgon' mean?

- **a** greetings
- **b** ladies and gentlemen
- **c** good morning

**9** Which line from the text is used to foreshadow the embarrassing language mistake?

- **a** Line 19: 'Little did I know that my optimism was unwarranted.'
- **b** Line 36: '"Good morning, toilets and urinals".'
- **c** Line 9: 'Dad's first lecture was booked for the second morning of our arrival.'

**10** How do we know the people in the audience reacted in different ways from one another to the mistake?

- **a** because of the words 'laughter', 'boos' and 'tittering'
- **b** because they applauded
- **c** because they answered the speaker when he'd said 'God morgon'

### Applied questions

*Hint: This question requires you to understand a text's implications to infer meaning from the text.*

**11** What does the word 'sheepishly' imply about the author's father's attitude in regard to the incident?

____________________________________________

*Hint: These questions require you to consider what information may be missing from the text.*

**12** We read in line 27, 'We met up with Dad at one of the cafés on campus later that day.' What does this tell us about the setting for the incident?

- **a** that the man's embarrassing mistake happened in a café
- **b** that it occurred at a university
- **c** that it happened at a camping ground

# NARRATIVE TEXT
## *Biography and autobiography*

**SPELLING WORK**

### List Words

All of the words in the box below appear in the text 'Bad Swedish'.

| | | | | |
|---|---|---|---|---|
| geological | auditorium | composed | unwarranted | campus |
| adventures | critique | dignified | pronunciation | sheepishly |
| audience | occasion | optimism | listeners | memorised |

**1** Rearrange these word fragments to form four list words.

| | | | | |
|---|---|---|---|---|
| iation | pro | ence | opt | occ |
| ism | audi | asion | im | nunc |

________________ ________________ ________________ ________________

We use the term **affixes** to refer to word parts that can be used at the beginning or ending of words. A fragment placed at the beginning of a word is called a **prefix** and one used at the end is called a **suffix**.

**2** Identify the correct list words to write in the spaces by using these clues about the meaning of their affixes.

**a** ________________ contains a prefix that means 'related to the Earth's crust'.

**b** ________________ contains a prefix that means 'related to the memory'.

**c** ________________ contains a prefix that means 'related to the sense of hearing'.

**d** ________________ contains a prefix that means 'related to the sense of hearing' and a suffix that means 'a space where people gather in large numbers'.

**e** ________________ contains a prefix that means 'not'.

**f** ________________ contains a suffix that means 'having the likeness of'.

**3** Write the base words of these list words. *Hint: Simplify the words into their smallest meaningful form.*

**a** listeners ________________ **b** adventures ________________

**c** dignified ________________ **d** sheepishly ________________

**e** unwarranted ________________ **f** memorised ________________

Sometimes when words change their **form**, their spelling also changes.

**4** Complete this activity to test your sharpness as a speller.

**a** The word *pronounce* is the base word of which list word? ________________

**b** Describe the irregularity in the spelling of this word in comparison to the base word.

____________________________________________

**c** The word *critic* is the base word of which list word? ________________

**d** Describe the irregularity in the spelling of this word in comparison to the base word.

____________________________________________

# NARRATIVE TEXT

## *Biography and autobiography*

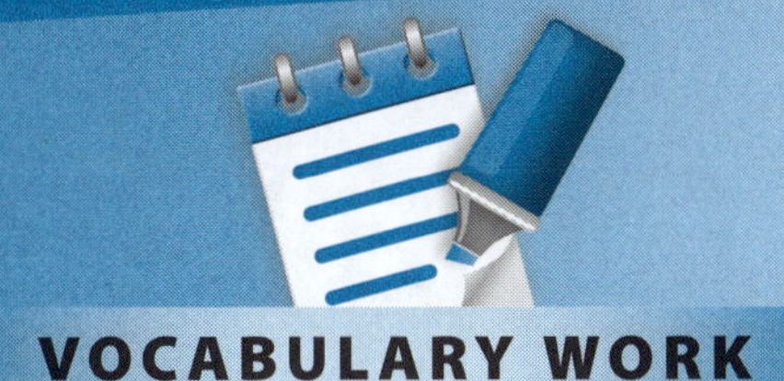

**VOCABULARY WORK**

**1** Complete these sentences by inserting one of these list words into each space.

| auditorium | campus | adventures | sheepishly | audience | memorised |
|---|---|---|---|---|---|

**a** The meeting was held in the large ______________________ on the university ______________________.

**b** The guest lecturer spoke about his ______________________ on safari in Africa.

**c** I was impressed that the speaker used no notes at all because he'd ______________________ his speech.

**d** Dad ______________________ admitted that he'd accidentally insulted the ______________________ at the lecture.

**2** Change these list words into different forms using the same base word.

| | | | |
|---|---|---|---|
| **a** geological | ______________y | ______________ists | ______________ally |
| **b** composed | ______________ure | ______________ing | ______________ition |
| **c** critique | ______________cise | ______________cal | ______________cally |
| **d** occasion | ______________s | ______________al | ______________ally |

**3** Which is the correct definition for the word 'unwarranted'? Circle one: not justified unwanted

**4** Which is the correct definition for the word 'sheepishly'? Circle one: shamefacedly shyly

An **idiom** is an expression that shouldn't be taken literally. Idioms are often understood by people who come from the same place, group or time period. Here are some sentences that contain idioms often heard in the educational setting.

**5** Write the meaning of each highlighted idiom.

**a** I got caught cheating and after suffering the consequences I certainly **learned my lesson**.

______________________________________________

**b** I memorised a poem **off by heart**.

______________________________________________

**c** He passed his aeronautics exam **with flying colours**.

______________________________________________

**d** The girl who sits next to me in class is a **copycat**.

______________________________________________

**e** They're new on campus and are still **learning the ropes**.

______________________________________________

**f** My sister is not very adventurous and always **does everything by the book**.

______________________________________________

**g** I hadn't prepared a speech so I thought I'd just **wing it**.

______________________________________________

# NARRATIVE TEXT

## *Biography and autobiography*

**GRAMMAR WORK**

### Prepositions

**Prepositions** enable us to make connections between words in a sentence. They tell us about the relationship between two things. Prepositions often appear before nouns and pronouns to show direction. Look at this example: *The boy was hiding under the table*. In this example, the boy's position is described in relation to the table. Look at this example: *The tomatoes were in the salad.* In this example, the preposition *in* shows the relationship between the tomatoes and the salad.

**1** Circle the prepositions in these sentences.

**a** Our family put most of our belongings into storage.

**b** I took a seat between my two brothers.

**c** I saw the host whisper something to Dad.

**d** We had never been out of our own country.

**e** We met Dad at a café.

**f** We all had a good laugh after the incident.

**2** Add prepositions so that these sentences make sense. *Hint: there may be more than one correct answer.*

**a** Uppsala is a city _______ Sweden.

**b** Dad took his place _______ the stage to deliver the lecture.

**c** We moved _______ Australia _______ Sweden.

**d** My brother sat in the chair _______ me.

**e** The audience sat _______ the auditorium.

**f** Dad cleared his throat _______ he began.

**3** Complete this puzzle grid by writing the prepositions in the spaces. Use the letter clues to help you solve it.

| | | |
|---|---|---|
| by | atop | between |
| beyond | over | in |
| out | beneath | with |
| around | at | inside |
| under | into | from |
| among | within | after |
| against | upon | near |
| above | through | beside |
| below | off | before |
| outside | on | amid |

**4** Using the word list in Question 3, write the opposites of these prepositions.

**a** below _______________

**b** off _______________

**c** outside _______________

**d** over _______________

**e** after _______________

# NARRATIVE TEXT
## *Biography and autobiography*

**PUNCTUATION WORK**

We use **colons** to introduce further information in a sentence. This information might be a list, a quotation, a definition or a series of connected ideas. For example, *Mum bought me all of my favourite treats: chocolate, chips and ice cream.*

**1** Insert a colon in the correct place in each of these sentences.

- **a** The university campus has great facilities modern lecture theatres, a large auditorium, a library and a café.
- **b** I know two Swedish phrases 'God morgon' and 'God natt'.
- **c** When we flew to Sweden, we had three stopovers Perth, Singapore and London.

We use **semicolons** to separate two equal parts of a sentence. Semicolons can be used in place of conjunctions and commas, or instead of using a full stop. They show that there is a connection between the two parts of a sentence. For example: *I won the raffle today; I collect the prize tomorrow.*

**2** Rewrite these pairs of sentences using a semicolon to join them into one. You will need to omit or change some words.

- **a** We came from Australia to Sweden. We came from a hot summer to a cold winter.

  ______________________________________________

- **b** Dad's skills as a geologist are great. Dad's skills as a linguist are not so great.

  ______________________________________________

We can also use **semicolons** to separate a list of items that are described in phrases rather than single words. For example: *My guinea pigs live in a house with a big, grassy outdoor area; a large bedroom with fluffy bedding; and a series of play tunnels made of pipes.*

**3** Complete these sentences by placing the colons in the correct places.

- **a** There are three children in our family Kai, Brynn and Morgan.
- **b** Five countries make up the region of Scandinavia Denmark, Norway, Sweden, Finland, and Iceland.
- **c** Dad's lecture tour took him to three other cities that year Stockholm, Gothenburg and Malmö.
- **d** On arriving in Sweden, I bought winter gear a pair of mittens, a warm woolly hat and waterproof snowboots.

**4** Circle the punctuation errors in this passage. *Hint: There are ten to find.*

Dad began his lecture by saying, a few words of greeting in swedish Some people could still be heard Tittering as the lecture went on. when dad sat down I saw; the host lean over. and whisper something to him? Until that day, Id' never seen my father blush so deeply.

**5** Rewrite the passage, using the correct punctuation.

______________________________________________

______________________________________________

______________________________________________

______________________________________________

______________________________________________

# NARRATIVE TEXT

## *Biography and autobiography*

**WRITING WORK 1**

### Biographies and autobiographies

**Biographies** and **autobiographies** are texts written about the life experiences and achievements of a particular person. This is why they are sometimes called life writing. Biographies are written by one person about another, whereas autobiographies are written about the author's own life. These texts may be classified as informative or narrative, depending upon the writer's purpose and the elements of style featured in the text.

### Structural features of a biography and autobiography

These forms of life writing have a similar **structure**, including these features:

- orientation
- a sequence of events presented in chronological order
- a section establishing the relevance of the person to society today
- photographs, maps, illustrations, reproductions of supporting documents and other visual content.

### Language features of a biography and autobiography

The text 'Bad Swedish' contains a number of specific **language features** that are common to the biography and autobiography forms of writing. They include:

- first or third person storytelling mode
- the past tense (and the present tense for current information about the subject if they were alive at the time of publication)
- highly descriptive language
- the active voice
- connectives that link paragraphs and chapters together in a chronological sequence
- foreshadowing
- emotive language
- direct quotes presenting people's exact words
- indirect speech paraphrasing things people have said
- highly detailed factual information including dates and the names of people, places and events
- reference to significant events drawn from the social and historical context of the subject.

**1** What is another name for the category of writing that includes biographies and autobiographies?

______________________________

**2** In which of the two forms do authors write about themselves?

______________________________

**3** What are two types of visual content often included in biographies and autobiographies?

______________________________

______________________________

**4** In which storytelling mode and tense are autobiographies usually written?

______________________________

**5** Which type of speech paraphrases things people have said, rather than using quotation marks?

______________________________

# NARRATIVE TEXT

## Biography and autobiography

**WRITING WORK 2**

### Language features in biographies and autobiographies

Biographies and autobiographies vary only slightly in their **language features**. The main difference is in their storytelling mode. For biographies, the only possible mode is the third person because the content is about another person. For autobiographies, the writer uses the first person mode because the content is presented from their personal perspective.

**6** Convert these sentences from the text into the first person mode, from the point of view of the author's father.

**a** He sheepishly told us that he was trying to impress the audience with his language skills.

________________________________________

**b** He'd asked us to attend and give him a critique on his performance.

________________________________________

Biographies and autobiographies are written in the **past tense**, since they are narrative events from the past. The writing takes on a different tone and effect when the tense is changed.

**7** Rewrite these sentences in the present tense.

**a** As Dad took to the stage, I was feeling rather proud of him.

________________________________________

**b** When Dad sat down I saw the host lean over and whisper something to him.

________________________________________

In life writing, it's not always possible for authors to recount the precise words someone spoke many years ago. Indirect speech may be used to convey the sense of what was communicated, rather than the exact words.

**8** Change this sentence to direct speech.

He'd simply memorised the words from the signs on the restroom doors to complete his prepared greeting.

________________________________________

________________________________________

**9** Which of these quotes from the text contain emotive language? Circle *emotive* or *objective* for each one.

| | | | |
|---|---|---|---|
| **a** | 'It was a two-year contract' | Emotive | Objective |
| **b** | 'we were excited about the adventures to come' | Emotive | Objective |
| **c** | 'we'd taken our seats several rows back' | Emotive | Objective |
| **d** | 'I was feeling rather proud of him' | Emotive | Objective |
| **e** | 'We were quite impressed' | Emotive | Objective |
| **f** | 'He sheepishly told us that he was trying to impress the audience' | Emotive | Objective |

# NARRATIVE TEXT

## *Biography and autobiography*

**WRITING SAMPLE**

Here is a sample text showing you how to structure and write an autobiography. Keep in mind that this is part of a chapter from an extended autobiography.

### Raffling nothing

* **Use an interesting heading** to attract the reader to the text. Here the heading's meaning is puzzling until later in the text.

For some years, my mother worked for a charity as President and Secretary. She enjoyed fundraising when we were children. Selling raffle tickets were her main means of bringing in the charity's much-needed funds.

* **Begin with the orientation:** one or more paragraphs that provide some context for the incident to be described. The text should be concise, since it functions primarily as an introduction. The narrative is delivered in the past tense first person mode which adds a sense of personal experience to the recounting of the details.

We kids would accompany her, selling tickets with great success. My father, a cabinet-maker, made and donated beautiful wooden toys, jewellery boxes and other lovely items as prizes.

* **Add supporting details** to expand the context. We are told of a general pattern of behaviour that has led up to the incident about to be described to amplify the contextual details. These details also provide more clues about the setting—the time and place in which the event occurred.

Now my sister was always coming up with 'good ideas', most of which didn't work out to plan. But that didn't deter her. She had many just waiting to be road-tested. When she was eight and I was just five, we devised a marvellous idea for a business venture. We decided we would sell raffle tickets for charity, and that charity was us!

* **Establish a cause and effect structure.** The 'good ideas' of the author's sister have been set up as the cause and the outcome of the story will tell of the effects. It has the effect of foreshadowing the trouble to come. The major plot point of the story, the fact that the raffle had no prize to win, is presented in the last line of this paragraph, setting up our expectations that this is the main focus of the story.

So one afternoon, we told our mother we were going to play in the park with our cousins as we did most days after school. But instead, we ventured off around the streets armed with a raffle book, a pen and a large cloth bag to carry the money.

* **Organise the narrative chronologically** so that the reader is easily able to move from the contextual details and the main plot point through a clear progression of events in a natural sequence that will lead to the conclusion. Here we see that as the adventure begins, the girls are unaware of the trouble they will be in later.

We'd accompanied our mother numerous times when she sold tickets legitimately, so people were familiar with us when we appeared at their doors. Despite the blank looks they received when asking about the prizes on offer, they were very generous. Although there were no actual prizes on offer, our mother's previous track record enabled us to sell nearly the whole book of raffle tickets. In fact, many of our neighbours were quite impressed that we were adventurous enough to go door-to-door on Mum's behalf, as they saw it.

* **Present detailed information** to build the sense that this was a real event that is being remembered with sufficient detail to convince the reader of its authenticity. Here we read of the actions of the two girls, the reactions of the people in the neighbourhood and the significant plot point that there were no prizes. It is in this passage that we realise they are selling bogus raffle tickets, and the title's meaning becomes clear.

Like a little pair of lottery winners, we strutted home and proudly showed off our takings.

* **Use similes or metaphors** to create visual descriptions. Look at the simile used here: 'like a little pair of lottery winners, we strutted home'.

But our enjoyment of this sudden wealth was short-lived, and our schemes for spending it quickly thwarted.

* **Use connectives to form links between paragraphs.** This sentence links the paragraph to the next one with a foreshadowing statement signalling consequences to come.

Our horrified mother took us back to every ticket buyer, making us apologise and give the money back. As I remember, most people thought it sweet and funny; but others were not so lenient and gave us a piece of their minds.

* **Present the effects or outcome of the major plot point introduced earlier.** This concludes the structural pattern of cause and effect. The personal pronoun 'I' is used to report the author's memories of the incident's outcome.

Children don't tend to get embarrassed in the way adults do, but I do remember my sister's entrepreneurial spirit dried up a bit after that.

* **Conclude with an ending that makes a summary comment.** Here we are told about the repercussions of the incident or chapter in the person's life, with a sense of looking back on it after some time has passed and they have grown older and wiser.

# NARRATIVE TEXT

*Biography and autobiography*

## WRITING YOUR OWN SAMPLE

Plan your sample on the lines provided.

- **Use an interesting heading** to attract the reader to the text.
- **Begin with the orientation:** one or more paragraphs that provide some context for the incident to be described. The text should be concise. The narrative should be delivered in the past tense first person mode.
- **Add supporting details** to expand the context. These details also provide more clues about the setting—the time and place in which the event occurred.
- **Establish a cause and effect structure.** You could create a foreshadowing effect through structure. The major plot point of the story should be presented toward the end of this paragraph, setting up the main focus of the story.
- **Organise the narrative chronologically** so that the reader is easily able to move through a clear progression of events in a natural sequence that will lead to the conclusion.
- **Present detailed information** to build the sense that this is a real event that is being remembered with sufficient detail to convince the reader of its authenticity. This may be a good point at which to make the title's meaning clear, if you've specifically chosen an ambiguous or obscure title.
- **Use similes or metaphors** to create visual descriptions.
- **Use connectives to form links between paragraphs.** The last sentence of one paragraph should link with the first sentence of the next one.
- **Present the effects or outcome of the major plot point introduced earlier.** This provides a neat conclusion to the structural pattern established earlier.
- **Conclude with an ending that makes a summary comment.** Add to the sense of the passage of time and the subject's growth in wisdom, making a reflective statement in which you interpret the event from a different perspective now that you're older.

# PERSUASIVE TEXT

## *Blog*

**READING WORK**

## Minecraft Megabuilds—your source for memorable Minecraft builds

FOLLOW THIS BLOG
Sign me up!
*Sign up with Facebook*
*Follow on Twitter*
Followers: 2,061
Comments: 354
Online now: 9

### Albatross House

December 12, 2016 by DarkWing71—2 comments

Heaps of players have been asking me for a while now to post a screenshot of the famous Albatross House, made using vanilla Minecraft. So here it is, megafans. You'll notice it's three storeys in the body but just one storey on each wing (but they're massive wings). And yes, you can walk inside the beak. It looks epic from the ground. [Read more …]

*The mighty Albatross House*

*Comments*
Isn't Big Bird supposed to be yellow?
----------------
Posted by LewChu9 4 days ago
Tagged: #stuffnoobssay

Haha. I'm gonna build a bigger one!
----------------
Posted by JorDee 3 days ago
Tagged: #stuffnoobssay

Archived under: Construction tips Best vanilla builds

### The Magnificent Palace

December 11, 2016 by DarkWing71—1 comment

Many of you guys have abandoned vanilla (unmodified) Minecraft in favour of tricky mods and texture packs. They transform the Overworld pretty nicely but I think there's lots of untapped potential for detailed builds without mods. It just takes some imagination! Playing unmodded vanilla in Creative mode is my thing. The Magnificent Palace (which took me two weeks to build) has everything from an ice-skating rink, theatre and garden maze to its very own zoo. Sure, the ocelots keep escaping and Endermen aren't technically animals, but it's still a cool project. Let me know what you think by posting comments on this thread. [Read more …]

*The Magnificent Palace, with maze and ice rink*

*Comments*
Too much time on your hands.
----------------
Posted by BlueFire 2 days ago
Tagged: #blockaddict

Archived under: Gardens Construction tips Best Vanilla builds

### Build to the Moon modpack

December 11, 2016 by DarkWing71—0 comments

Well, BlueFire has managed to get our server up and running. So far it's glitch-free. It has around ten new biomes to explore and should provide a great intro to newbies who aren't quite ready for PvP just yet. We've selected some great mods (including *Harvestfest, Tinker's Creations* and *Botanica*) that open up many cool new possibilities. There's a communal garden to get you started. Just make sure you re-plant anything you use. Please note, we have a strict policy on griefing—do it and you're blacklisted. Join us on the server—the more, the merrier. [Read more …]

Archived under: Modpacks Multiplayer servers

**Best vanilla builds Construction tips Modpacks Multiplayer servers**

© J & D Richards, 2016

DISCLAIMER: Not officially endorsed by Minecraft ®TM or Mojang/Microsoft

- The blog title is created using an **alliterative effect** with repeated 'm' sounds, a common device used to make attention-grabbing headlines.
- An **advertisement** from the site host or sponsor is featured at the beginning of the blog's main page.
- **Invitations** are extended to users to follow the blog using the social media sites Facebook and Twitter.
- Each topic is given a **thread heading** to identify it and to present it as distinct from the other topics in the blog.
- The **starting date of the thread** is provided, along with the number of comments posted on the thread since the starting date.
- The **blogger's username** is given. Usernames rarely conform to the usual rules of spelling and punctuation. They rarely contain spaces and may be composed of special characters and numbers as well as letters and punctuation marks.
- A **comment counter** is presented with links to archived comments that can be accessed by users with a single click.
- To maintain highly relevant content, the **newest comments are displayed first**.
- Advice is provided about **how the images are stored** on the blog, with live links for users to follow if they wish to access related material.
- **Informal language** such as 'you guys' is used to create a tone that makes the blogger appear to be addressing users directly in a conversational, friendly manner.
- **Slang and jargon** relating to the specific topic is used, including terms such as 'mods and texture packs'.
- The use of **personal pronouns** ('my' and 'me') in the present tense adds a sense of inclusion to the blog.
- **Jargon** specific to the topic is used, including 'ocelots' and 'Endermen', making the blog very specific to the game of Minecraft.
- We are presented with an invitation linking to the full text of the thread which is not featured on the main blog page in order to save space for other threads.
- Text that **identifies the poster**, the date posted and relevant metatags is presented to enable user-friendly access to other areas of the site.
- **Abbreviations** specific to the topic are used, including the term 'PvP' and 'newbies'.
- The use of the **personal pronoun** 'you're' provides a sense of the blogger directly addressing the user.
- This is the **site navigation bar**.
- Here we see the **statement of copyright.**
- **Disclaimer** stating that the blog is not an official product of the legal owners of the Minecraft game and brand name.

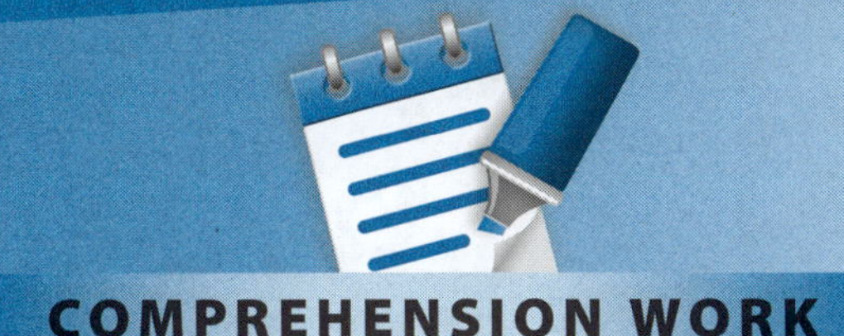

# PERSUASIVE TEXT

*Blog*

COMPREHENSION WORK

## Literal questions

1 What is the username of the owner and writer of this blog?

**a** LewChu9 **b** Endermen **c** DarkWing71

2 What does the 'disclaimer' tell us?

**a** That the blog and its content is officially endorsed by or associated with the copyright owners of Minecraft.

**b** That the blog and its content is not officially endorsed by or associated with the copyright owners of Minecraft.

**c** Minecraft Megabuilds—your source for memorable Minecraft builds

3 What is the punishment for 'griefing' on the multiplayer server?

**a** blacklisting **b** glitch-free game play **c** a monetary prize

4 Name three mods mentioned in the text. ____________________

5 What are three features of the Magnificent Palace?

____________________

## Interpretive questions

*Hint: These questions require you to combine facts and details to synthesise the meaning.*

6 What modifications were made to the original Minecraft software to build the Albatross House?

____________________

7 To which children's television character does LewChu9 compare the Albatross House?

____________________

*Hint: Only one answer option is correct. Use the process of elimination to work through the options.*

8 Does this blogger appear willing to share their knowledge with new players? Explain your answer.

____________________

9 What does the blogger feel is 'untapped' by gamers who've abandoned the original game?

**a** the potential for detailed builds **b** the potential for transformation of the Overworld

**c** the potential for being blacklisted

10 Using the context, what is the most likely definition of the word 'biomes' in line 37?

**a** servers **b** environments **c** new players

## Applied questions

*Hint: This question requires you to understand a text's implications to infer meaning from the text.*

11 What does the statement, 'And yes, you can walk inside the beak' in line 8 imply?

**a** that the beak has three storeys

**b** the blogger is inviting people to visit the house, which exists in the real world

**c** that the blogger has expected this question will be asked

12 How do we know that the blog contains advice about building gardens in Minecraft?

____________________

# PERSUASIVE TEXT

## *Blog*

**SPELLING WORK**

### List Words

All of the words in the box below appear in the text 'Minecraft Megabuilds'.

| | | | | |
|---|---|---|---|---|
| memorable | followers | famous | construction | thread |
| abandoned | imagination | technically | storeys | archived |
| potential | managed | possibilities | server | communal |

**1** Find words from the text that have these letters as their endings:

**a** ally ______________ **b** ilities ______________

**c** icy ______________ **d** bies ______________

**e** unal ______________ **f** tre ______________

**2** How many syllables are in the following list words? *Hint: The suffix* tion *is pronounced as a single syllable.*

**a** imagination ________ **b** abandoned ________

**c** communal ________ **d** construction ________

**e** server ________ **f** thread ________

**3** Complete these sentences by crossing out the misspelt list word from each set of parentheses.

**a** Most (gaming / gameing) communities are happy to welcome new players.

**b** Minecraft is a sandbox game where the (goal / gaol) is to survive in a hostile environment.

**c** In Creative mode, players have many different (vareties / varieties) of building blocks to use.

**d** The best way to learn how to play a new game is to (participate / participant) in online forums.

**4** Which of these words from the text ending in *s* are just plurals and which should have apostrophes? Read the words in their context then circle *apostrophe* or *plural* for each one.

| | | | | | |
|---|---|---|---|---|---|
| **a** heaps (line 5) | Apostrophe | Plural | **b** wings (line 7) | Apostrophe | Plural |
| **c** theres (line 22) | Apostrophe | Plural | **d** animals (line 26) | Apostrophe | Plural |
| **e** its (line 36) | Apostrophe | Plural | **f** theyre (line 7) | Apostrophe | Plural |
| **g** weeks (line 24) | Apostrophe | Plural | **h** isnt (line 10) | Apostrophe | Plural |

**5** Correct the spelling in this passage. Rewrite the misspelt words in the spaces.

Our new servar is up and running and we're waiting for new players to join us.

There are new funcshons to explore and our silection of frigtening enemies

should keep you busy for ours. If you are knew to the game, don't worry.

There are plenty of tipps and hints that will unable you to enjoy yourselv

as you learn. There are so many cool new posabilities for bilding large

structurs, either individully or as a team.

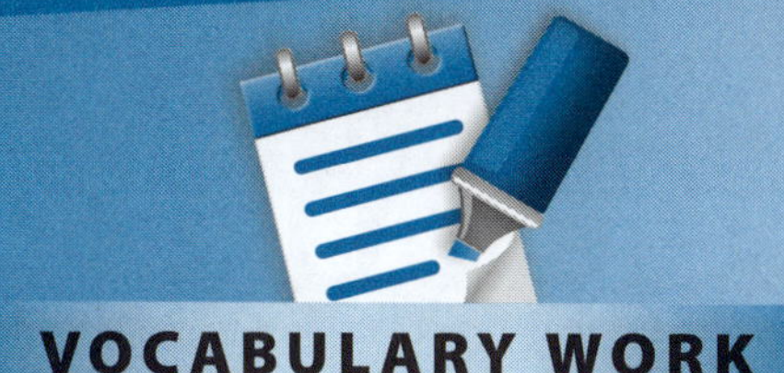

# PERSUASIVE TEXT

## Blog

**VOCABULARY WORK**

Look at these words in the text and use their context to help you work out their meanings.
*Hint: Try not to use words from the same family as the word being defined.*

**1** Complete definitions for the highlighted words by adding appropriate words and phrases to these sentences.

- **a** A **screenshot** is ______________________________ of something displayed on the monitor or screen of a device.
- **b** A **megafan** is a person who is a ______________________________ fan of a particular game or online product.
- **c** A **storey** is a ____________________ of a building.
- **d** If something is described as **epic**, it is really ______________________________.
- **e** The word **mods** is short for ______________________________, which are made to software programs.
- **f** If a program is **glitch-free**, it means there are no ______________________________.
- **g** A **newbie** is a person who is ______________________________.
- **h** The abbreviation **PvP** means 'player versus ________________', and refers to games where players compete against each other.

**2** The term 'griefing' refers to players of online games who purposely destroy or mess up someone else's building, points or resources. What does the base word 'grief' mean?

______________________________________________________________

An **idiom** is an expression used by speakers from a particular place, group or time period. Here are some idioms and slang terms that are commonly used in online gaming.

**3** Complete the definitions by writing in the missing letters.

| | |
|---|---|
| **a** h _ _ dc _ re | playing the most difficult levels where you're likely to be killed and lose your game progress |
| **b** m _ ds | modifications to the original game software |
| **c** noo _ | short for 'newbie', a person who is still learning the game (or 'new' to it) |
| **d** v _ t _ _ an | a person who has mastered the game and plays at a high level of achievement |
| **e** s _ aw _ | anything that is born or spontaneously appears in the game, including your own avatar |
| **f** b _ ss mob | the most difficult enemy character to defeat. The term 'mob' is short for 'mobile' and is pronounced to rhyme with 'robe' |
| **g** want to _ _ y | began as a legitimate request to purchase something in-game but is now an expression of jealousy, even in games where there is no purchasing |
| **h** b _ ff | to increase your strength or player stats |
| **i** n _ rf | to decrease your strength or player stats |

# PERSUASIVE TEXT

## *Blog*

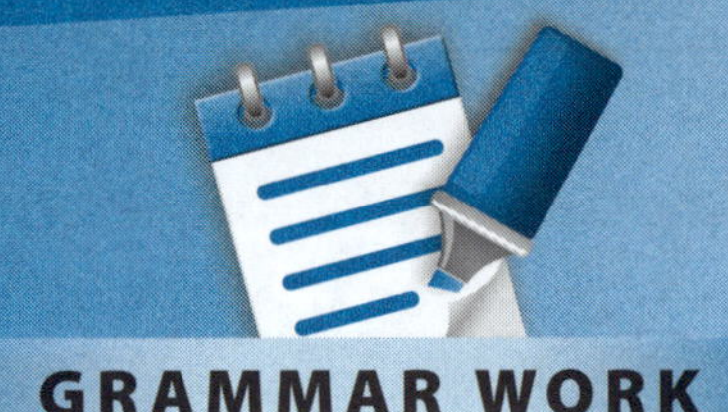

**GRAMMAR WORK**

In writing, we should aim to use the best word for the job. **Precise choices** in **language** lead to clear, economical writing that is engaging and interesting to read.

**1** Select the best word for 'a little bit' of each of these nouns. The first one has been done for you. Use the process of elimination to work through the options in the word bank, crossing off the ones you use as you go.

**Word bank**

| whiff | speck | kernel | sip | scrap | blade | flake |
|---|---|---|---|---|---|---|
| ray | grain | thread | sprig | splinter | smear | puff |

**a** a ______speck______ of dust　**b** a __________ of water

**c** a __________ of grease　**d** a __________ of cotton

**e** a __________ of herbs　**f** a __________ of corn

**g** a __________ of skin　**h** a __________ of paper

**i** a __________ of wood　**j** a __________ of sand

**k** a __________ of grass　**l** a __________ of light

**m** a __________ of powder　**n** a __________ of perfume

**2** Complete these precise nouns in the same way, using the letter clues. These do not refer to tiny pieces; instead they refer to single items.

| spoonful | dose | wisp | coat | lump | sheet | scoop |
|---|---|---|---|---|---|---|
| shard | bolt | slice | wedge | cake | sprinkling | length |

**a** a __________ of medicine　**b** a __________ of iron

**c** a __________ of lightning　**d** a __________ of paint

**e** a __________ of smoke　**f** a __________ of pizza

**g** a __________ of rope　**h** a __________ of toast

**i** a __________ of glass　**j** a __________ of dough

**k** a __________ of ice-cream　**l** a __________ of soap

**m** a __________ of sugar　**n** a __________ of salt

Nouns that have been made from another part of speech are called **nominalisations**. We can make these words from verbs, adjectives and adverbs. Nominalisations are **abstract nouns**. They can replace whole phrases and therefore reduce wordiness in writing. For example, instead of writing the way people behave, we could simply use the expression *behaviour*.

**3** Turn these expressions into nominalisations by filling in the missing letters.

**a** violent actions in games　_ _ _ l _ _ ce

**b** the games I chose　my c h _ _ _ _ s

**c** the avatar I selected　s _ l _ _ tion

**d** the way my Dad plays games all the time　his g _ _ _ _ g

# PERSUASIVE TEXT

## Blog

**PUNCTUATION WORK**

### Parentheses

**Parentheses** are used to enclose extra information in a sentence. Parentheses are also (incorrectly) called brackets. They are sometimes called 'round brackets'. You might present an example, a personal comment or additional details in parentheses to help explain the main content. For example, *When my father was nineteen (in 1978) he joined the army.* Text presented in parentheses should help clarify meaning without interrupting the flow of ideas.

**1** In the blog entry on the Albatross House, which two phrases appear in parentheses?

---

**2** Why is the word '*Botanica*' presented in italics?

---

**3** Where in the text are ellipses used?

---

**4** What does the © symbol at the bottom of the page represent?

---

**5** What do you notice about the punctuation of the username 'DarkWing71'?

---

**6** Rewrite these sentences, correcting the punctuation.
*Hint: Look for incorrectly used apostrophes, capital letters, commas and full stops.*

**a** in minecraft my sister Built a house. thats shaped like a bird

---

**b** the best thing about playing, minecraft is the FREEdom player's have to do whatever they want,

---

---

**c** ive been playing game's on our. private server all Afternoon

---

**d** player's will be, blacklisted, if they destroy anyone elses property in the game

---

**e** the unmodified Version of mineCraft is known as. 'vanilla' among gamers.

---

A **navigation bar** is a feature on a website that enables users to move from one page to another by clicking icons that link to the various pages. It may be horizontal or vertical in its alignment.

# PERSUASIVE TEXT

## Blog

**WRITING WORK 1**

### Blogs

A **blog** is a website that consists of individual journal-style entries that may be linked by a common topic or theme, or that may be entirely unrelated to one another. Blogs began as personal diary pages, but with their rise in popularity and the enormous amount of online traffic they generate, blogs have now transformed into tools of advertising. Bloggers make income by hosting links on their site to other sites. Each time users 'click through' to the advertiser's site from the blogger's site the blogger earns a small payment.

The term 'blog' is a shortened version of the phrase 'web log'. A 'log' is a sequence of diary or journal entries that was once used primarily for record keeping. Some blogs feature mostly textual content, while others focus on art, videos or music.

1 Of which two words is the term 'blog' a contraction? ______________________________

2 What were the earliest blogs like? ______________________________

3 How do bloggers make income from their websites?

______________________________

______________________________

4 Who owns the sites to which users can 'click through' from a blog? ______________________________

5 List three common topics or areas of interest covered by different blogs.

__________________ __________________ __________________

### Structural and interactive features of blogs

Although **blogs** vary widely in their style of presentation, most include:

- a blog title
- an avatar, image or photograph of the blogger
- thread headings
- a structure presenting the most recent posts at the top
- a facility for visitors to make comments on the posts
- a structure presenting the most recent comments at the top of the page
- a comment counter
- counters for number of followers and number of users currently online
- an archive of older posts accessible through links
- links to video content or embedded video clips
- short blocks of text
- a navigation bar
- a statement of copyright
- condensed or limited text displays with 'read more …' invitations
- photos and captions.

# PERSUASIVE TEXT

*Blog*

**WRITING WORK 2**

Tumblr and WordPress are two of the world's largest blogging platforms. Twitter is considered a 'microblogging' service, a condensed version of a regular blog. Multi-author blogs are written by many authors employed to contribute to the blog. Multi-author blogs (MABs) have now become popular. MAB hosts hire freelance bloggers to write for their sites, with many different people contributing content to the blog.

**6** Name two of the world's biggest blog hosting sites.

________________ and ________________

**7** What is the difference between an ordinary blog and a MAB?

________________________________

## Language features of blogs

**Blogs** vary so widely in type, form and content that it is virtually impossible to list **language features** which they all share. The style of language found in a blog depends upon the target audience to which it is aimed, the composer's purpose and the context in which it arose. Some features of language to look out for in blogs are:

- informal expressions
- personal observations
- personal pronouns
- slang, idioms and colloquial expressions that online users understand
- emotive language that describes the blogger's feelings and reactions
- jargon specific to the topic
- interactive features that vary according to the device used to access the blog
- dates, timestamps and other specific factual details describing or logging usage statistics
- calls to action to encourage users to visit more pages on the site.

**8** The text 'Travel for good' contains a number of specific language features that are common to blogs. Find one example of each language feature listed below. Write one example under each feature.

**a** an informal expression

________________________________

**b** a personal observation

________________________________

**c** a personal pronoun

________________________________

**d** a colloquial expression

________________________________

**e** an emotive expression

________________________________

# PERSUASIVE TEXT

## Blog

WRITING SAMPLE

Here is a sample text showing you how to structure and write a blog.

### Travel for Good

> ✱ **Create a blog title.** This tells users specifically what the blog is about.

> ✱ **Include an advertisement from the sponsor or site host.** This provides the blogger with a means of making money if users 'click through' to the advertised site.

Following: 75     Online now: 4

Hi, blog faithful! Thanks for travelling with me and Angie as we fundraise our way around the mighty U.S. of A. for Multiple Sclerosis research. Read all about our Travel for Good campaign and find out how you can donate or embark on your own charity trek here.

> ✱ **Make a call to action.** The user is asked to sign up or log in using social media sites and to donate to the cause (if there is one).

**Day 1 New York City**—December 26—*3 comments*
Well, we're here! What a great first day in the USA! We got to Times Square about half an hour ago. I'm writing this in an Italian restaurant while we wait for a table. There are squillions of people here in New York. I hugged a big Elmo and this guy in a Statue of Liberty costume. After Angie took this photo of us, he demanded payment. How rude! To be fair, he threw us some loose change when he heard that we're here for Travel for Good. [Read more …]

> ✱ **Use a logical structure.** The most recent posts appear at the top of the page.

*Times Square*

*Hot apple cider in Bryant Park, NYC*

> ✱ **Display a photograph of yourself.**

COMMENT ✍

> ✱ **Display a facility for users to comment.** Links are provided to an archive of stored comments.

**Day 7 Niagara Falls**—January 1—*0 comments*

> ✱ **Use a thread heading.** A name, a place and/or a date provide a way of organising the thread topics.

> ✱ **Use a comment counter.** This keeps track of remarks and discussion points raised by other visitors to the site.

Niagara Falls is in the middle of the Super Storm, which is awesome for us coz we really wanted to see some snow. My feet have been freezing since we touched down in Buffalo, so I just bought the first pair of waterproof snow boots I could find. Champion sales assistant made a Travel for Good donation! Loving my comfy, fur-lined boots. That snoring you can hear is my feet. They've gone to bed. [Read more …]

> ✱ **Write blocks of body text to present the content.** In a personal blog like this one, the language is usually informal and reflects ordinary speech.

> ✱ **Include some featured images relating to the content or topic of the blog.**

*Niagara Falls.*     *Oh America, how I love your breakfasts!*

> ✱ **Add captions that identify the subject of the images.**

COMMENT ✍

**Day 10 Washington DC**—January 4—*2 comments*
At last, we've hit Washington. We've had some fine days in DC, and have packed in a lot of fine dining (and walking it off!). A 'highlight' was being apprehended at the entrance to the Capitol Building by security guards, guns drawn, who suspected that my water bottle was a deadly weapon. Needless to say, I meekly complied. [Read more …]

COMMENT ✍

> ✱ **Give an invitation for the user to read more about the topic.** The full text is not displayed on the main page of the blog so that users can see multiple threads at once, making them more likely to find a topic that interests them on the blog.

Boston | New York | Niagara Falls | Washington | Miami

> ✱ **Make a navigation bar to organise posts and photos.** This consists of a menu of clickable hyperlinks that encourages users to click through the pages and potentially click on the paid advertisements.

*© Kate Maskin 2016*

> ✱ **Add a statement of copyright.** This asserts the writer's ownership of the intellectual property on the site.

# PERSUASIVE TEXT

*Blog*

## WRITING YOUR OWN SAMPLE

Plan your sample on the lines provided.

- **Create a blog title.** This tells users specifically what the blog is about.
- **Include an advertisement from the sponsor or site host.**
- **Make a call to action.** Persuade the user to sign up or log in using social media sites.
- **Use a logical structure.** Ensure that the most recent posts appear at the top of the page.
- **Display a photograph of yourself.**
- **Display a facility for users to comment.** Provide links to an archive of stored comments.
- **Use a thread heading.** You could use a name, a place and/or a date, providing a way of organising the thread topics.
- **Use a comment counter.** Keep track of remarks and discussion points raised by other visitors to the site.
- **Write blocks of body text to present the content.**
- **Include some featured images relating to the content or topic of the blog.**
- **Add captions that identify the subject of the images.** You could also add a personal comment about each picture's context.
- **Give an invitation for the user to read more about the topic.**
- **Make a navigation bar to organise posts and photos.**
- **Add a statement of copyright.** This covers the text of your blog posts, your own comments and your photos.

# PERSUASIVE TEXT

## *Magazine cover*

**READING WORK**

- The **masthead** shows the name of the magazine in large typeface with a special decorative feature in the letter *O* that depicts a mountain scene.
- The **background colour** of the masthead and footer are both violet, providing a sense of visual unity and symbolising the region's name.
- The **subheading** tells us about the magazine's purpose and headquarters so the title makes sense. The season (rather than the date) is given. The retail price is also shown.
- The **background image** creates a serene mood that reminds us of autumn. Pale text allows the article titles to stand out clearly on the darker background.
- The **title of the feature article** is shown in larger lettering. It contains alliteration and the subtitle contains rhyme to capture interest.
- **Other article titles** and subtitles contain alliterative effects that help build a consistent mood of nature's mystical wonders. The typefaces of the headings are simple and easy to read.
- **Images** feature items drawn from nature, including peaches and other round-shaped fruit.
- **Imagery** is created to appeal to each of the physical senses.
- **Descriptive language** reinforces the themes of nature, including words like 'birdsong', 'fireflies', 'ecotourism', 'mountain', 'wonders', 'fruitful' and 'peachy'.
- A **free product** is advertised as being inside the magazine, encouraging people to buy it.

# PERSUASIVE TEXT

*Magazine cover*

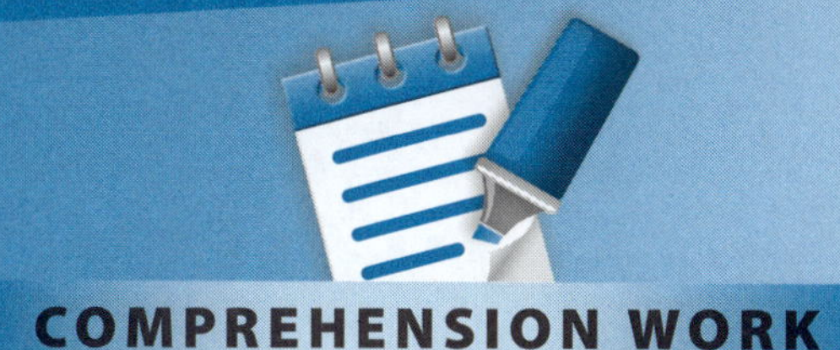

COMPREHENSION WORK

## Literal questions

*Hint: Use the process of elimination to work through the options.*

**1** According to the magazine cover, what are 'nature's candles'?

**a** stars **b** fireflies **c** homemade beeswax candles

**2** Why is Harry Houdini mentioned on the cover of the magazine?

**a** because he currently lives in the Violet Lakes area

**b** because he once visited the Violet Lakes area

**c** because he has been interviewed for the feature article of this magazine

**3** From which state and country does the magazine originate?

**a** Lake Victoria, Tanzania **b** British Columbia, Canada **c** Victoria, Australia

## Interpretive questions

*Hint: These questions require you to combine facts and details to synthesise the meaning. Read the text carefully to locate specific facts and details.*

**4** What type of product is 'Cocoa Mist Mocha' most likely to be?

______________________________

**5** How do we know that the fruit and pinecones featured in the table decorations image are not freshly picked?

______________________________

**6** Which articles are particularly designed to appeal to people interested in craft?

______________________________

**7** What can we assume about the physical geography of the Violet Lakes region, based on the text and imagery on the magazine cover?

______________________________

**8** What is the double meaning of the word 'peachy' in one of the subtitles?

______________________________

**9** Which literary technique is present in the title 'The Mountain Magic Festival' and the subtitle 'wonders in wax'?

**a** onomatopoeia **b** assonance **c** alliteration

**10** How many issues of this magazine are published each year, according to the clues on the cover?

**a** four **b** three **c** twelve

## Applied questions

*Hint: This question requires you to understand a text's implications to infer meaning from the text.*

**11** What type of printed resources might be offered to readers in the section on handwoven fabrics?

**a** patterns for making fabrics **b** jams **c** magazines

**12** Describe the target audience for *Violet Life* magazine, considering the clues on the cover.

______________________________

______________________________

# PERSUASIVE TEXT

## *Magazine cover*

**SPELLING WORK**

### List Words

All of the words in the box below appear in the text '*Violet Life*'.

| | | | | |
|---|---|---|---|---|
| publication | festival | collaboration | visual | articles |
| magazine | autumn | antique | unifying | aromatic |
| decorative | sachet | distilli | fruitful | entrepreneur |

**1** These sentences contain spelling mistakes that have been circled. Write the correct spelling for each word. *Hint: Refer to the list words to help you.*

- **a** A magazine contains a variety of **articels** that appeal to the interests of the target reader. ______________
- **b** It's important to use only the ripest fruit when you're **distiling** juice for making syrups. ______________
- **c** I have a collection of **anteke** items that I hope to sell at the markets on the weekend. ______________
- **d** The **pulication** of the magazine occurs four times per year. ______________

**2** Each of these sentences contains two spelling mistakes that have not been circled. Write the correct spelling for each misspelt word.

- **a** The autum colours in the images have a unifing effect on the cover.

  ______________ ______________

- **b** The magezine has an article on how to create aramatic candles.

  ______________ ______________

- **c** We had a fruitfull meeting with the organisers of the festavel.

  ______________ ______________

Spelling can be easier when we recognise that some difficult words are made up of simple elements. Many words have a **base word** containing the meaning, with other parts added to refine that meaning further.

**3** What is the simplest base word identifiable in each of these list words? *Hint: They may have very different letters than those in the list words.*

- **a** publication ______________
- **b** distilling ______________
- **c** decorative ______________
- **d** fruitful ______________
- **e** collaboration ______________
- **f** aromatic ______________

**4** Which list words contain silent consonants? *Hint: There are three.*

______________ ______________ ______________

**5** Find two words where the letters *ch* do not make their usual sound.

______________ ______________

**6** Find four compound words on the magazine cover. *Hint: A compound word is a single word made from two separate ones.*

______________ ______________

______________ ______________

# PERSUASIVE TEXT
## *Magazine cover*

**VOCABULARY WORK**

**1** Look at the magazine cover and answer these questions about the vocabulary used to create the text by circling *true* or *false*.

| | | |
|---|---|---|
| **a** Fireflies are described as nature's candles. This is a metaphor. | True | False |
| **b** Alliteration is used in the expression 'aromatic wonders in wax'. | True | False |
| **c** The subtitle 'The history and the mystery' rhymes. | True | False |
| **d** The product Cocoa Mist Mocha contains an example of personification. | True | False |

**2** List all the words that specifically build sensory images of the natural world in autumn.

______________________________

**3** List all the words that add to the idea of 'magic'.

______________________________

### Abbreviations and initialisms

The fictitious 'Violet Lakes region' is supposedly located in Victoria. When we write the names of Australian states and territories, we're dealing with two types of terms. First, there are words that are simply **abbreviations** of the full name, such as *Vic.* (*Victoria*). The other kind are called **initialisms** and are formed from the first letters of each word, such as *SA* (*South Australia*). When punctuating state and territory abbreviations, add a full stop unless the last letter of the abbreviation is also the last letter of the name. For example, *Queensland* ends in a *d*, so its abbreviation (*Qld*) takes no full stop. In contrast, *Victoria* (*Vic.*) is abbreviated with a full stop.

**4** Write the abbreviations and full names of two other Australian states that are abbreviations rather than initialisms.

______________ ______________

**5** Write the initials and full names of four Australian states and territories not already mentioned in this activity. *Hint: Remember to follow the rules about abbreviations and initialisms.*

______________ ______________

______________ ______________

An **idiom** is a figurative expression used by speakers from a particular place, group or time period. Idioms differ widely across regions and cultural groups. Australians share many common idioms. For example, one name we have for people born in Queensland is a *banana bender.*

**6** Here are some Australian idioms for people that depend upon the state or territory in which they were born. Write in the correct abbreviations to complete the idioms.

| WA | Qld | NSW | Tas. | Vic. | ACT | NT | SA |
|---|---|---|---|---|---|---|---|

**a** Sandgropers are from ______________.

**b** Cane Toads are from ______________.

**c** Cabbage Patchers are from ______________.

**d** Apple-eaters are from ______________.

**e** Cockroaches are from ______________.

**f** Territorians are from ______________.

**g** Croweaters are from ______________.

**h** Actarians are from the ______________.

# PERSUASIVE TEXT

## Magazine cover

GRAMMAR WORK

**1** Nouns can be converted into adjectives to make our writing more specific. Complete these two tables of adjectives made from nouns, following the pattern shown in the example. The first one has been done for you. *Hint: Adjectives describe nouns.*

| Noun | Adjective |
|---|---|
| taste | tasty |
| magic | **b** ______ |
| fire | **d** ______ |
| aroma | **f** ______ |
| peach | **h** ______ |

| Noun | Adjective |
|---|---|
| **a** ______ | autumnal |
| history | **c** ______ |
| **e** ______ | natural |
| treasure | **g** ______ |
| mystery | **i** ______ |

**2** Separate these words into nouns, verbs and adjectives and write them in the table.
*Hint: Look at how the words are used in the context of the magazine cover.*

| | | | | | |
|---|---|---|---|---|---|
| violet | community | mountain | entrepreneur | fruitful | fabrics |
| new | destinations | visiting | tasting | distilling | making |
| historical | make | aromatic | free | festivals | |

| Nouns | Verbs | Adjectives |
|---|---|---|
| | | |
| | | |
| | | |
| | | |
| | | |
| | | |

Compound words are formed when we make a single word from two separate ones. Complete these compound word puzzles.

**3** Which four-letter word can be written on the line to make three compound words?

**a** _ _ _ _ →woven →made →crafted

**b** _ _ _ _ →stone →castle →paper

**c** _ _ _ _ →flies →place →light

**4** **a** Which five-letter word can be written on the line to make six compound words?

grape→ →cake
passion→ _ _ _ _ _ →bowl
kiwi→ →fly

**b** Which five-letter word can be written on the line to make fourteen compound words?

star→ →house
torch→ _ _ _ _ _ →weight
moon→ →year
street→ →speed
foot→ →bulb
fire→ →box
sun→ →scape

# PERSUASIVE TEXT

## PUNCTUATION WORK

### Punctuating sentences

We can end a **sentence** using one of three **punctuation** marks: a full stop, a question mark and an exclamation mark. Full stops end sentences that are statements. Obviously we use question marks to end sentences that are phrased as questions and we use exclamation marks to end sentences that are exclaiming in an emotional way. Impressions of emotions such as delight, anger, excitement or surprise can be indicated by exclamation marks.

**1** Add the correct end punctuation mark. *Hint: Rhetorical questions may not require an answer but they're still questions all the same.*

**a** A magazine's masthead appears at the top of the front cover____________________

**b** Decorative typefaces add interest to magazine cover designs____________________

**c** Our client absolutely hated the design of the new cover____________________

**d** Who would've predicted how famous this magazine would become____________________

**e** Do people in the Violet Lakes region generate enough news to fill a magazine

**2** The punctuation in these sentences is all wrong. Correct the punctuation by rewriting each sentence.

**a** The 'background' image is a Mountain scene that Reminds us of autumn?

________________________________________

________________________________________

**b** do the Typefaces you've selected make, the headings simple and easy to read

________________________________________

________________________________________

**c** Wev'e chosen Images of fresh peaches to feature On the cover of violet lifes autumn edition!

________________________________________

________________________________________

**d** we are offering a free product! to encourage people to buy our magazine,

________________________________________

**3** Write the names of these punctuation marks.

**a** ; ________________ **b** ’ ________________ **c** , ________________

**d** … ________________ **e** ( ) ________________ **f** ‘ ’ ________________

**g** : ________________ **h** / ________________

**4** The article titles on the magazine cover are presented in all caps (capital letters). Work out how this title would be punctuated if it was written in a regular sentence rather than on the cover. Rewrite the sentence and adjust the punctuation so it is in the correct form.

This weekend, we're going to Violet Lakes for THE MOUNTAIN MAGIC FESTIVAL.

________________________________________

________________________________________

**5** List all of the proper nouns found on the magazine cover. *Hint: Look for words that would ordinarily begin with a capital letter, such as the names of people, places and special events.*

________________________________________

# PERSUASIVE TEXT

## Magazine cover

**WRITING WORK 1**

### Magazine covers

**Magazine covers** are a highly specialised type of persuasive text. They use a combination of text and images to capture and maintain the interest of their target audience. The aim of magazine publishers is primarily to persuade people to pick up and explore, and hopefully buy, the magazine and each new issue.

### Structural features of a magazine cover

**Magazine covers** contain the following **structural features**:

- a masthead
- the issue number, date or season of publication
- the recommended retail price
- article titles
- subtitles that summarise the content of some articles
- imagery that appeals to the senses and emotions.

### Language features of magazine covers

The persuasive **language** used in **magazine covers** is designed to encourage people to buy the product. **Features** include:

- sensory images that appeal to the physical senses
- emotive language
- sensationalised language to create a sense of drama and action
- short phrases for titles that are quick to read
- simple sentences for subtitles that are easy to comprehend
- alliteration
- rhyme
- buzzwords
- repetition
- a call to action with an insistent tone, urging the responder to further explore the magazine.

**1** What is the recommended retail price of *Violet Life* magazine? ____________________

**2** How many times is the word 'magic' mentioned on the magazine cover? ____________________

**3** Identify two buzzwords on the magazine cover that are commonly seen in persuasive texts.

____________________ and ____________________

**4** What call to action is present on the cover? ____________________

**5** On the magazine cover, nature is a strong focus. Can you describe what 'ecotourism' might be, based on the target audience for the magazine and its other content?

____________________

____________________

**6** How are the five physical senses engaged by five features of the cover of *Violet Life* magazine?

**a** sight ____________________

**b** hearing ____________________

**c** smell ____________________

**d** touch ____________________

**e** taste ____________________

# PERSUASIVE TEXT

## Magazine cover

**WRITING WORK 2**

### Visual language features of magazine covers

The main **visual language features** of **magazine covers** are:

- the main background image
- supporting images
- titles of feature articles shown in larger print
- visual imagery
- a colour scheme carefully chosen to reflect a particular mood
- a carefully designed layout that uses vector lines to attract the eye
- light and shade effects
- creative use of typography.

The text '*Violet Life*' contains a number of specific language features peculiar to the writing and designing of magazine covers.

**7** Imagine you have the task of colouring the magazine cover. What palette of colours would you select for the following elements? Explain your answer.

**a** the sky ______________________________

______________________________

**b** the foliage on the trees ______________________________

______________________________

**c** the peach slices ______________________________

______________________________

**d** the bottle of peach syrup ______________________________

______________________________

**e** the table decorations ______________________________

______________________________

**f** the masthead and footer ______________________________

______________________________

**8** Think of two topics that would be suitable for *Violet Life* magazine's Spring issue. Write titles for each article.

______________________________

______________________________

**9** Describe one photo you would expect to see inside the magazine to illustrate each of these three articles.

**a** Fireflies ______________________________

______________________________

**b** The Great Houdini ______________________________

______________________________

**c** The Mountain Magic Festival ______________________________

______________________________

# PERSUASIVE TEXT

## *Magazine cover*

**WRITING SAMPLE**

Here is a sample text showing you how to structure, design and write a magazine cover.

Pigstars

*For all things guinea pig*

September 2017

$4.50

$1000 Photo Competition

All about COLOURS

Guinea pig games

Outdoor hutches

Growth chart

Learn how to speak my language

10 benefits of ALFALFA HAY

BREED OF THE WEEK: Banded smooth coats

- **Create a masthead that clearly shows what the magazine is about.** Use an attractive typeface and design, ensuring that the text can be read clearly against the background.
- **Use a subheading that tells us about the magazine's purpose.**
- **Show the date of this issue, along with the retail price.**
- **Include a special feature that makes the reader want to buy the magazine.** Here they are offered a competition where they can win a cash prize.
- **Feature a large image relevant to the topic of the magazine.** Here we see a picture of a cute guinea pig. It's facing the camera and the position of its head draws our eye into the middle of the page layout.
- **Add smaller images to create visual interest.** Here a bright dandelion has been used.
- **Present article titles in a list in clear typeface.** It's advisable to ensure that one of the images relates directly to the feature article (main article).
- **Think of unusual visual techniques to present extra information.** Here we have direct speech shown in this speech balloon from the guinea pig.
- **Present at least one item as a 'regular feature'.** This emphasises that the magazine has a well-established format and readership.
- **Choose a background that contrasts sufficiently with the text to enable the titles to be read clearly.**

# PERSUASIVE TEXT

## WRITING YOUR OWN SAMPLE

Plan your sample in the space provided.

- **Create a masthead that clearly shows what the magazine is about.** Use an attractive typeface and design, ensuring that the text can be read clearly against the background.
- **Use a subheading that tells us about the magazine's purpose.**
- Show the date of this issue, along with the retail price.
- **Include a special feature that makes the reader want to buy the magazine.**
- **Feature a large image relevant to the topic of the magazine.**
- **Add smaller images to create visual interest.**
- **Present article titles in a list in clear typeface.** It's advisable to ensure that one of the images relates directly to the feature article (main article).
- Think of unusual visual techniques to present extra information.
- Present at least one item as a 'regular feature'.
- Choose a background that contrasts sufficiently with the text to enable the titles to be read clearly.

UNIT 11

# PERSUASIVE TEXT

## *Formal letter*

**READING WORK**

### A letter from the Department of Dental Affairs

Paul Molar
Chief Minister of Teeth
Department of Dental Affairs
101 Government Road
Canberra ACT 2600
17 October 2015

James Lewis
Top bunk
Boys' bedroom
144 Station Street
Ipswich Qld 4305

Dear Mr Lewis,

It has come to our attention that you lost a tooth on Wednesday, 16 October. According to the records of this office, a lower front tooth (your right-hand side) was expected to come out this month, so we are pleased to advise that your tooth loss is right on schedule.

We are writing to send our apologies for the Tooth Fairy's failure to arrive at your house on Wednesday night to do her duty. Since taking up the position with the Department of Dental Affairs, the Tooth Fairy has proven to be quite unreliable. She has failed in her responsibilities to children across Australia more than once. Consequently we would like to inform you that the Tooth Fairy has been dismissed from this office because of her forgetfulness.

We have organised for a replacement Tooth Fairy to visit your home this evening. We sincerely hope that this visit will ease the distress caused on Thursday morning. We have been working hard to ensure that you are not further inconvenienced in this matter.

The Department pays the same fixed sum for every tooth lost, regardless of size, to ensure fairness to all children. To be eligible to collect your Tooth Money, it is important to ensure that you deal with the lost tooth according to Department policy by following these three steps:

1 Please wrap the tooth in a tissue for safekeeping.
2 Please remember to place the wrapped tooth under your pillow.
3 You must try to go to sleep immediately so that the Replacement Tooth Fairy can do the exchange quickly, as she has a busy schedule and cannot be expected to spend time waiting until you drift off.

We hope to contact you again soon when your upper front lateral teeth come out. Should they both happen to fall out simultaneously, you will be eligible to receive a double payment. Please *do not* wobble or wiggle any loose teeth in an effort to speed up the process. This can damage the tooth and it is our policy to refuse payment for inferior quality teeth. We only collect and pay for teeth that are in topnotch condition so remember to brush them each and every night.

Once again, we are very sorry for any inconvenience caused by the delay in the delivery of your Tooth Money.

Kind regards,

*Paul Molar*

Paul Molar
Chief Minister of Teeth
Department of Dental Affairs

- The **sender's name and address** appears at the top of the page on the left-hand side.
- The **date that the letter will be posted** is given, followed by two lines of space.
- The **recipient's full name and address** is presented, followed by two blank lines.
- A brief and polite **greeting** is presented. Called the 'salutation', it is most often composed of the word 'Dear' and the recipient's name, followed by a comma.
- In the introduction, we find a **summary** that clearly presents the main reason the sender is writing.
- After the introduction, we find the beginning of the **main body** of paragraphs.
- In a formal letter, the writer uses accurate **punctuation**, including the proper use of capitals.
- The word 'consequently' is a **connective word** that signals a cause-and-effect relationship between the Tooth Fairy's failure and her dismissal.
- In the middle section, we find **background information** presented about the issue.
- A series of facts are presented and supported by **specific details**.
- Here we see economical but **formal language** used.
- The word 'please' is often present in letters as an expression of **politeness**.
- **Precise language** is used to convey information clearly, with the use of **numbered points**.
- The word 'must' is a **high modality verb** used to add force to the advice.
- **Uncontracted words** are used in formal language, such as 'cannot' rather than 'can't'.
- The phrase 'upper front lateral teeth' is an example of dental **jargon** (specialised language) about tooth loss.
- This is an **uncontracted word** ('do not' rather than 'don't').
- This is the **conclusion**.
- Here we read a final **summary sentence** that reiterates the statement at the start and expresses apologies.
- This is a **sign-off phrase** finishing with a comma, followed by four lines of space.
- There is a **handwritten signature** just above the printed name.

## Literal questions

*Hint: Read the text carefully to locate specific facts and details.*

**1** What event prompted Paul Molar to write the letter to James?

______________________________________________

**2** What action was taken as a result of the Tooth Fairy's negligence?

______________________________________________

**3** What is the Department of Dental Affairs's policy about where lost teeth should be placed for collection?

______________________________________________

## Interpretive questions

*Hint: These questions require you to combine facts and details to synthesise the meaning.*

**4** Which of James's other teeth are due to fall out, according to the Chief Minister of Teeth?

______________________________________________

**5** What habit will help to ensure that James will receive payment for his lost teeth in the future?

______________________________________________

**6** What is the significance of the name 'Paul Molar'? ______________________

**7** What is the main purpose of this text?

**a** to inform kids about tooth loss in an entertaining way **b** to criticise the Tooth Fairy

**c** to make Paul Molar more popular with children

**8** Why is the Department's policy about not paying for damaged teeth stated in the letter to James?

**a** to enable him to receive more money than other kids for his teeth

**b** to discourage him from looking after his teeth

**c** to ensure that he doesn't hurt himself by trying to loosen his teeth too early

**9** One reason we know that this text is written in the style of a formal business letter because

**a** it is from Canberra. **b** it contains formal language. **c** it was intended for a child.

**10** What does the inclusion of the detail about the 'distress caused on Thursday morning' reveal?

**a** James was disappointed when he awoke to find that there was no Tooth Money.

**b** James's tooth was rejected by the Tooth Fairy as it was damaged, causing him to be upset.

**c** The loss of James's tooth caused him pain and misery that lasted until Thursday morning.

## Applied questions

*Hint: This question requires you to understand a text's implications to infer meaning from the text.*

**11** Why might the letter advise James to 'try to go to sleep immediately' in Step 3?

**a** because the Tooth Fairy is shy **b** so that the Tooth Fairy isn't seen

**c** because Paul Molar goes to bed early

*Hint: This question requires you to make an informed judgement based on the evidence.*

**12** What can we reasonably assume about the original source of this letter?

**a** that it was written as a bit of fun by one of James's parents or another family member who forgot to give him his Tooth Money when he'd lost a tooth

**b** that it is a genuine letter from an official government department **c** that James wrote the letter to himself

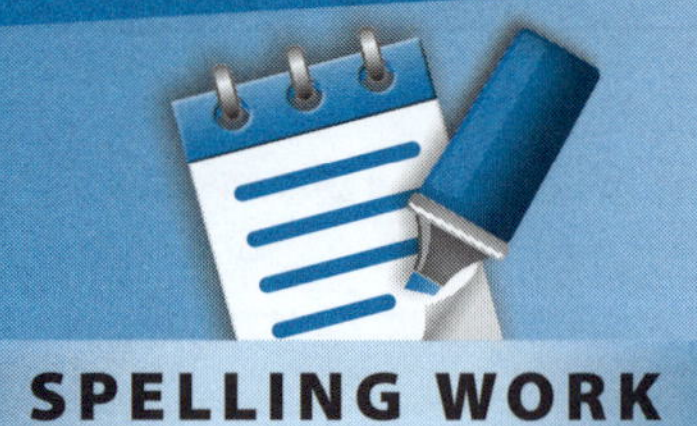

# PERSUASIVE TEXT

## *Formal letter*

## SPELLING WORK

**List Words** All of the words in the box below appear in the text 'A letter from the Department of Dental Affairs'.

| | | | | |
|---|---|---|---|---|
| department | schedule | apologies | unreliable | dismissed |
| forgetfulness | organised | sincerely | inconvenienced | eligible |
| simultaneously | loose | damage | condition | inferior |

**1** Look at these misspelt words and rewrite them with the correct spelling. Refer to the list words to help you spot the errors.

**a** scedule ______________ **b** forgetfullness ______________

**c** inconvienced ______________ **d** sincerely ______________

**e** eligible ______________ **f** inferor ______________

**2** Select the correct spelling from these sets by circling your choice.

| | | | |
|---|---|---|---|
| **a** | condition | condishon | condision |
| **b** | damige | damage | damadge |
| **c** | stimultaneously | simultaneously | simultanously |
| **d** | dissmissed | dismist | dismissed |
| **e** | inferiour | inferior | inferrior |
| **f** | unrelyable | unrelieble | unreliable |

The word *syllabification* refers to breaking a word up into its individual syllables.

**3** Write these list words so that the dashes (–) break them into their syllables. For example, the word *delay* has two syllables: de–lay. *Hints: Every syllable must have a vowel. Prefixes and suffixes should remain intact.*

**a** apologies ____–____–____–____ **b** organised ____–____–____

**c** condition ____–____–____ **d** loose ________–____

**e** eligible ____–__–____–____ **f** department ____–____–____

**g** simultaneously ____–____–____–__–____–____

**4** Convert these expressions from informal to formal language, suitable for inclusion in a formal letter.

**a** haven't ______________ **b** won't ______________

**c** he's ______________ **d** can't ______________

**e** shouldn't ______________ **f** might've ______________

**5** Convert these expressions from formal to informal language.

**a** they will ____________ **b** I have ____________ **c** she had ____________

**d** we would ____________ **e** could have ____________ **f** you are ____________

**6** Tick the correct boxes to answer these questions

**a** In one of the list words, is *ment* used as a prefix or a suffix? ☐ Prefix ☐ Suffix

**b** In one of the list words, is *un* used as a prefix or a suffix? ☐ Prefix ☐ Suffix

**c** In one of the list words, is *ed* used as a prefix or a suffix? ☐ Prefix ☐ Suffix

**d** In one of the list words, is *ly* used as a prefix or a suffix? ☐ Prefix ☐ Suffix

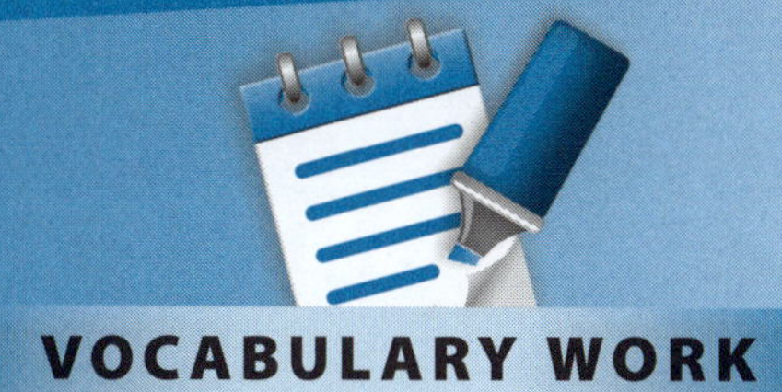

# PERSUASIVE TEXT
## *Formal letter*

**VOCABULARY WORK**

We can often work out the meanings of words by reading them within their context in a text. Use that strategy to work out the meanings of these list words.

**1** Tick the correct boxes to define these words.

| | | |
|---|---|---|
| **a** The word 'department' means | ☐ a division of an organisation | ☐ a small container |
| **b** The word 'dismissed' means | ☐ allowed or asked to leave | ☐ punished |
| **c** The word 'inconvenienced' means | ☐ suffered disadvantage or delay | ☐ caused pain |
| **d** The word 'loose' means | ☐ misplace | ☐ not tight or firm |
| **e** The word 'condition' means | ☐ change | ☐ state of repair |
| **f** The word 'apologies' means | ☐ expressions of regret | ☐ computer science |
| **g** The word 'schedule' means | ☐ pre-organised plan | ☐ regular |

**2** Complete these sentences by making list words and writing the word fragments in the correct order.

**a** The Tooth Fairy proved to be quite ____________ as an employee. re un able li

**b** Paul Molar works for the ____________ of Dental Affairs. ment part de

**c** The Chief Minister advises against the wobbling of ____________ teeth. ose lo

**d** James's payment was delayed due to the Tooth Fairy's ____________. ful get ness for

**3** Write list words that are synonyms for these words.

**a** substandard ____________ **b** breakage ____________ **c** wobbly ____________

**d** arranged ____________ **e** fired ____________ **f** timetable ____________

**g** untrustworthy ____________ **h** truly ____________

**4** Insert these two list words into the following sentence: condition, eligible

To be ____________ for a payment for lost teeth, they need to be in top ____________.

**5** Insert these two list words into the following sentence: forgetfulness, apologies

Paul Molar expressed his ____________ about the Tooth Fairy's ____________.

**6** Insert these three list words into the following sentence: loose, inferior, damage

It is unwise to wobble ____________ teeth in case you ____________ them because you cannot collect payment for teeth that are kept in an ____________ condition.

**7** Underline all the plural nouns in this extract from the text.

We are writing to send our apologies for the Tooth Fairy's failure to arrive at your house on Wednesday night to do her duty. Since taking up the position with the Department of Dental Affairs, the Tooth Fairy has proven to be quite unreliable. She has failed in her responsibilities to children across Australia more than once.

**Jargon** is specialised language that relates to a specific subject. It is often related to a particular profession, work or academic setting.

**8** List four words and/or phrases related to teeth and dental care that appear in the text.

**a** ____________ ____________ ____________ ____________

List three words and/or phrases related to government departmental jargon.

**b** ____________ ____________ ____________

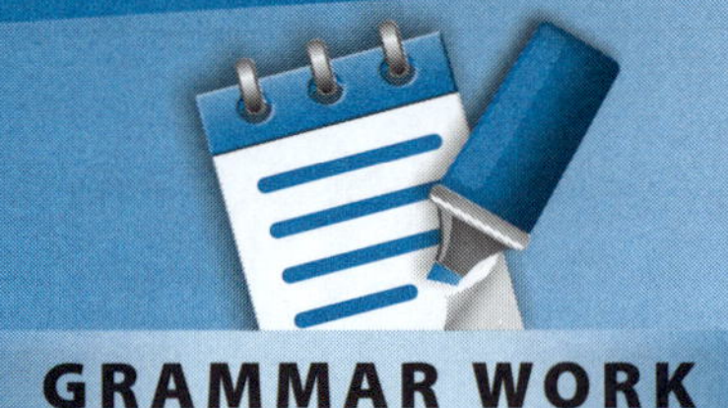

# PERSUASIVE TEXT

## Formal letter

GRAMMAR WORK

### Pronouns

**Pronouns** take the place of nouns that have already been mentioned in a text. There are different types of pronouns.

- **Personal** pronouns refer to specific people, such as *I, we, he, she* and *they*.
- **Possessive** pronouns show ownership, such as *mine, yours, his, hers, its, ours* and *theirs*.
- **Relative** pronouns show the relationship between two or more nouns in a sentence, such as *who, whom, that* and *which*.

*Hint: Pronouns do not need apostrophes—not even* its.

**1** Circle the two pronouns in this sentence.

The Tooth Fairy lost her job because she failed to visit James Lewis on time.

**2** What type of pronouns are these? Circle your choice. personal relative possessive

mine hers ours them

**3** Which word in this sentence is a possessive pronoun? Circle your answer.

The Department of Dental Affairs will pay Tooth Money according to its usual policy.

**4** Complete this table of personal pronouns, following the pattern shown in the example.

| | | |
|---|---|---|
| I | my | mine |
| she | ______ | hers |
| they | their | ______ |
| ______ | our | ours |
| you | your | ______ |
| ______ | his | his |

**5** Underline all of the pronouns (of all types) in these sentences.

**a** Wiggling your wobbly teeth could prevent you from receiving your Tooth Money.

**b** Our lateral teeth are the two positioned on either side of our two central teeth.

**c** Wrapping a lost tooth in a tissue is the best way to protect its surface before collection.

**d** I still remember my first visit from the Tooth Fairy, whom I never believed in as a child.

**e** James's new teeth will have grown to their full size by his ninth birthday.

**6** **a** Underline the pronoun in this sentence. *Hint: When selecting a pronoun, note whether the subject is singular or plural.*

The boy who lost a tooth was disappointed when the Tooth Fairy failed to visit.

**b** What type of pronoun is it? Circle your choice. personal relative possessive

**7** Cross out the incorrect pronoun for these sentences.

**a** After childhood, people no longer lose their / they teeth and grow new ones.

**b** The best thing about brushing my teeth is the clean feeling it gives you / me.

**c** When I was a child, my / mine teeth fell out on schedule.

**d** Your toothbrush should be changed before his / its bristles wear down too far.

**e** The toothpaste who / that I use has a peppermint flavour.

**f** The dentist that / who works on my teeth told me I need to brush them more often.

# PERSUASIVE TEXT

*Formal letter*

## PUNCTUATION WORK

### Commas

A comma is a punctuation mark with multiple uses. Commas can be used:

- to signal a pause
- to separate items in a list
- to separate two or more adjectives
- to separate two or more adverbs
- to mark off a person's name or title, both before and after it appears in a sentence.

Commas help to make meaning clearer by separating certain parts of a sentence. It's the *meaning* of a sentence not its *length* that determines how many commas are needed.

**1** Place one or more commas in each of these sentences to make the meaning clearer.
*Hint: In lists there is no comma between the second last and the last noun. The word* and *is used as the separator in place of the comma.*

**a** Regular brushing flossing and rinsing are important aspects of good dental hygiene.

**b** I loved getting my Tooth Money as a child although it was usually only twenty cents back then.

**c** Four children lost their front teeth this week—Brad Amy Chris and Kate.

**d** The Tooth Fairy a made-up character comforts children who are anxious about losing their teeth.

**Commas** are also used when we write **direct speech**. Follow these rules when using commas to punctuate direct speech.

- Use a comma to mark the end of a piece of direct speech before the closing quotation mark.
- If the speaker resumes again after the phrase that attributes the words to a speaker, use another comma before the beginning quotation mark of the next spoken phrase.

For example, note where the commas fall in this sentence with two instances of direct speech:
'There is no Tooth Fairy,' Grandpa said gruffly, 'and we shouldn't tell kids such silly stories.'

**2** Add two commas in these sentences.

**a** 'It's coming out' said Mia wobbling her loose tooth.

**b** 'If the Tooth Fairy doesn't come tonight' James announced 'I'm going to write a letter of complaint.'

**3** Add the missing pair of commas to these sentences.

**a** The Chief Minister of Teeth Mr Paul Molar told us he couldn't accept damaged teeth.

**b** An eight-year old boy James Lewis lost a tooth on Wednesday evening.

**4** Punctuate this passage properly by placing full stops and commas in the appropriate places.
*Hint: There are five full stops and five commas missing.*

James Lewis was disappointed on Thursday morning after failing to receive his Tooth Money The Tooth Fairy forgot to collect and pay for the lost tooth James who had placed the tooth under his pillow with great anticipation awoke to find that the tooth was still there much to his annoyance. Upon checking the post James was pleased to find a letter waiting for him from the Department of Dental Affairs an organisation of which he'd never heard He was delighted to read that the replacement Tooth Fairy would be visiting him that very evening with his Tooth Money.

# PERSUASIVE TEXT

## Formal letter

WRITING WORK 1

### Formal letters

**Formal letters** are informative texts that enable people to communicate about a particular topic. Until digital media gave us email, everyone relied on letters sent through the postal system as the main way to send and receive information across distances. Formal letters are used in business, law, government, medicine, education and many other sectors. They differ from informal letters, which are usually written by ordinary people for personal or private reasons.

### Structural features of a formal letter

**Formal letters** follow certain conventions. They contain the following specific **features**:

- an introduction, a body of paragraphs and a closing section
- the sender's address
- the date the letter will be posted
- the recipient's address
- a brief and polite greeting (called the 'salutation')
- a summary that clearly presents the main reason you are writing
- a clear description of what the recipient needs to know or do
- a sign-off phrase, such as *Yours faithfully* or *Yours sincerely*, finishing with a comma
- your first and last name, your position or official role, and the organisation or business you represent.

### Language features of a formal letter

To write an effective **formal letter** we must:

- rely on strong paragraph structure, rather than subheadings
- include facts supported by specific details
- use economical but formal expression
- use connective words and phrases to create a unified effect
- use uncontracted expression (not contractions)
- use high modality verb phrases
- address people by their formal names and titles
- describe details with precision
- use jargon, if relevant
- use accurate punctuation
- use expressions of politeness.

**1** Look at the letter from Paul Molar to James Lewis and identify three structural features that mark it out as a formal letter. Describe each feature.

______________________________

______________________________

______________________________

**2** What are some differences between a formal and an informal letter?

______________________________

______________________________

**3** Think of two situations that might require official letters to be sent. Describe them here.

______________________________

______________________________

**4** Why do you think the sender's address is shown at the top of a formal letter?

______________________________

# PERSUASIVE TEXT

## Formal letter

## WRITING WORK 2

**5** The text 'A letter from the Department of Dental Affairs' contains a number of specific language features that are common to most formal letters. To complete this activity match the language feature with an example from the text. Write the letter of the language feature next to the extract it models. *Hint: Use the annotations on the original text to help you.*

| | | |
|---|---|---|
| **a** economical language | **b** formal expression | **c** connective words and phrases |
| **d** uncontracted expressions | **e** high modality verb phrases | **f** formal names and titles |
| **g** describe details with precision | **h** use jargon, if relevant | **i** use accurate punctuation |
| **j** expressions of politeness | | |

**a** 'your upper front lateral teeth …' _____

**b** 'do not' (rather than 'don't') _____

**c** 'Please remember to …' _____

**d** 'Wednesday, 16 October' (instead of 'last night') _____

**e** 'Consequently …' _____

**f** 'simultaneously' (rather than 'at the same time') _____

**g** 'It has come to our attention …' (rather than 'We know') _____

**h** 'the Tooth Fairy' (shown with proper initial capitals) _____

**i** 'Mr Lewis' _____

**j** 'You must try to go to sleep immediately …' _____

**6** Look at the language features shown in the table. When you have completed the previous question, fill in the second and third columns. The second column should contain the same examples as in Question 5.

| Language feature | Example from the text | Effect in the text |
|---|---|---|
| **a** economical language | | |
| **b** polite expression | | |
| **c** connective words and phrases | | |
| **d** uncontracted expressions | | |
| **e** high modality verb phrases | | |
| **f** formal names and titles | | |
| **g** describe details with precision | | |
| **h** use jargon, if relevant | | |

# PERSUASIVE TEXT

## *Formal letter*

**WRITING SAMPLE**

Here is a sample text showing you how to structure and write a formal letter.

|  |  |
|---|---|
| Anthony Drake<br>Scout Leader<br>Kingston Sea Scouts<br>22 Parry Street<br>Kingston Tas. 7050 | **Write your (the sender's) name and address at the top left-hand corner of the page.** This includes the street address, town, postcode and state. We see the sender's formal name, title and the name of the organisation they represent. |
| 3 August 2015 | **On the left-hand side write the date the letter was written.** It is under the sender's address followed by two blank lines of space under the date. |
| Mrs Janice Roberts<br>14 Bridge Street<br>Kingston Tas. 7050 | **Write the recipient's address on the left-hand side.** Below the street name, write the suburb, the abbreviated name of the state, then the four-digit postcode. Underneath the recipient's address leave two blank lines. |
| Dear Ms Roberts, | **Write a polite greeting (called the 'salutation'), followed by a comma.** The writer calls the recipient 'Dear Ms Roberts' because it's seen as polite to use the word 'dear' in a formal letter. If you don't know the recipient's name, you can use *Dear Sir* or *Dear Madam*. If you don't know their gender you could say *Dear Sir/Madam* or use their job or role title, such as *Dear Teacher*. |
| I am writing to let you know that I ran over your dog on Friday afternoon. | **Summarise the main reason you are writing to the recipient.** Anthony is writing to let the recipient know that he was the person who ran over the dog and that he intends to cover any costs and wishes to apologise. |
| The accident occurred at the junction of Ocean Drive and Bridge Street, directly in front of the RSL Club. | **Ensure that you use accurate punctuation to make the message clear.** The street names have initial capitalisation. |
| On that Friday, one of our members had suddenly fallen ill at the Scout Hall. I telephoned her doctor and described the symptoms, and he requested that she be brought to the Emergency Department immediately. | **Provide some background to the topic.** This will aid the reader's understanding of the wider issues raised. Here they are presented in logical order to explain why the driver wasn't able to stay at the scene of the accident. |
| He told me he suspected that my student's appendix had ruptured and expressed to me the extreme urgency of the situation. | **Include facts supported by specific details that are highly relevant to the recipient.** Because the emergency was related to a possibly life-threatening condition, the driver's actions are understandable. |
| I had to get her to the hospital quickly. | **Use economical but formal language to ensure that the message is brief and to the point.** For example, 'quickly' is used instead of a wordier phrase like *as soon as possible*. |
| During the trip I passed by your house. Suddenly your dog ran out into the road and into my front bumper bar. In response, I stopped the car and ran around looking for the dog but it had run away. I knocked on your door but I could see that no-one was home. | **Use connective words to create a sense of flow between the ideas and coherence among the paragraphs.** Here connectives reveal the order of the events (for example 'during the trip', 'suddenly', 'in response'). |
| I could not see where the dog had gone, and with my student so ill I had no choice but to leave the scene and continue my journey. | **Use uncontracted words to retain the tone of formality.** For example, 'could not'. |
| I fully intend to pay for the veterinarian bill. I would be grateful if you could make a list of any costs you may have incurred because of this incident. | **Clearly describe what the recipient needs to know using precise language.** For example, 'make a list'. |
| Please collect and forward me any such bills at the address shown on this letter. | **Use expressions of politeness.** For example, 'please' softens the effect of the command to 'collect and forward me any such bills'. |
| Your neighbour informed me that your dog sustained a fracture to the left foreleg and a mild concussion. | **Include relevant jargon.** Here we find medical jargon that adds a sense of authority and expertise (e.g. 'fracture', 'left foreleg', 'concussion'). |
| You must allow me to pay for his medical care. I intend to visit him to offer my apologies in person. | **Use high modality verbs to describe what the recipient needs to do in response to the letter.** For example, 'must'. |
| Again, I truly regret the sorrow caused by this unfortunate accident and send my best wishes to little Snowy. | **Conclude with a final sentence that summarises your reason for writing.** Reiterate the statement at the start. Here the sender expresses his apologies, regrets and best wishes to the dog. |
| Yours faithfully, | **Write a sign-off phrase on the left-hand side of the page.** A common sign-off is 'Yours faithfully', followed by a comma. |
| *Anthony Drake* | **Handwrite your signature on the left-hand side.** It goes just above the printed name. |
| Anthony Drake<br>Scout Leader<br>Kingston Sea Scouts | **Include your first and last name, your position or official role, and the organisation or business you represent.** Here we see Anthony's position as Scout Leader and his organisation, the Kingston Sea Scouts. |

Plan your sample on the lines provided.

- **Write your (the sender's) name and address at the top left-hand corner of the page.**
- **On the left-hand side write the date the letter was written.**
- **Write the recipient's address on the left-hand side.**
- **Write a polite greeting (called the 'salutation'), followed by a comma.** We call the recipient 'Dear Mr …', 'Dear Ms …' (or another name prefix) in a formal letter. If we don't know the name of the recipient or their gender, we use the salutation 'Dear Sir or Madam'.
- **Summarise the main reason you are writing to the recipient.**
- **Ensure that you use accurate punctuation to make the message clear.**
- **Provide some background to the topic.** This is not essential information but it aids the reader's understanding of the wider issues raised by the letter.
- **Include facts supported by specific details that are highly relevant to the recipient.**
- **Use economical but formal language to ensure that the message is brief and to the point.**
- **Use connective words to create a sense of flow between the ideas and a sense of coherence among the paragraphs.** Often connectives reveal cause-and-effect relationships.
- **Use uncontracted words to retain the tone of formality.**
- **Clearly describe what the recipient needs to know using precise language.** Use bullet points or numbers to aid clarity.
- **Use expressions of politeness.** Even though the tone created by high modality verbs in commands may be rather strong, the polite terms soften the effect.
- **Include relevant jargon.** Specialised language about the topic adds a sense of authority and expertise.
- **Use high modality verbs to describe what the recipient needs to do in response to the letter.**
- **Conclude with a final sentence that summarises your reason for writing.** Express some emotion—such as joy, anticipation, apologies, regret—that is associated with the topic.
- **Write a sign-off phrase on the left-hand side of the page.** Use a term like *Yours faithfully* or *Yours sincerely*, followed by a comma.
- **Handwrite your signature on the left-hand side.**
- **Include your first and last name, your position or official role, and the organisation or business you represent.**

# PERSUASIVE TEXT

## *Advertising script*

**READING WORK**

### Discovery Cruises television commercial script

**Campaign: Discovery Cruises Family Packages**

Project: 30 sec TVC

Version: Draft 3

| SCENE | TIME | VISION | AUDIO |
|---|---|---|---|
| 000 | 00:00 | | *MUSIC TRACK BEGINS AND CONTINUES THROUGHOUT* |
| 001 | 4 secs<br>00:04 | Onscreen text: Fade in the word 'Discovery' in light blue, stylised, wavy text. Slow zoom on smooth ocean's surface as ship comes into focus.<br>*Transition: fast dissolve* | VO<br>A Discovery Cruise invites you to discover how it feels to leave your stress behind. |
| 002 | 3<br>00:07 | Zoom continues to a medium close-up focus on woman relaxing on a sun lounge on the deck.<br>*Transition: fast dissolve* | Rediscover a better version of yourself. |
| 003 | 5<br>00:12 | Montage of scenes showing families rock climbing, ice skating, surfing and enjoying fine dining.<br>*Transition: fast cut* | VO<br>Discover new horizons and wow-factor shipboard experiences you've only ever dreamt about. |
| 004 | 6<br>00:18 | Vox pops of locals from four ports saying the names:<br>'Venice welcomes you!'<br>'Come to Athens!'<br>'Relax in Corfu!'<br>'Explore Barcelona!'<br>*Transition: fast cuts* | VO<br>Enjoy onshore tours of discovery at each exciting port. |
| 005 | 3<br>00:21 | Grab from the current shipboard stage show.<br>*Transition: fast cut* | You'll discover that our cruise ships are destinations in themselves. |
| 006 | 5<br>00:26 | Footage of a smiling, uniformed staff member at a cabin door handing a pillow to a happy customer.<br>*Transition: fast cut* | Discover our award-winning onboard service. Let us help you discover how to create memories that will last a lifetime. |
| 007 | 4<br>00:30 | Onscreen text:<br>Voted Best Family Cruise Operator in 2016.<br>To book, go to www.discoverycruises.com | VO<br>Why not discover it all for yourself? |

- This is the **name** of the advertising campaign.
- This describes the **type of project** ('TVC' means 'television commercial').
- This is the **version number** of this draft of the script.
- These are the **scene numbers**.
- We are given the **length of each scene** in seconds plus the running total of the ad's duration.
- 'VO' stands for **'voice over'** delivered by an unseen narrator.
- This is the **text that will appear** on the screen.
- Here the **brand name** is mentioned and is reinforced by the on-screen text.
- A **personal pronoun** creates a sense of inclusion of the viewer.
- The specific **focal movement of camera** is described.
- The word **'transitions'** describes the way the scenes change. To 'dissolve' means to slowly fade the image down and the next scene's first image up.
- Here we see **repetition of the keyword**, 'discover', in a new form.
- A **clichéd** holiday image helps viewers imagine themselves in the scene.
- A **'montage'** is a group of short scenes that briefly summarise a theme or topic, usually to show the passage of time.
- **Words specific** to ocean-going ships reinforce the setting and mood, suggesting that the viewer will experience life differently at sea.
- This phrase **reinforces** the sea voyage theme.
- **'Vox pops'** are short clips recording ordinary people on the street. Here they suggest personal invitations from 'friends you haven't met yet', who live in exotic locations the ship will visit.
- **Emotive language** suggests opportunities for positive experiences.
- A **'grab'** is a short piece of footage to be edited into the clip.
- This adds a **professional dimension** to your image of a dream holiday.
- The keyword alludes to the **award** won by the company in 2016.
- An item is mentioned that suggests the crew have your personal comfort as their top priority.
- The words 'memories' and 'lifetime' tap into **what people truly value.**
- **Transitions** speed up to maximise the screen time available for shots.
- A **call to action** is direct, phrased as a rhetorical question, prompting viewers to ask themselves 'Why not?'.
- The on-screen text **points viewers to the website** where they can book.

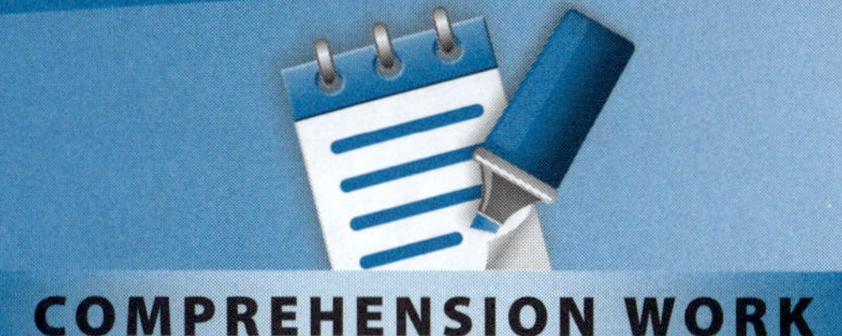

## Literal questions

*Hint: Read the text carefully to locate specific facts and details.*

**1** What is the first camera movement mentioned in the text? ______

**2** How many ports are mentioned in the text? ______

*Hint: Only one answer option is correct. Use the process of elimination to work through the options.*

**3** How many times has this script been drafted?

**a** once　**b** twice　**c** three times

**4** Which activity is not advertised in this television commercial?

**a** ice-skating　**b** rock climbing　**c** skydiving

## Interpretive questions

*Hint: These questions require you to combine facts and details to synthesise the meaning.*

**5** How do we know that Discovery Cruises travel to Europe?

______

**6** As which part of speech is 'award-winning' used in the text?

______

**7** If scenes 004 and 006 were removed, for how long would the commercial run?

**a** 19 seconds　**b** 22 seconds　**c** 11 seconds

**8** What is a 'grab'?

**a** a theft　**b** a short piece of footage　**c** a zoom shot

**9** Identify two visual techniques in the text that are designed to persuade viewers to book a Discovery cruise.

______

______

**10** What is the intended effect of using vox pops?

**a** It makes the local people sound friendly and welcoming of tourists.

**b** It teaches viewers how to pronounce unfamiliar placenames.

**c** It shows us friendly crew members from the ship.

## Applied questions

*Hint: This question requires you to understand a text's implications to infer meaning from the text.*

**11** Why is footage from a stage show in the television commercial?

**a** to emphasise the opportunities for exercise on the ship

**b** to offer information about a show currently being performed in New York

**c** to prove that the cruise ship has many activities that are exciting and entertaining

**12** What is one implication of the line 'Rediscover a better version of yourself'?

______

______

# PERSUASIVE TEXT

## SPELLING WORK

**List Words** All of the words in the box below appear in the text 'Discovery Cruises television commercial script'.

| surface | transition | horizon | current | lifetime |
|---|---|---|---|---|
| discovery | version | experiences | destinations | operator |
| continues | throughout | dreamt | memories | exciting |

**1** Fix the spelling errors in this passage and write them out correctly.

In the television commercial script, we see the camera zoom across the serface of the ocean, heading toward the horizen, where a gigantic cruise ship comes into view. In this vershen of the script, four exiting destanations are mentioned. The voice over continues to repeat the key word 'discoverry' as a way of reinforcing the brand name. The commercial appeals to viewers who have dreamd about taking a trip of a lifetime that will leave them with great memorise of their experiencers.

**Synonyms** are words that have the same meaning as each other. **Antonyms** are words with opposite meanings.

**2** Answer *true* or *false* for each of these statements. Circle your response.

**a** A synonym for the word 'surface' is 'horizon'. True False

**b** The antonym for the word 'exciting' is 'boring'. True False

Variations of the list words appear in these questions.

**c** The words 'find' and 'discover' are synonyms. True False

**d** The words 'exciting' and 'exiting' are synonyms. True False

**e** The words 'transitioning' and 'unchanging' are synonyms. True False

**f** The words 'operative' and 'inoperative' are antonyms. True False

**g** The words 'past' and 'current' are synonyms. True False

**Homonyms** are words that are the same in some way. One type of homonyms are **homophones**—words that sound the same as each other, although they may have different spellings and meanings. The other type of homonyms are **homographs**—words that are written in the same way but have different sounds and meanings.

**3** Answer *true* or *false* for each of these statements. Circle your response.

**a** The words 'current' and 'currant' are homophones. True False

**b** A homophone for the word 'memories' is 'memorise'. True False

**c** A homophone for the word 'throughout' is 'thorough'. True False

**d** The words 'read' and 'reed' are homographs. True False

**e** The word 'add' and the abbreviation 'ad' have the same meaning. True False

**f** The word 'cruise' and the plural 'crews' are homophones. True False

**g** The word 'grease' and the name of the country 'Greece' are homonyms. True False

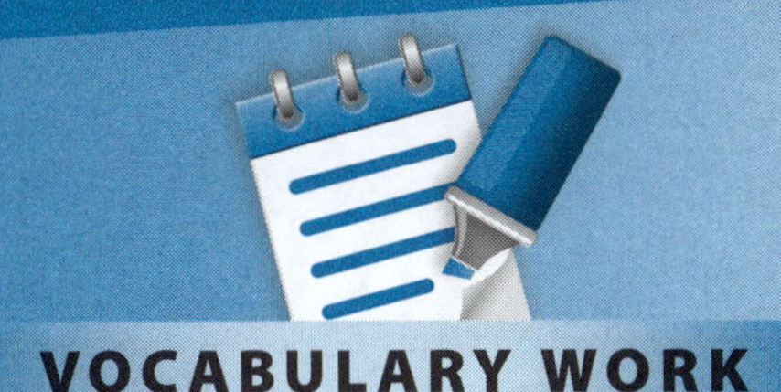

# PERSUASIVE TEXT

## Advertising script

## VOCABULARY WORK

**1** Write these terms used in television scripts from the text next to their meanings.

| scene | secs | onscreen text | zoom | dissolve |
|---|---|---|---|---|
| grab | montage | vox pops | VO | track |

**a** ______________________ an abbreviation that refers to a recording of a person's voice

**b** ______________________ an abbreviation for units of time

**c** ______________________ a type of transition where one scene fades into the next

**d** ______________________ to focus in tightly on the subject with a camera lens

**e** ______________________ a piece of footage that has been prerecorded

**f** ______________________ footage of ordinary people on the street making impromptu remarks

**g** ______________________ a piece of music

**h** ______________________ a group of shots

**i** ______________________ writing that appears overlaid on the visual image in a scene

**j** ______________________ a group of scenes that summarise the passage of time

**2** In which European countries are these cities?

**a** Venice ______________ **b** Athens ______________ **c** Barcelona ______________

### Idioms and abbreviations

Sometimes students become confused about whether an expression is an **idiom** or an **abbreviation**. Abbreviations are just shorter forms of words, whereas idioms are sayings that are not meant to be understood literally.

**3** Decide whether these expressions are idioms or abbreviations. Tick one box to answer each of the following.

**a** If something is dead or no longer works, it is 'cactus'.

idiom ☐ abbreviation ☐

**b** To leave suddenly is to 'shoot through'.

idiom ☐ abbreviation ☐

**c** The 'Gabba' is the Brisbane cricket ground at Wooloongabba.

idiom ☐ abbreviation ☐

**d** Another term for a kangaroo is a 'roo'.

idiom ☐ abbreviation ☐

**e** Australians call budgerigars 'budgies'.

idiom ☐ abbreviation ☐

**f** A kangaroo is a 'boomer'.

idiom ☐ abbreviation ☐

**4** Answer these questions about true idioms.

**a** To travel from Australia to New Zealand is to 'cross the ditch'. What is 'the ditch'?

______________________________________________

**b** Someone who's acting strangely because of the heat is said to have 'gone troppo'. What word does 'troppo' stand for? ______________________________

**c** A country person who moves to the city is said to have gone to 'the big smoke'. Why is it called the 'big smoke'? ______________________________

# PERSUASIVE TEXT

## GRAMMAR WORK

**Modality** refers to the strength with which we make a statement. Expressions with low modality often have the words *could*, *may* or *might*, in comparison to high modality expressions that use *should*, *must* or *will*.

**1** Place these modal verbs in the correct spaces to indicate their strength.

| | | | | |
|---|---|---|---|---|
| won't | must | might / may | will | may be |
| can, could or may | is | mightn't | has to | may have to |

| High modality | Medium to low modality |
|---|---|
| must | **a** |
| **b** | can, could or may |
| is | **c** |
| **d** | mightn't |
| has to | **e** |

High modality terms allow writers to express a strong degree of certainty, which adds a sense of authority to a text.

**2** Write the opposites of these modal verb expressions.

**a** cannot ____________ **b** couldn't ____________

**c** should ____________ **d** will be ____________

**e** mustn't ____________ **f** will have to ____________

To make adverbs from base words ending in *y*, we need to change the *y* into an *i* before adding the suffix.

**3** Change these words into adverbs.

**a** necessary ____________ **b** messy ____________

**c** day ____________ **d** happy ____________

**e** busy ____________ **f** hungry ____________

**g** noisy ____________ **h** tidy ____________

**i** steady ____________ **j** lazy ____________

**4** Fill in the missing letters to complete these adverbs that describe time.

**a** h _ _ _ ly **b** _ ai _ y **c** y _ _ _ _ y **d** m _ _ t _ _ _

**5** Rewrite these sentences, changing the modality from low to high.

**a** You **could** go to Corfu for a holiday.

**b** You **may have** some fun in the Greek Islands.

**c** You **may not** get tickets if you don't call today.

# PERSUASIVE TEXT

## PUNCTUATION WORK

**Contractions** are made by joining two words that are commonly used together in sentences. The apostrophe marks the place where letters have been omitted from the second word.

**1** Rewrite these modal expressions as contractions, using apostrophes in the correct places.

**a** must not ______________________ **b** should have ______________________

**c** cannot ______________________ **d** does not ______________________

**e** have not ______________________ **f** need not ______________________

**g** did not ______________________ **h** were not ______________________

**2** Check that you understand how to punctuate sentences by rewriting these sentences using correct full stops, capital letters, apostrophes, commas and question marks.

**a** discovery cruises use Persuasive Techniques to encourage, people to book a holiday with their company,

______________________________________________

**b** the're are numerous destination Cities to explore, including Athens and Barcelona?

______________________________________________

**c** kids of all age's have access to a whole range of Activities designed just for them.

______________________________________________

**d** sunbathing is One Way, in which people relax and enjoy themselve's on a cruise.

______________________________________________

**3** Punctuate this passage properly by placing apostrophes in the right places.
*Hint: There are eight apostrophes missing.*

Taking a cruise is a great way to see some of Europes greatest cities. The city of Athens is one of the Mediterranean Seas most popular ports. Athens is the gateway to the Greek Islands. Athenss remarkable history draws thousands of tourists each year. The capital of the ancient Greeks, the citys landmarks include the Parthenon, which sits high on the hill called the Acropolis. The columns of the Parthenon are one of the ancient worlds great marvels. They demonstrate the genius of mathematicians and engineers who lived and worked thousands of years ago. Each columns shape helps us perceive the building as perfectly square, although in reality the pillars have slightly curved lines. A tourists experience of Athens would not be complete without a brisk walk up to the Parthenon, one of the Greek civilisations most enduring icons.

**4** Which unit of time is shown in abbreviated form in the script for the television commercial? ______________

**5** Which punctuation mark appears after the word 'Transition' in most scenes? ______________________

**6** Rewrite this fragment, correcting the punctuation so that it appears the same as it does in the text.

voted best family cruise operator in 2016. ______________________________

# PERSUASIVE TEXT

## *Advertising script*

**WRITING WORK 1**

### Advertising scripts

Television commercial **scripts** are persuasive texts that provide a written plan for a clip's filming and production. They include numerous elements including textual, visual and audio features. The text, footage and audio content are designed to persuade the target audience to respond to the product, service or idea being presented.

### Structural features of a television commercial script

**Television commercial scripts** share some common **features**, including:

- layout in visual and audio columns
- scripted dialogue
- scripted voice over
- on-screen text
- directions for camera work—shots, angles and movements
- descriptions of footage
- descriptions of audio content including music and sound effects.

1 How is a television commercial script laid out on paper?

______________________________________________

2 What two elements of a script are intended to be spoken out loud?

______________________________________________

3 What are three types of camera work involved in filming a television commercial?

______________________________________________

4 What does the abbreviation 'VO' stand for in making a television commercial? ____________

5 What are two types of audio content described in scripts?

______________________________________________

6 What is a 'transition'?

______________________________________________

**Editing** is the process of selecting and organising the shots into scenes and the scenes into a particular sequence. In a short television commercial, every second of footage and audio must count. It's not a long time to get a message across.

7 How many seconds long is the clip advertising Discovery Cruises? ____________

8 How many scenes are in the commercial, according to the script? ____________

### Language features of television commercial scripts

The **language** used in **television advertising** is designed to appeal to a particular target audience and varies according to the product, service or idea being promoted.

Most television commercial scripts include:

- abbreviations related to filmmaking, such as *VO* (voice over) or *PTC* (presenter to camera)
- jargon related to filmmaking, such as *transitions, montages, vox pops* and *grabs*
- scene numbers
- timing advice
- personal pronouns
- descriptive language
- emotive language
- rhetorical questions
- repetition
- high modality words
- imperatives (a call to action).

# PERSUASIVE TEXT

## *Advertising script*

**WRITING WORK 2**

The text 'Discovery Cruises' contains a number of **specific language features** that are common to scripts written to produce **television commercials**. They feature persuasive language, incorporating textual, visual and audio features.

**9** Comment on the use of repetition in the commercial. How effective is it?

**10** What is the call to action at the end of the commercial?

**11** Who seems to be the target audience? What evidence can we use to support this view?

**12** What emotions are being manipulated in the script?

Imagine you are the director tasked with making the script for the 'Discovery Cruises' commercial into a finished clip ready for television. Answer these questions. *Hint: Use the annotations on the original text to help you.*

**13** What ideas about holidays will you highlight that are particularly suited to this target audience?

**14** What sound effects could you use to add realism and excitement to the clip?

**15** Draw a three-frame storyboard in which you summarise the visuals of the first three shots of the television commercial, as you imagine them.

# PERSUASIVE TEXT
## *Advertising script*

**WRITING SAMPLE**

Here is a sample text showing you how to structure and write a script for a television commercial. This one is persuading viewers to become involved in rescuing marine mammals.

**Campaign: Sea Sentinels recruiting**
Project: 30 sec TVC
Version: Draft 1

| SCENE | TIME | VISION | AUDIO |
|---|---|---|---|
| 000 | 00:00 | | *SLOW, SAD, EMOTIVE MUSIC TRACK BEGINS AND CONTINUES UNTIL 004* |
| 001 | 4 secs<br>00:04 | Footage of a dying whale thrashing on the beach, with a red light flashing in the background. | *SIREN SOUND EFFECT*<br>Presenter to camera (PTC):<br>How would it feel to know that you've saved a whale from dying? |
| 002 | 3 secs<br>00:07 | Footage of people clapping and cheering as a stranded whale is refloated and swims out to sea. | Well, with the right equipment on hand, we can rescue these magnificent creatures when they become stranded on the beach. |
| 003 | 5 secs<br>00:12 | Presenter holding out her hands to the camera, appealing for help. | PTC:<br>All we need is a little money. Can you find it in your heart to give us a helping hand? |
| 004 | 6 secs<br>00:18 | Montage of people holding out $20 and $50 dollar notes toward the camera. | *MUSIC BRIGHTENS AND SPEEDS UP TO CREATE AN UPLIFTING MOOD*<br>Join with the thousands of Aussies who've already handed us donations so we can get on with this vital task. |
| 005 | 3 secs<br>00:21 | On-screen text:<br>Sea Sentinels<br>with logo (whale inside a protective circle) | PTC:<br>We're the Sea Sentinels.<br>We're always out there, watching over Australia's precious marine mammals. |
| 006 | 5 secs<br>00:26 | Footage of a speeding rescue boat crashing through waves at night with red lights flashing. | *SIREN SOUND EFFECT*<br>Ensuring the safety of our Humpback and Southern Right Whales is a national emergency. |
| 007 | 4 secs<br>00:30 | On-screen text:<br>Please visit<br>www. seasentinels.com.au | VO:<br>Join hands with us and donate today. |

- **Reference information.** This can include the name of this advertising campaign, the type of project ('TVC' means 'television commercial') and the version number of this draft of the script.
- **Make headings to identify the purpose of each column.** This provides clear details about the two components of audio and visual content for the commercial.
- **Include a description of sound elements.** Here we have a music track and special sound effects.
- **Describe how the text will be presented and accompanied by visual imagery.** This image is a graphic and upsetting one designed to appeal to viewers' emotions. A persuasive technique (rhetorical question) is used to personally involve people.
- **Use contrasting footage for emphasis.** Here it implies that the potential for such a joyous rescue is in the hands of the viewers. Emotive terms like 'rescue' and 'stranded' are used, and the whales are described as 'magnificent'.
- **Use the presenter to make a verbal and physical appeal to the viewers.** By having the presenter reach out her hands, we reinforce the desperate nature of the situation.
- **Change the soundtrack to draw a contrast.** Here the contrast is between the sad fate of dying whales and the delight of rescuers who have saved them. The word 'hand' is repeated throughout to imply that the power is in the viewer's 'hands'. The cash shown is in large notes to encourage sizeable donations.
- **Introduce the name of the organisation at the end to maximise the effect on the viewers' memory.** This technique also gives the impression of humility and the word 'sentinels' suggests they are trustworthy and solemn guardians.
- **Give specific names or details to add a sense of authority.** Here two whale species known to live in Australian waters are named.
- **Finish with a strong call to action.** Here the call is to 'join hands' in an act of unity, which sounds very positive and community-spirited. The word 'today' encourages people to act now.

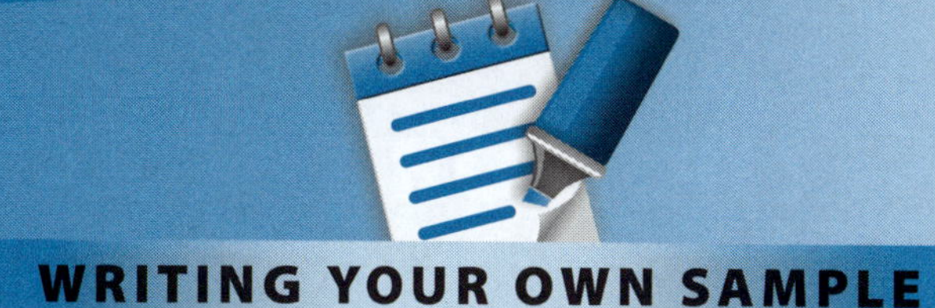

# PERSUASIVE TEXT

## Advertising script

WRITING YOUR OWN SAMPLE

Plan your sample in the spaces provided.

**Campaign:**
Project:
Version:

| SCENE | TIME | VISION | AUDIO |
|---|---|---|---|
| 000 | | | |
| 001 | | | |
| 002 | | | |
| 003 | | | |
| 004 | | | |
| 005 | | | |
| 006 | | | |
| 007 | | | |

- **Reference information.** Include the name of this advertising campaign, the type of project and the version number of this draft of the script.
- **Make headings to identify the purpose of each column.** Provide clear details about content in both the audio and visual columns.
- **Include a description of sound elements.** Consider what specific emotive effects you are intending to create through sound.
- **Describe how the text will be presented and accompanied by visual imagery.** Consider using a rhetorical question, repetition or another persuasive language technique.
- **Use contrasting footage for emphasis.** Use emotive terms in the audio content.
- **Use the presenter to make a verbal and physical appeal to the viewers.** Think about how you could use the physical gestures of the presenter to appeal to the viewers on an emotional level.
- **Change the sound track to draw a contrast.** Emphasise the positive outcome you require for the organisation.
- **Introduce the name of the organisation at the end to maximise the effect on the viewers' memory.** Think about what your choices of words suggests to the viewers.
- **Give specific names or details to add a sense of authority.**
- **Finish with a strong call to action.** Try to appeal to the viewers' sense of community spirit and encourage them to act immediately.

# TIPS FOR THE SAMPLE TESTS

STUDY TIPS

## Know what to expect

- Find out from your teacher what knowledge and skills will be assessed in the sample test.
- Find out what format is being used for the sample test.

## Revise and rehearse

- Revise the relevant knowledge and skills.
- Write some practice analysis paragraphs about sample texts.

## Read carefully

- Read all instructions on the test paper.
- Note the mark allocations. These indicate how much you should write and how much time you should spend on each answer.
- Read the questions before the texts so that when reading the texts you know what to look for.

## Make your answers count

- Use handwriting that is clear (not too large, too small or too cursive).
- Use all of the answer spaces provided.
- Be specific in your answers and don't use padding or repetition to make them look longer.

## Re-read and check

- Once you have completed a response, re-read it to make sure it actually answers the question. This will only take a few seconds.
- Edit quickly and clearly. If you need to, make corrections using single cross-out lines (not scribbles).

## Manage your time

- Write legibly but quickly.
- Ensure you are working through the test efficiently and not spending too much time on each question, or you may not finish the test.
- If you finish early, don't waste the leftover time. Spend that time checking, editing and possibly extending your answers.

## Be ready

- Always study English actively. This means using a pen and paper to make notes. It also involves recording grammar rules, language features and definitions of difficult terms.
- If you have prepared thoroughly for the test, you do not need to be nervous. Tests are not designed to trap you, but to give you an opportunity to show how much you know.

## Part A Reading and comprehension

Read the following texts and answer the questions that follow on page 125.

### Text 1: Informative text—News article

**Pets behaving badly**

They may be guilty or they may just be misunderstood but all of them are busted! Here are some pets that make your dog look like an angel!

**Polly and the police**

They say that just about anything can happen in South America but this story is still a 'what the?!'. A parrot in Argentina was accused of withholding information and interrogated by police for five days.

Neighbours Jorge and Roberto both claimed to own Pepo the parrot. A judge sent the bird to prison and held it in custody until it admitted who its real owner was. Five days later, Pepo squawked 'Jorge!' and then sang the anthem of the San Lorenzo soccer club. An ecstatic Jorge said, 'I knew he wouldn't let me down! He's a true friend … and we support the same football team!'

**KFC: Kill the Freaky Chook**

Pepo's story had a happy ending, but not all feathered felons escape the law as easily. At least there's the rule of innocent until proven guilty … or until it lays an egg.

In the 1400s in Basel, Switzerland, a chicken laid an egg. WOW, right? Unfortunately, someone thought she was a rooster. The poor fowl was arrested, then sentenced to be burned at the stake for her 'heinous and unnatural crime'. Witches were thought to use 'rooster eggs' (no, they don't exist) in their spells, and this hen looked suspiciously rooster-like. It's not too tragic: she was probably destined for the barbecue anyway!

**Cat the Ripper**

Did you know you might be living with a homicidal maniac? Just because she's soft and furry doesn't mean she isn't making plans involving your liver … or your appendix, in this case.

Kitka, a Himalayan cat and surgeon-in-the-making, picked open her owner Brad's appendectomy stitches in the middle of the night with her scalpel-sharp claws. Brad did not wake during the 'procedure' due to the heavy painkillers still in his system after his real surgery. Imagine Kitka's surprise when she opened him up only to find his appendix missing!

When choosing your next pet, don't settle for boring! Jailbird parrots, witchy chicks and killer kitties are a small sampling of the marvellous menagerie of pets on offer. Just keep some emergency funds ready for legal fees.

## Part A Reading and comprehension

### Text 2: Narrative text—Novel

**Extract from *The Secret Garden* by Frances Hodgson Burnett**

She looked at the key quite a long time. She turned it over and over, and thought about it.

It was because it had been shut up so long that she wanted to see it. It seemed as if it must be different from other places and that something strange must have happened to it during ten years.

Besides that, if she liked it she could go into it every day and shut the door behind her and she could make up some play of her own and play it quite alone, because nobody would ever know where she was, but would think the door was still locked and the key buried in the earth. The thought of that pleased her very much.

One of the nice little gusts of wind rushed down the walk, and it was a stronger one than the rest. It was strong enough to wave the branches of the trees, and it was more than strong enough to sway the trailing sprays of untrimmed ivy hanging from the wall.

Mary had stepped close to the robin, and suddenly the gust of wind swung aside some loose ivy trails, and more suddenly still she jumped toward it and caught it in her hand. This she did because she had seen something under it—a round knob which had been covered by the leaves hanging over it. It was the knob of a door.

She put her hands under the leaves and began to pull and push them aside. Thick as the ivy hung, it nearly all was a loose and swinging curtain, though some had crept over wood and iron.

What was this under her hands which was square and made of iron and which her fingers found a hole in?

It was the lock of the door which had been closed ten years and she put her hand in her pocket, drew out the key and found it fitted the keyhole. She put the key in and turned it. It took two hands to do it, but it did turn.

And then she took a long breath and looked behind her up the long walk to see if anyone was coming. No one was coming. No one ever did come, it seemed, and she took another long breath, because she could not help it, and she held back the swinging curtain of ivy and pushed back the door which opened slowly—slowly.

Then she slipped through it, and shut it behind her, and stood with her back against it, looking about her and breathing quite fast with excitement, and wonder and delight.

She was standing inside the secret garden.

**Part A** Reading and comprehension

**Text 3: Persuasive text—Formal letter**

Anthony Drake
Scout Leader
Kingston Sea Scouts
22 Parry Street
Kingston Tas 7050

3 August 2015

Mrs Janice Roberts
14 Bridge Street
Kingston Tas 7050

Dear Ms Roberts,

I am writing to let you know that I ran over your dog on Friday afternoon.

The accident occurred at the junction of Ocean Drive and Bridge Street, directly in front of the RSL Club.

On that Friday, one of our members had suddenly fallen ill at the Scout Hall. I telephoned her doctor and described the symptoms, and he requested that she be brought to the Emergency Department immediately.

He told me he suspected that my student's appendix had ruptured and expressed to me the extreme urgency of the situation.

I had to get her to the hospital quickly.

During the trip I passed by your house. Suddenly your dog ran out into the road and into my front bumper bar. In response, I stopped the car and ran around looking for the dog but it had run away. I knocked on your door but I could see that no-one was home.

I could not see where the dog had gone, and with my student so ill I had no choice but to leave the scene and continue my journey.

I fully intend to pay for the veterinarian bill. I would be grateful if you could make a list of any costs you may have incurred because of this incident.

Please collect and forward me any such bills at the address shown on this letter.

Your neighbour informed me that your dog sustained a fracture to the left foreleg and a mild concussion.

You must allow me to pay for his medical care. I intend to visit him to offer my apologies in person.

Again, I truly regret the sorrow caused by this unfortunate accident and send my best wishes to little Snowy.

Yours faithfully,

Anthony Drake
Scout Leader
Kingston Sea Scouts

# SAMPLE TESTS

## PAPER 1

### Part A Reading and comprehension

Answer the following questions:

#### Text 1

1 Who was interrogated by police for 'withholding information'? (1 mark)

2 What are 'rooster eggs' used for? (1 mark)

3 Why is Kitka called a 'surgeon-in-the-making'? (1 mark)

#### Text 2

4 Of what two materials is the hidden door made? (1 mark)

5 Why does it please Mary very much that people believe the key is still buried? (1 mark)

6 Why might the key take two hands to turn in the lock? (1 mark)

#### Text 3

7 Why is Mr Drake writing to Ms Roberts? (1 mark)

8 What was the 'extreme urgency of the situation'? (1 mark)

9 List, in order, the four key events that occurred after Mr Drake hit Snowy. (1 mark)

Your Score

/9

## Part B Language conventions

Answer the following questions:

### Text 1

1 While this text is informative, it is also entertaining. Give two pieces of evidence that show this. (2 marks)

### Text 2

2 A language technique often used in narratives like this one is personification. Give one example of personification from the text and explain its effect. (2 marks)

### Text 3

3 Through his letter, Mr Drake wants to persuade Ms Roberts to let him pay for Snowy's vet bills. What else might he want to persuade Ms Roberts to think or do? (2 marks)

Your Score

/ 6

## Part C Comparing texts

Answer the following questions:

Use the number of lines and the allocated marks as a guide to the length of your answer.

1 What differences in structure do you see in Text 1 and Text 2? (2 marks)

**2** Re-read the following short sentences from Texts 2 and 3: (2 marks)

Text 2: 'She put the key in and turned it.'
Text 3: 'I had to get her to the hospital quickly.'

What is the effect of these short sentences in each text? Remember that Text 2 is a narrative and Text 3 is a persuasive letter.

Text 2: ______________________________

Text 3: ______________________________

**3** What do Texts 1, 2 and 3 have in common? Make specific references to the texts. (4 marks)

______________________________

______________________________

______________________________

______________________________

Your Score

/8

## Part D Themes and meaning

Answer the following question:

**1** Choose one of the three texts (1, 2 or 3) and write a paragraph about its messages or lessons. These messages do not need to be stated directly in the text—they can be suggested as you read it. (7 marks)

______________________________

______________________________

______________________________

______________________________

______________________________

Your Score

/7

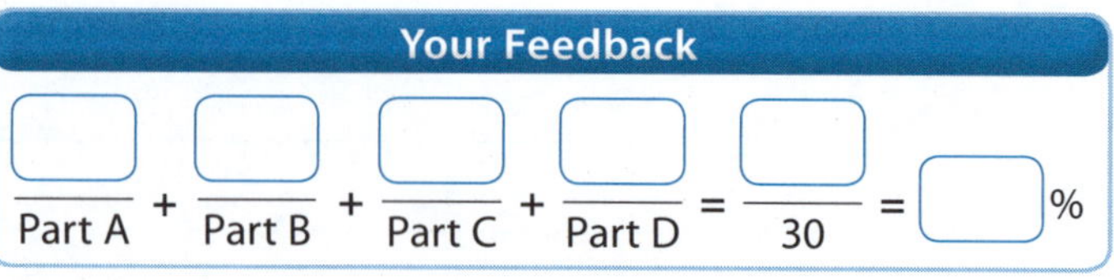

## Part A Reading and comprehension

Read the following texts and answer the questions that follow on page 131.

### Text 1: Informative text—Online news piece

**Tree limbs spear through caravan**

*by Sarah Duck*

Holiday-makers at Brookeside caravan park came within inches of losing their lives in the early hours of Wednesday morning. The force of high winds caused two large gum tree limbs to snap off, one of which came crashing through the roof of Hamish and Natasha Harrison's caravan. The other narrowly missed the van, slamming onto a concrete slab nearby.

Mrs Harrison reported that as the couple lay awake listening to the howling winds they became very worried about the trees overarching their van site. They were glad they'd decided to park their car across the road, rather than in its usual spot on the cement next to the van. The larger of the limbs, almost a metre in diameter, fell in tandem with one that speared its branches through the roof in two places. One piece went through ceiling of the kitchen area, while the second sheared through the bedroom, missing the bed where they were sleeping by inches.

'It mustn't have been our time to go,' Mrs Harrison concluded as she showed neighbours the damaged interior of the van. 'We'd only just returned from the amenities block when it happened. Had we not been back in bed, it could have been much worse.' The bed area was the only space in the van that was spared. The ceiling of the caravan was crushed inwards, leaving two massive holes in the roof letting in the rain and the daylight.

Mr Harrison, from Wauchope, NSW, identified the tree as a swamp gum. 'It has a very brittle interior. When the wind hit it at that speed, instead of flexing it just snapped like a carrot. Natasha and I are lucky to escape with our lives, that's for sure.'

The noise of Tuesday night's violent winds caused many Brookeside residents a sleepless night. Some have expressed concerns over Rosewood Street's tall trees, which have limbs dangerously overhanging many houses. Only last week, the electricity company sent a representative to the location to mark out branches which are leaning perilously close to overhead powerlines. Several trees are already scheduled for lopping.

High above the ground in the offending tree, a koala was found clinging in the easing wind and rain, just below the point where the limbs broke off.

Seth Josson from the local Koala Hospital came to assess the animal for any injuries, but it appeared unharmed and was later released. Mr Josson said that it's important that members of the public keep an eye out for wildlife that may have been injured in the storms. 'Our treatment service operates cost-free and is staffed entirely by volunteers. We'd like to encourage people to make reports so that we can rehabilitate the animals and birds that have been displaced.'

State Emergency Service crew member, Ian Towers, supervised the removal of the tree limbs from the caravan park, after attending a number of other scenes of tree damage to residential properties. Mr Towers reports that there has been an unprecedented number of houses and businesses damaged by the storm, including the local health-food store, which had its roof completely torn off. Repair work will continue for several months.

## Part A Reading and comprehension

### Text 2: Narrative text—Ballad

**'The *Alice Jean*' by Robert Graves**

One moonlit night a ship drove in,
  A ghost ship from the west,
Drifting with bare mast and lone tiller;
  Like a mermaid drest
In long green weed and barnacles
  She beached and came to rest.
All the watchers of the coast
  Flocked to see the sight;
Men and women streaming down
  Through the summer night,
Found her standing tall and ragged
  Beached in the moonlight.

Then one old woman looked and wept:
  'The *Alice Jean*? But no!
The ship that took my Dick from me
  Sixty years ago
Drifted back from the utmost west
  With the ocean's flow?
'Caught and caged in the weedy pool
  Beyond the western brink,
Where crewless vessels lie and rot
  In waters black as ink,
Torn out again by a sudden storm –
  Is it the Jean, you think?'

A hundred women stared agape,
  The menfolk nudged and laughed,
But none could find a likelier story
  For the strange craft
With fear and death and desolation
  Rigged fore and aft.
The blind ship came forgotten home
  To all but one of these,
Of whom none dared to climb aboard her:
  And by and by the breeze
Sprang to a storm and the *Alice Jean*
  Foundered in frothy seas.

Part A Reading and comprehension

**Text 3: Persuasive text—Magazine cover**

Pigstars
*For all things guinea pig*

September 2017

$4.50

$1000 Photo Competition

All about
COLOURS

Guinea pig games

Outdoor hutches

Growth chart

Learn how to speak my language

10 benefits of
ALFALFA HAY

**BREED OF THE WEEK:**
**Banded smooth coats**

# SAMPLE TESTS

## PAPER 2

## Part A Reading and comprehension

Answer the following questions:

### Text 1

**1** Why were the Harrisons worried when they heard the 'howling winds'? (1 mark)

**2** Why could it have 'been much worse' if the Harrisons weren't back in bed when the tree limbs fell? (1 mark)

**3** On which street is Brookeside caravan park located? (1 mark)

### Text 2

**4** What poetic technique is used to depict the *Alice Jean* as a mermaid? (1 mark)

**5** How long ago did the *Alice Jean* sink? (1 mark)

**6** Why is it that 'no-one dared to climb aboard her'? (1 mark)

### Text 3

**7** How much does this issue of *Pigstars* cost? (1 mark)

**8** What are two articles that will help readers to understand and communicate with their guinea pigs? (1 mark)

**9** What does the article on alfalfa hay suggest about the people reading this magazine? (1 mark)

Your Score

/9

# SAMPLE TESTS

## PAPER 2

### Part B Language conventions

Answer the following questions:

#### Text 1

1 Apart from the damage to the caravan park, what else are readers told about in this informative article? (2 marks)

#### Text 2

2 Choose one sound technique used by Robert Graves in his poem. What is the technique and what is the effect of the sound or sounds it creates? (2 marks)

#### Text 3

3 What is the most persuasive feature of this magazine cover? (2 marks)

Your Score

/6

### Part C Comparing texts

Answer the following questions:

1 We know that the general purpose of Text 1 is to inform and the general purpose of Text 2 is to narrate (tell a story). What is a more specific purpose of each text? (2 marks)

Text 1:

Text 2:

2 Text 1 and Text 2 both include references to animals. What are readers of these texts encouraged to do regarding animals? Be specific and give details. (2 marks)

**3** **a** While the writers of the three texts have different readers in mind, Texts 1 and 2 are likely to attract a similar type of reader. Describe them. (2 marks)

**b** Who do you think would be most likely to read Text 3? Give specific reasons. (2 marks)

Your Score ___ / 8

## Part D Themes and meaning

Answer the following question:

**1** Choose one of the three texts and write a paragraph about at least two of its themes. Name the themes and give examples of where or how they are presented in the text. (7 marks)

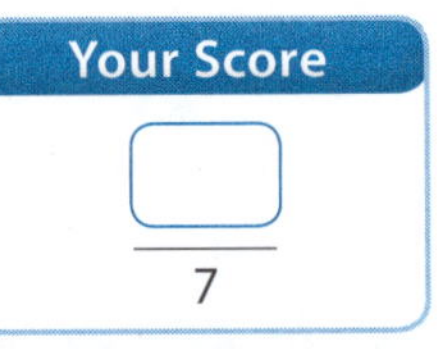


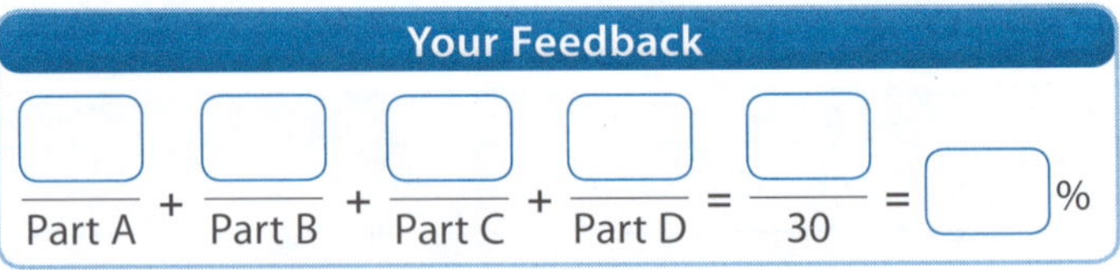

# ANSWERS

CHECK YOUR ANSWERS

## UNIT 1: INFORMATIVE TEXT—NEWS ARTICLE

INFORMATIVE TEXT
### Comprehension Work
page 3

**1** an assault with a dangerous weapon
This is a **literal** question. We read that 'The poodle-wielding driver was charged with … assault with a dangerous weapon' *(line 13)*. All we do is locate this fact from the text.

**2** The teacher had violated a law against housing animals other than traditional pets.
This is a **literal** question. We read that a snooping passer-by reported the lamb to the authorities, who claimed that 'the teacher had violated a law against housing animals other than traditional pets' *(lines 28–29)*. All we do is locate this fact from the text.

**3** a fine
This is an **interpretive** question. We read that the man 'faces a possible jail sentence and a certain fine' *(lines 40–41)*. This means that the fact that he will be fined is certain but he may also be handed a jail sentence. The question requires us to understand the contrasting meanings of the words 'possible' and 'certain' as used in this context. In this line, 'certain' means 'definite'.

**4** to summarise the content of the story
This is an **interpretive** question. We read that 'The poodle-wielding driver was charged with … dangerous weapon' *(lines 12–13)*. When we interpret the meaning in this sentence we notice that the author has given general information about what the article is about and then gives specific information in the next sentences. This is typical of articles written in the journalistic style, where readers are given a preview of the main idea in the story—which engages their interest more effectively.

**5** He pulled over voluntarily, pretending that he wanted to give himself up.
This is an **interpretive** question. We read that the officer 'was pursuing a dangerous driver, who suddenly pulled over, pretending that he wanted to give himself up. But when the officer approached the car to make the arrest, the driver thrust a tiny black poodle into his face' *(lines 6–9)*. When we interpret the meaning of the phrase 'pretending to give himself up', we notice that the writer realises that the driver was pretending. This can only mean that he had a different motive from what his behaviour would suggest. We can infer that he must have planned to attack the officer.

**6** Her owners contacted them.
This is an **interpretive** question. We read that 'Twinkle Toes … has an unusual place in the *Guinness Book of Records*' *(lines 17–18)*. This implies that the *Guinness Book of Records* must have been alerted to the cat's condition. It is logical to conclude that the owners, who gain publicity from the listing, would be the most likely people to have contacted them. Our knowledge from outside the text also tells us that this is the process by which such records are published.

**7** **d** This is an **interpretive** question. We know from our experience that few preschool teachers would bring truly dangerous animals into contact with children.

**8** **b** This is an **interpretive** question. We read that 'The dog … has since been adopted by a nice, law-abiding family' *(lines 13–15)*. When we interpret this sentence we notice the text doesn't say that the dog owner went to prison. So Answer **a** is incorrect. Answer **c** is incorrect because the text does not tell us how the dog was taken from the scene of the crime. However, it does tell us that the pet has a new family so we can infer that it was confiscated by the authorities and rehomed.

**9** **a** This is an **interpretive** question. We read about 'a fully fenced yard' *(line 30)* which reveals that the teacher took safety seriously. This means that she was not irresponsible, so Answer **b** cannot be right. Answer **c** cannot be correct since there is no mention of the teacher having an alternative profession as a farmer and having a lamb as a pet is not the exclusive province of farmers.

**10** **a** This is an **interpretive** question. Both of the other texts feature the animal as a key aspect of the story. The cat with extra toes and the use of a poodle to attack a police officer form the major part of the story, whereas the snake killer story tells of the aftermath of a man killing a snake.

**11** **c** This is an **applied** question. We read two key facts in—that Twinkle Toes has twenty-five toes, and that her mother had twenty-one toes *(lines 18–20)*. We need to do a simple calculation to find the answer: 25 minus 21 equals 4. This means she has four more toes than her mother.

**12** **c** This is an **applied** question. We need to consider the offences committed in the three texts and compare them. We read of the teacher 'beating the charge' *(line 34)*, which means that a court found she did not commit any crime. We read that the snake killer thought he was 'doing a "good deed"' *(lines 37–38)*, so although he committed a minor offence against a technical law he was motivated by good. We can read beyond the lines to realise that the worst crime is to act with violence against a person and we read that the poodle-owner 'thrust a tiny black poodle' *(lines 8–9)* into the police officer's face. A second crime was his dangerous driving, mentioned in line 6.

# ANSWERS

## CHECK YOUR ANSWERS

INFORMATIVE TEXT
### Spelling Work page 4

1 **a** shortage **b** legal **c** unfortunate
2 **a** eighteen **b** venomous **c** loses **d** legal
3 **a** trouble **b** shortage **c** bizarre **d** assault
4 **a** LEGAL/EIGHTEEN/LOSES **b** SHORTAGE/TROUBLE/BIZARRE
**c** PTERODACTYL/ASSAULT/VIOLATED
**d** APPARENTLY/WIELDING/VENOMOUS
5 **a** pursuing **b** lawsuit **c** wielding **d** unfortunate
6 dangerous, lawsuit, prosecutor, authorities

INFORMATIVE TEXT
### Vocabulary Work page 5

1 **a** wielding **b** pursuing **c** bizarre **d** assault **e** violated **f** apparently
2 **a** true **b** false **c** false **d** true
3 **a** appearances **b** dangerous **c** minus **d** broke
4 **a** pull a pistol **b** serve time **c** media spotlight **d** wacko

INFORMATIVE TEXT
### Grammar Work page 6

1 common nouns
2 teacher, animals, preschool
3 Hollywood
4 Common nouns: pistol, toes, animals, handcuffs
Proper nouns: USA, Bob Richards, Australia, Thursday
5 Jeep Grand Cherokee, Brisbane
6 people, pets and houses
7 Twinkle Toes, *Guinness Book of Records*.
8 weirdos, wackos, headlines, animals

INFORMATIVE TEXT
### Punctuation Work page 7

1 **a** the snake **b** the children **c** the teacher **d** the animals **e** the cat
2 **a** driver's **b** preschoolers' **c** Twinkle Toes's **d** man's **e** cat's **f** driver's
3 **a** Apostrophes not required in *weirdo's* and *wacko's*.
**b** There should be no capital *D* for *Dog*, and there is an unnecessary open parenthesis.
**c** The hyphen appears in the wrong place in *pass-erby* (passer-by), and there is an unnecessary comma after *reported*.
**d** The sentence should begin with a capital *T*, and there should be no comma in the four-digit numerical figure.
**e** An apostrophe is missing in *Ive* (I've), and there is an extra open quotation mark after *cars* in the quote.
4 **a** He was pursuing a dangerous driver, who suddenly pulled over, pretending that he wanted to give himself up.
**b** The poodle-wielding driver was charged with 'assault with a dangerous weapon'.
**c** Her mother has twenty-one toes, which is also above average.
**d** The prosecutor in the case told the media, 'This lady is out of control.'
**e** Instead of a bravery award, the unfortunate hero was presented with handcuffs.

INFORMATIVE TEXT
### Writing Work page 8

1 Answers will vary, but should feature at least two of the animals mentioned, perhaps a preschool class or teacher, and a police car or police officer.
2 Roundups are much shorter; they cover a wider variety of content by bringing multiple news stories together; they contain only the major details of each story.
3 Suggested answers: police reports about local crimes; celebrity gossip; community events; sports reports.
4 Roundups require less time and focused attention; they are written in a fast, engaging style; they offer only the most exciting details, so they require less commitment to read.
5 The writer intends to inform readers about interesting news snippets in a lighthearted manner.
6 The sentence means that each item in a roundup must be as interesting and amusing as the other items. No irrelevant material should be included, since the form is so short and concise.
7 **a** 'I've had a guy pull a pistol on me.'
**b** idiom
**c** 'there's', 'I've', 'that's'
**d** 'Instead of a bravery award, the unfortunate hero was presented with handcuffs'; 'A brave man in the USA is in trouble with the law after doing a "good deed".'

**e** The addition of a pun presents the writer as playful and signals that we are not to take the content too seriously.
**f** This metaphor is an economical way of creating a visual image in the reader's mind to add impact to the article.
**g** direct speech
**h** 'Mary had a little lawsuit'
**i** 'She might next decide to bring in a fifteen-foot killer python, poisonous bugs or killer bees.'
**j** alliteration
**k** 'weirdos and wackos'

## UNIT 2: INFORMATIVE TEXT—BROCHURE

INFORMATIVE TEXT
### Comprehension Work

page 13

**1** Goat Island
This is a **literal** question. All you do is look for simple facts in the text. We notice that in the feature about Bennelong *(line 49)*, the text says that Goat Island was known by the local Indigenous people as 'Mamila'.

**2** a rock engraving
This is a **literal** question. It simply requires you to find a fact in the text. We read in the map key that there is a whale engraving site located at Balls Head *(line 25)*. The text also mentions this fact in the passage about engravings *(line 37)*.

**3** We know the shelter was used by families to eat their meals because of primary historical evidence of charcoal pits and smoke stains.
This is a **literal** question. All you do is look for facts in the text. We read that 'rock overhangs, like the one at Balmoral Beach, were used as shelters by Indigenous people of the past. At living sites like this one, you'll see charcoal pits and smoke stains on the ceilings … where families ate their meals.' *(line 9)*. The phrase 'living sites like this one' comes immediately after the site is named—Balmoral Beach. From these facts, we can determine that the writer is making a link between the site at Balmoral Beach and the evidence of families eating meals in the cave shelter there.

**4** **a** This is an **interpretive** question. It requires you to synthesise the meaning of a common literary technique. You need to read the text carefully and decide whether it is meant to be taken literally. Logically tourists today would not literally be walking in someone's footprints. This expression is just a figurative way of saying that they will be walking in the same areas as ancient people walked. Answer **b** cannot be correct because no emotive words are used in the statement. Emotive words describe feelings, which is not evident here. The answer is not **c** because the punctuation and the grammar indicates that this is not phrased as a question of any kind.

**5** the governor
This is an **interpretive** question. You need to read the text closely to find the correct details and also evaluate the context to make an interpretation of those details. Then you can synthesise the meaning. Sometimes it is helpful to read around the specific detail to get a clearer picture of the wider context. Although the text says that Arabanoo died from disease, before this fact appears in the text we read that 'the abduction was a failed effort at facilitating communications with the local Indigenous people' *(lines 43–44)*. We then read that this 'tragically resulted in Arabanoo's death' *(line 45)*. The emotive word 'tragically' implies that his death from disease was a result (directly or indirectly) of his abduction. He was probably exposed to a new range of diseases from contact with Europeans for which he had no natural immunity.

**6** They tell us that the people enjoyed a varied diet that included meat and shellfish.
This is an **interpretive** question. It requires us to put facts together and use logic to interpret the meaning of the text. The historical sources related to diet are fossilised animal bones and discarded shells. These sources tell us that the people ate fish, wallabies, kangaroos and wombats *(line 10)*. We can conclude from this that the people enjoyed a rich and varied diet with plenty of food available from multiple sources.

**7** They are faint because they are very old, have been exposed to weathering and erosion and were made of chalky pigments mixed with water that has faded over time.
This is an **interpretive** question. It requires you to notice the details about how the hand stencils were made *(lines 32–33)*, then apply your logic to make an interpretation about the durability of the materials used to create them and the conditions in which they have existed for thousands of years.

**8** **b** This is an **interpretive** question. It requires you to find a detail in the text and then interpret the reason for its presence. We read in the list of sites that there is a living site at Bennelong Point *(line 22)*. We can use logic to interpret this fact to mean that evidence of people living at the site must have been discovered. For the other sites mentioned, such evidence includes food remains and fire remains; therefore Answer **b** must be correct. Answer **a** cannot be correct because the whale

engraving is located at Balls Head. Had there been another one at Bennelong Point, it would likely have been listed. Answer **c** cannot be correct because we know that Arabanoo was not the traditional owner of Bennelong Point and also that Indigenous Australians had no written language in which they could have recorded their names in writing.

**9** **c** This is an **interpretive** question. It requires you to use skills in synthesis to determine the impact of these names on the meaning of the text. The three names reveal that multiple groups of people lived in the area over the years, and they had distinctly different identities. Answer **a** cannot be correct because the text states that the individuals from these three people groups each owned land in the area so they probably were not nomadic. Answer **b** cannot be correct because the three famous people were all from different people groups, which implies they were not related to one another.

**10** **b** This is an **interpretive** question. You need to understand the implications of the title, the introduction and the content of the text. We can use our logic and wider experience to reach some conclusions about the purpose from these elements. The focus of the writer seems to be to encourage people to visit and value the heritage sites because they reveal Sydney Harbour's rich history from before European involvement. The phrases 'the city's rich Indigenous heritage' and 'thrived here' point to the writer's admiration of the sites for their historical and cultural value. Answer **a** cannot be correct because the rock art is only featured at a few sites, yet many other sites are listed. The writer does not focus more on Bennelong than the other two featured people, so Answer **c** cannot be correct.

**11** **a** This is an **applied** question. We need to consider the writer's purpose in presenting the map in this particular way. Most maps, being informative texts, show intricately detailed roads, public infrastructure, and the names of suburbs and streets. The presentation of the land and waters as an undivided area with heritage sites dotted around the coastline illustrates the state of the region before European contact—unchanged during thousands of years of habitation. The lack of artificially imposed separations makes it clear that our organisation of the area is arbitrary and very recent. The lack of names, roads and infrastructure implies that the land and waters have their own majestic existence, quite apart from our attempts at taming them and exploiting them. In addition, the lack of names respects the older traditional names assigned to various places by the traditional owners of these places. Another indicator that Answer **a** is correct is in the reference to three Indigenous Australian people groups by name, revealing the author's intention to feature the original names and not the European ones. Therefore Answer **c** cannot be correct. By using the process of elimination, we can arrive at the most logical answer. Answer **b** cannot be correct, because although it is a big place, the size is never mentioned in the text as a feature of the area.

**12** **c** This is an **applied** question. We need to consider the text as a whole, including its parts: the map, the list of sites, the feature boxes and the main text. We can consider all of these facts together and apply reasoning to conclude that the answer must be Answer **c** because the map is a representation of Sydney Harbour from an ancient Indigenous perspective. We can see that the inclusion of the Sydney Harbour Bridge, the Tunnel and the relevant roadways would look jarring in the context of the completely natural landscape of the overall scene. Answer **b** cannot be correct, because there is no such creature as a two-tailed snake and the drawing is not a realistic representation of a snake. Answer **a** cannot be correct because the drawing is clearly symbolic and the objects it represents do not look 'exactly like a snake' in reality.

INFORMATIVE TEXT

## Spelling Work

page 14

**1** **a** continuous: hard; ochre: hard; centuries: soft; abduction: hard

**2** specific, precinct

**3** **a** southern **b** continuous **c** governor **d** ochre **e** fossilised

**4** continuous, numerous

**5** **a** continuous **b** fossilised **c** centuries **d** numerous **e** specific **f** traditional

**6** **a** 2 **b** 4 **c** 5 **d** 4 **e** 3 **f** 2 **g** 3 **h** 2

**7** **a** 'er' as in 'her' **b** 'u' as in 'cut'

INFORMATIVE TEXT

## Vocabulary Work

page 15

**1** **a** Indigenous: native to a particular place
**b** variety: range of different
**c** etching: scratching with a sharp tool
**d** stencils: outlines of shapes or objects

**2** **a** southern and centuries
**b** valuable and specific
**c** precinct and fossilised
**d** numerous and occasionally
**e** abduction and mediator

**3** **a** mediates **b** century **c** government

# ANSWERS

CHECK YOUR ANSWERS

**4** **d** Gammon: refers to something that is pretend or false.
**c** Deadly: means 'really awesome', 'wicked' or 'mad'.
**e** Unna: means 'ain't it?' or 'isn't it?'
**a** Aunty and uncle: terms of respect for people who may not be relatives.
**b** Sorry business: refers to mourning and funerals for the dead.

INFORMATIVE TEXT
## Grammar Work page 16

**1** **a** proper noun **b** common noun
**c** common noun **d** proper noun
**e** proper noun **f** proper noun **g** proper noun

**2** **a** barangaroo **b** gadyan **c** cadigal
**d** wallaby **e** mamila **f** wangal

**3** occasionally, southern, specific, specifically, tradition, traditionally

**4** **a** on **b** at **c** behind **d** under **e** into

INFORMATIVE TEXT
## Punctuation Work page 17

**1** **a** Lower case **b** Capital **c** Lower case **d** Capital
**e** Capital **f** Lower case **g** Capital

**2** We should preserve historical sites because:
- they have cultural significance to many people
- we can learn a lot from the past
- they can never be replaced
- it is respectful to those who've gone before us.

**3** **a** city's *(line 3)* **b** you'll *(line 5)*
**c** mounds of discarded shells and food waste *(line 13)*
**d** 'Mamila' *(line 49)*
**e** Sydney Opera House and and Sydney Harbour Bridge *(lines 48 and 54)*

INFORMATIVE TEXT
## Writing Work page 18

**1** Suggestions: subheadings, bullet point lists, visual features

**2** Suggestions: photographs, drawings, graphic organisers, diagrams, tables, charts, maps

**3** Answers will be individual.

**4** the map, the key, the photograph, the text boxes

**5** The key shows people how to interpret the visual symbols shown on the map.

**6** **a** Indigenous Sydney
**b** Indigenous heritage sites around Sydney Harbour
**c** middens **d** smooth rock surfaces
**e** hand stencil rock art

**7** **a** Dobroyd Head, Manly Cove, Balmoral Beach, Bennelong Point, Goat Island
**b** Arabanoo, Barangaroo, Cadigal, Cammeraygal
**c** silcrete, chert, ochre

**8** Suggestions: any of the specific places named in the text: sandstone rock overhangs, shelters, living sites, charcoal pits, smoke stains, fossilised bones, middens, axe-grinding grooves, stone tools or artefacts, other rock art, ochre, a hand, drilled holes and etching lines, engravings, the Whale engraving, and individuals such as Arabanoo, Bennelong and Barangaroo.

**9** Answers will vary, but should include the colours most traditionally associated with Indigenous Australian culture and artwork—ochres made from earth pigments, such as brown, red, orange, yellow, black and white. Reasoning could include reference to the flag, the colours of the environment and the usual colours seen in dot painting and other art and craft.

## UNIT 3: INFORMATIVE TEXT—ONLINE NEWS PIECE

INFORMATIVE TEXT
## Comprehension Work page 23

**1** **c** This is a **literal** question. All you need to do is locate a fact in the text. When the sketch's owner is first mentioned, he is referred to as 'Private Jack Shelley' *(line 10)*. We know the answer is not Answer **a** Captain nor Answer **b** Major because the very first time the man is mentioned we are told his full title was 'Private Jack Shelley'.

**2** Christmas carols
This is a **literal** question. You need to find a specific detail in the text. We read in the text that the significant event around the time of the truce was Christmas and that the men 'sang carols'.

**3** The tales about the unofficial truces enjoyed by soldiers from both sides at Christmas in 1914.
This is a **literal** question. You need to use your comprehension to find details in the text. We read the phrase 'the tales of enemy soldiers socialising together' *(line 13)* which tells us what the tales were about.

**4** at mealtime, exercise time and work time
This is a **literal** question. All we need to do is read the text to locate facts. We read of 'unofficial agreements between the sides to refrain from shooting at mealtimes, during stints of exercise and

even at times when soldiers were working in the open.' *(lines 31–33)*

5 December 1914
This is an **interpretive** question. It requires you to synthesise meaning by putting various facts together to reach a conclusion. We read that Jack 'had at least two buttons from German uniforms that he told us were exchanged between the men involved in the Christmas Day Truce' *(lines 23–25)*. Because Christmas falls in December, the name 'Christmas Day Truce' tells us that the month was December. The text states that the year it took place was 1914.

6 **b** This is an **interpretive** question. It requires us to interpret the meaning of facts and details. We read that 'the family lost track of the artwork after Jack's possessions were moved during the sale of his estate when he died' *(lines 13–19)*. The phrase 'when he died' and the word 'possessions' imply that the term 'estate' must relate to someone's possessions disposed of or inherited by relatives after death. We know Answer **a** can't be correct, because a body would not be among items sold by the family. We know Answer **c** can't be correct because the word 'neighbourhood' doesn't fit logically into the context and could not be described as a 'possession'.

7 because the British fought alongside Australians as allies
This is an **interpretive** question. You need to think about the implications of certain words and phrases, such as the term 'Allied soldiers' *(line 7)*, which reminds us that the British and Australians fought side by side in World War I.

8 **c** This is an **interpretive** question. You have to think about the connotations of words. The term 'kickabout' implies that the feet are used in the sport, which means that neither Answer **a** basketball nor Answer **b** tennis can be correct.

9 **b** This is an **interpretive** question. You need to scan the text to look for a synonym for 'great personal value', which is 'prized'. We read that the sketch is 'Jack's prized possession' *(line 15)*. We know that Answer **a** is not correct because the word 'socialising' does not mean 'great personal value' and the context does not apply to Jack's valuing of the sketch. Answer **c** cannot be correct because 'fond' is too weak a word to mean 'great personal value', and again, the context is irrelevant to the question.

10 **b** This is an **interpretive** question. You need to consider multiple aspects of the text at once. We know that Answer **a** is not correct because, even though the buttons being gold would make them valuable, the article is about an item of sentimental value so we can infer that monetary value is irrelevant. We know that Answer **b** is not correct because this is a misrepresentation of the relationships described in the text: Jack is the grandfather mentioned.

11 **a** This is an **applied** question. It requires you to read beyond the lines to find additional meaning beyond the words. The artwork shows a friendly football game and sport is commonly viewed as a symbol of cooperation and international friendship, which explains why it is viewed as a symbol of hope. Answer **b** can't be correct because there is no mention of the sketch saving Jack's life in the war. And Answer **c** can't be correct because the sketch's subject matter reveals nothing about who won the war.

12 because the person who'd inherited it had no idea of its historical authenticity and significance
This is an **applied** question. It requires you to make an informed judgement based on evidence from the text. We read that Jack Shelley's family lost track of the sketch *(line 18)*, and we can infer that they presumed it had been lost among small, insignificant items from his estate. We can infer, then, that without a knowledge of the sketch's origins, the new owner wouldn't attach any value to the text. This also implies that the sketch was not labelled or marked with a name or date.

## INFORMATIVE TEXT
## Spelling Work page 24

1 **a** soldier **b** possession **c** exchanged **d** uniforms **e** remarkably **f** occurred **g** violent **h** descendants

2 **a** three **b** three **c** four **d** two

3 **a** memory **b** history **c** agree **d** defend **e** possess **f** social **g** occur **h** descend

4 **a** uni **b** re **c** co **d** west **e** art **f** grand **g** un **h** foot

5 soldeirs, hungar, condishon, extendid, trenchs, outbrakes, dissease, dificulties, continul, sircumstances, feet

## INFORMATIVE TEXT
## Vocabulary Work page 25

1 **a** commemoration **b** refrain **c** dozen **d** amid **e** prevail **f** stints

2 **a** official **b** peace **c** enemy **d** young or youthful

3 **a** 'No-man's land' was the space between the two opposing trenches that was literally controlled

by nobody. Being caught there meant certain death, as you would be exposed to enemy fire immediately.

**b** A 'kickabout' is an informal game where two teams composed of any number of players simulate a soccer game with a ball or other item.

**4** **a** raw **b** galah **c** sheep **d** stump **e** cooee **f** gun **g** Blue or Bluey **h** smoko **i** diggers

INFORMATIVE TEXT
## Grammar Work
page 26

**1** four (his, he, his, he)

**2** Jack's

**3** four (he, he'd, he, he)

**4** I, me, my

**5** 'We were really pleased when the Australian War Memorial staff told us that they wanted to put our great-grandfather's items on display.'

**6** soldiers, trenches, food, drinks, cigarettes, gifts

**7** Australian War Memorial's, Christmas Day Truce, Canberra

INFORMATIVE TEXT
## Punctuation Work
page 27

**1** **a**

**2** **a** 'Private Shelley's items have attracted a lot of public interest,' said the spokesperson.
**b** 'We are laying a wreath at the commemoration service,' an army cadet told me.

**3** **a** Indirect speech: My great-grandfather told me not to read his personal letters.
**b** Direct speech: 'Our ancestor was a talented sketch artist,' the German soldier's grand-nephew told me during our interview.

**4** **a** Incorrect **b** Correct **c** Incorrect **d** Correct **e** Incorrect

**5** 'I wrote to Mum telling her of the rumours that the war would soon be over, but by the time the letter reached her I was already home,' Private Burke said.

INFORMATIVE TEXT
## Writing Work
page 28

**1** headline, subheading

**2** by-line

**3** **a** facts **b** quotations **c** awareness **d** logical **e** images

**4** Answers will be individual.

**5** **a** Authoritative **b** Opinion **c** Opinion **d** Authoritative

**6** Suggested answers:
**a** This headline is not sufficiently specific. It doesn't provide any context about the war, the subject matter or the historical importance of the find.
**b** This one is more specific, but is not suitable for a wide audience. Anyone not familiar with the Perth area would not know the suburb name 'Lockridge'. Further, the garage sale where the piece was first discovered is not really relevant to the story and is a minor detail that is only briefly mentioned in the text.
**c** This is a more specific headline, but is still not ideal because Private Shelley was not a well-known person and therefore the name wouldn't be likely to attract much interest. Further, the headline is ambiguous, and could be interpreted in another way. It sounds as if the artwork was created by Private Shelley, rather than given to him by someone else.
**d** This is a very appropriate headline as it is specific and describes a piece of irony. The idea of war enemies enjoying a relationship of mateship is an interesting news angle that would attract readers' attention. The phrase 'long-lost' implies a sense of mystery and rediscovery that adds drama. The naming of the artefact as a sketch is also intriguing, revealing that the subject matter must undeniably provide visual evidence of friendship between enemies in a war famous for its brutality.

# UNIT 4: INFORMATIVE TEXT—WEB PAGE

INFORMATIVE TEXT
## Comprehension Work
page 33

**1** Three: Queensland, the Northern Territory and Western Australia.
This is a **literal** question. All you do is look for simple facts in the text. We notice that the subheadings of the text each name a location *(lines 6, 15 and 27)*. There are three locations, each one in a different state, totalling three states.

**2** The two creatures are wild birds and turtles.
This is a **literal** question. It simply requires you to find two facts in the text. We read in the second table that two animal products from the land and the sea are wild birds' eggs and turtle eggs *(lines 19 and 22)*.

# ANSWERS

## CHECK YOUR ANSWERS

**3** the flowers, seeds, stems and roots
This is a **literal** question. All you need to do is closely read the text to find the correct details. In the text associated with the waterlily icon, we read that all of these parts of waterlilies 'can be eaten raw' *(line 32)*.

**4** **c** This is a **literal** question. To answer it, you need to find some basic facts in the table *(lines 5–17)*, perform a simple calculation (addition) and match the sum to one answer option. You can also use the process of elimination to dismiss the incorrect answers. The question asks how many plant foods in total are listed. This means that **a** is not correct because this only includes land-based plants. Answer **b** is not correct because this only includes sea-based plants. Answer **c** is correct because all nine plants from the land, sea and freshwater must be totalled together.

**5** **b** This is a **literal** question. To answer it, you need to find a basic fact in the text, this time looking for an Aboriginal word *(line 29)*. Match the word to one answer option. You can also use the process of elimination to dismiss the incorrect answers. Answer **a** is not correct because it is the name of an insect from the Kimberley region not a fruit from Arnhem Land. Answer **c** is not correct because it is a species of Western Australian fish.

**6** The composer appears to admire the ingenuity of Indigenous Australians in finding and learning ways to prepare bush tucker.
This is an **interpretive** question. It requires us to use our vocabulary to interpret the tone (the composer's attitude toward the topic) by synthesising the meaning of particular inclusions. The composer uses expressions like 'incredibly knowledgeable and resourceful Wanjina–Wunggurr people' *(lines 36–37)*. Also mentioned is the 'wisdom the Yolngu people have faithfully passed down for millennia' *(line 28)*, a positive statement of affirmation. In reference to the Kimberley region, the writer states that the foods 'make your survival in the wilderness a breeze, according to the … Wanjina–Wunggurr people' *(lines 36–37)*. This carries the implication that one of the harshest desert environments on Earth posed no obstacle to the thriving of these nation groups. Each of these statements conveys an admiring and praising tone.

**7** The target audience for this text is ordinary Australians interested in finding out more about bush tucker.
This is an **interpretive** question. It requires you to notice that the text is written in a friendly, accessible style using everyday language and simple structure. The vocabulary is suitable for advanced younger readers but is most appropriate for adult readers. When we synthesise the meaning and the overall effect of the text, we can see that the references to places and creatures of Australia mean that the composer had an Australian audience in mind when writing the text.

**8** **b** This is an **interpretive** question. It requires you to find a detail in the text and then interpret the reason for its presence. We can use logic to interpret the reason for the name's inclusion—which is that it helps us to identify the exact species of bird. 'Bush turkey' could just be a generic name for all species of turkey-like birds in the bush, whereas 'Australian bustard' is an exact term for the species. The answer cannot be Answer **a** because the text shows that Indigenous Australians call the creature the 'bush turkey'. They would be unlikely to know or use its scientific name, attributed to it by (European) authorities. The answer cannot be Answer **c** because the text is about bush tucker, not professional food preparation.

**9** The answer is No. This is an **interpretive** question. It requires you to notice the logic behind the order in which the steps are presented *(lines 45–47)*. We can use the process of elimination to work through the possibilities. The first step cannot be changed, as the bees must be found before they can be followed. The second and third steps must follow in the order shown, as the tree is first located only after the bees have entered inside. Steps 4 and 5 may seem reversible until we consider the fact that the hollow part of the trunk must be located before the plug can be searched out. Finally, the draining step can only occur after the plug is removed.

**10** **a** This is an **interpretive** question. You need to understand the implications of the multiple uses for the different parts of the boab tree and how they were discovered. We can use our logic and wider experience to conclude that the people were motivated to find multiple uses for the products, which reveals that they highly valued their resources. Answer **b** cannot be correct because the information in the text has come from Indigenous people themselves. It is European Australians who are ignorant of the tree's usefulness. The answer cannot be Answer **c** because the principal resource provided by the tree is fresh drinking water, an absolutely essential resource in the desert.

**11** **c** This is an **applied** question. We need to consider the writer's purpose in presenting only three

# ANSWERS

areas of Australia. It isn't logical that there is no bush tucker to be found in Tasmania so Answer **a** cannot be correct. Many of the listed plants and animals are native to Tasmania as well as to mainland Australia. It doesn't seem likely that all of the bush tucker mentioned can be found in every area of Australia so Answer **b** cannot be correct. For example, barramundi are a species of fish only found in northern Australian waters and would not be able to survive in Tasmania. By using the process of elimination, we can arrive at the most logical answer.

**12** **c** This is an **applied** question. We need to make an informed judgement based on the evidence in the text. First, we must consider the fact that Indigenous Australians would not have encountered the word 'sugar' until Europeans came to Australia. After 1780, the English word 'sugar' would have been associated with sweet-tasting foods. The English word 'bag' was also introduced by Europeans. Therefore the name 'sugarbag' must have been in usage after the 1780s after some Indigenous people learned to speak English. We can consider all of these facts together and apply reasoning to conclude that Answer **c** must be correct. Answer **a** cannot be correct, because we know that neither 'sugar' nor 'bag' are words from Indigenous Australian languages. Answer **b** cannot be correct because the name 'sugarbag' is actually a highly effective and logical description of the sweetness and shape of the object it describes, and can therefore not have been randomly assigned.

## INFORMATIVE TEXT
## Spelling Work page 34

**1** **a** echidnas **b** wilderness **c** species **d** millennia

**2** **a** wallabies **b** medicinal **c** oysters **d** bream

**3** **a** wild **b** medicine **c** plenty

**4** **a** add the suffix *able* **b** add the prefix *in* **c** add the suffix *ful* **d** add the suffix *ine*

**5** **a** echidnas **b** indigenous

## INFORMATIVE TEXT
## Vocabulary Work page 35

**1** **a** True **b** False **c** False **d** True **e** False **f** False **g** True **h** True **i** False **j** False

**2** **a** shellfish **b** insect **c** plant **d** bird **e** fish **f** reptile **g** plant **h** fish

**3** **a** taste **b** gathering **c** flying **d** plants

**4** **a** wild bees **b** boab trees **c** lemon myrtle **d** mussels **e** lilly pilly **f** tamarind

**5** **a** becoming stuck in an isolated or remote location without a means of transport
**b** the kind of exaggerated ideas that occur to you in frightening dreams

## INFORMATIVE TEXT
## Grammar Work page 36

**1** plentiful, knowledgeable, Indigenous, seasonal, medicinal

**2** **a** blue flax lily **b** dark pink lilly pilly **c** white waterlily roots **d** green plums

**3** Answers will vary. Suggested answers appear below:
**a** kangaroo: red, grey, brown, furry, large
**b** mudcrab: clawed, hard-shelled, brown, buried
**c** yam root: long, crunchy, pale, dirt-covered
**d** wild birds: feathered, noisy, lively, skittish
**e** turtle: patterned, tough, wrinkled, submerged
**f** wild grapes: dark, black, purple, furry-skinned, tart
**g** yabbies: shelled, whiskered, fragile, hidden, tasty
**h** bunya nuts: solid, impenetrable, brown, shiny-skinned
**i** echidna: spiky, short, long-nosed
**j** bream: shiny, scaly, silver

**4** **a** sugarbag **b** mussels **c** tamarind **d** boab nuts

**5** **a** medicine **b** watery **c** clean **d** fresh **e** health **f** nutty **g** plenty **h** regional **i** useful

## INFORMATIVE TEXT
## Punctuation Work page 37

**1** **a** Correct
**b** Incorrect (*Glasshouse Mountains* should have initial capital letters)
**c** Incorrect (the *Gubbi Gubbi* people should have initial capital letters)
**d** Correct
**e** Incorrect (the word *tea* should not have a capital letter)
**f** Incorrect (the *Kimberley* takes an initial capital letter)
**g** Correct

**2** Queensland, Kakadu plums, vitamin C

**3** Arnhem Land turtle, the Northern Territory, Australian bush

**4** **a** I enjoy Aussie bush tucker when I am camping.
**b** It seems I'll need to light a fire very soon.
**c** I've had a really interesting outback adventure.

**d** Why couldn't I find my way back to my Ford Ranger?

**5** **a** Secrets of the Amazing Boab Tree
**b** How to Find Sugarbag and Other Bush Tucker Sweets
**c** I Survived in the Australian Desert
**d** Camping and Cooking in the Kimberley

INFORMATIVE TEXT
### Writing Work page 38

**1** **a** True **b** False **c** True **d** True **e** False **f** True **g** False **h** True **i** True

**2** Suggestions: to ensure that the user's attention is captured and maintained; to make the page visually interesting by creating a good balance between text and other elements.

**3** headings

**4** page title

**5** hyperlinked keywords

**6** Estimates will vary. Students should give reasons for their opinion based on the preceding guidelines.

**7** Increasing space between lines (called 'leading') makes the text easier to read onscreen. It also gives blocks of text a more visually pleasing layout.

**8** Graphic organisers help composers vary the look of information on a web page. They can add variety to a page that helps capture and hold the user's attention. Graphic organisers appeal to the user visually.

**9** fast, speed, organise, locate

## UNIT 5: INFORMATIVE TEXT—RECOUNT

INFORMATIVE TEXT
### Comprehension Work page 43

**1** **a** This is a **literal** question. All we do is look for a fact. We read that she'd been 'sent marching back' to her room to fix her hair *(line 5)*. We know that Answer **b** is not correct because civilian clothes are not mentioned in the text. Answer **c** is not correct because shoes are not mentioned at all in the text.

**2** **b** This is a **literal** question. All you have to do is locate a fact in the text. We read that she changed from her 'grey overalls' into the white dress uniform *(lines 18–19)*. We know that Answer **a** is not correct because the text says she changed 'into' not out of the white dress uniform. There is no mention of other clothes, such as jeans and a T-shirt in the text, so Answer **c** cannot be correct.

**3** The writer shook hands with a Vice Admiral just as a piece of chicken fell out of her sleeve and into the handshake.
This is a **literal** question. It requires you to summarise the main incident in the story using just one sentence. This is a test of your ability to use words economically to make a summary of the most important elements. It is also testing whether or not you can identify the most important element of the story. The title of the text contains a clue, mentioning the 'meat' (chicken) and 'greet' (handshake). When we read the text, we see that the key incident is described in the last paragraph. All we do is retell the incident very briefly.

**4** blue anchors
This is an **interpretive** question. It requires you to read a detail from the text and make an interpretation. We read that the bunk had to be made using a particular side of the blanket—with the 'blue anchors' facing upwards *(line 18)*. This tells us that the pattern on the blanket featured blue anchors.

**5** the idea that it is considered an honour for new recruits to dine with a Vice Admiral
This is an **interpretive** question. It requires you to combine facts and details to synthesise the meaning. The details of the word 'privileged', the phrase 'top brass' and the description of the Vice Admiral as having 'humbled himself' tells us that the recruits were intended to think of the presence of the dignitaries at their tables as an honour.

**6** because he was surprised and puzzled to feel a piece of chicken in someone's hand while he was shaking it
This is an **interpretive** question. To answer it, you must locate a fact from the text then make an interpretation of its meaning. We read that the Vice Admiral didn't say a word but he did raise his eyebrow *(line 47)*. This tells us that even though he said nothing about the chicken, he felt it. Logically we must conclude that he'd be wondering how it got there.

**7** **b** This is an **interpretive** question. It requires you to put various facts and details together and make an interpretation. We read that the chicken was 'a little on the tough side' so Answer **a** isn't correct. We read that the writer dropped her bread roll, so Answer **c** cannot be correct. We know there must've been other meal choices available because of the phrase 'I chose the roasted chicken' *(line 26)*, where the verb implies that there were other choices.

**8** **a** This is an **interpretive** question. You can use the process of elimination to answer it. There is nothing in the paragraph that suggests the writer laughed and joked with the Vice Admiral so Answer **b** isn't correct. The writer shook hands with the Vice Admiral in the last paragraph so Answer **c** cannot be correct.

**9** that it is governed by rules that many people would find strange and petty, and that the writer did not fit into the naval way of life at all
This is an **interpretive** question. To obtain the answer, we need to consider multiple facts drawn from the text. We read a list of troubles experienced by the writer in the first paragraph, which tells us that the writer didn't obey the rules. The writer's mocking tone suggests that the rules are petty and difficult to follow for everyday people.

**10** **c** This is an **interpretive** question. You need to combine the details of each incident's timing throughout the day. We read the words 'first ten minutes', 'breakfast', 'lunch', 'afternoon' and 'dinner', which tell us that the order is chronological. Answer **a** is not correct because the incidents cannot be explained in single words so they cannot be alphabetically ordered. Answer **b** cannot be correct because the events move forward in time throughout the day, which is obvious by the writer's references to mealtimes.

**11** **a** This is an **applied** question. It requires you to consider the combined effects of certain details as well as their implications to arrive at the answer. We read the words 'for daring to make my freezing cold bunk up with an electric blanket' *(line 15)*. The desire not to be cold in bed is not extreme so we must conclude that the navy puts rules above luxuries. Logic tells us that the overalls and uniforms supplied by the navy are designed to keep recruits warm so Answer **b** cannot be correct. The use of the word 'daring' echoes the tone of the officer who reprimanded the writer. This word implies that the writer thinks the rules are too rigid so Answer **c** is not correct.

**12** to help new recruits grow accustomed to life on board a ship
This is an **applied** question. We need to use logic to interpret the implications of the text in order to arrive at the answer. The clue about this answer is found in lines 9 to 10, where the matter of saluting the quarterdeck is explained.

## INFORMATIVE TEXT
## Spelling Work
page 44

**1** **a** custom **b** office **c** respect **d** privilege **e** resist **f** annoy **g** dignity **h** consider

**2** **a** *ary* **b** *ally* **c** *fully* **d** *ed* **e** *ed* **f** *ance* **g** *aries* **h** *ably*

**3** **a** considers, consideration, considerate, considerable, inconsiderate, considerately, considering
**b** respectful, respected, respectfully, respecting, disrespect

**4** **a** admiral **b** parade **c** grateful **d** solidarity **e** privileged **f** mesmerised **g** impeccable **h** solemnly

**5** **a** impeccable **b** officially **c** parade **d** dignitaries

**6** officially, parade, privileged, resisted, respectfully, solemnly, solidarity

## INFORMATIVE TEXT
## Vocabulary Work
page 45

**1** **a** outdoor area used for marching, drills and inspections
**b** the officer in charge of a group of cadets
**c** the formal uniform (complete with badges and insignias) used on official occasions in the military
**d** a non-military person; an ordinary citizen
**e** disobedient to a command or higher ranking person
**f** unity among military personnel

**2** **h**, **d**, **a**, **g**, **i**, **c**, **f**, **j**, **e**, **b**

**3** **a** synonym: initial, beginning; antonym: last
**b** synonym: freezing, chilly, icy, cool, bitter; antonym: hot
**c** synonym: tidy; antonym: messy, untidy, disheveled, unkempt

## INFORMATIVE TEXT
## Grammar Work
page 46

**1** **a** plural noun **b** plural noun **i** plural noun **j** plural noun **l** plural noun

**2** **a** grateful **b** respectfully **c** solemnly **d** dignitaries **e** officially **f** admiral

**3** **a** aces **b** boats **c** cards **d** disease **e** elephants **f** fish **g** galaxies **h** hay **i** infants **j** jets **k** knights **l** lions **m** mosquitoes **n** names **o** owls **p** poems **q** quail **r** rabbits **s** storm clouds **t** trees **u** uniforms **v** voters **w** witches **x** x-rays **y** yarn **z** zombies

## INFORMATIVE TEXT
## Punctuation Work
page 47

**1** **a** would not **b** could have **c** had not **d** she will **e** we had or we would **f** they are **g** have not **h** we are

**2** **a** they will **b** are not **c** I will **d** wouldn't **e** haven't

**3** **a** We're, who've **b** There's, you're **c** they're, they've **d** I've, I'm, hasn't

# ANSWERS

CHECK YOUR ANSWERS

INFORMATIVE TEXT
## Writing Work
page 48

1 to retell a true story, often to entertain and sometimes just to inform

2 chronological order (real-time order)

3 the text appeals to the reader's emotions, eliciting a 'felt' response

4 through the use of connective phrases that create transitions such as cause and effect structures

5 to set the scene for the embarrassing incident; to show us that she had already struggled with military protocols, which creates a sense of suspense

6 **a** The use of a pun on the common phrase 'meet and greet' makes the title particularly attention-grabbing.

**b** By using the first person mode to tell the story, the writer creates a sense that the events really occurred. It also enables the writer to provide a unique insight into how the events made them feel and what they were thinking, planning and experiencing as the events unfolded.

**c** Examples of contractions from the text include I'll, I'd, hadn't, he'd and didn't.

**d** Jargon terms in the text include Vice Admiral, New Entry Officer's course, Division Officer, quarterdeck, deck, cabins, commanding officer, bunk, mess hall and top brass (also a colloquialism).

**e** Examples of colloquial language are 'top brass' and 'I didn't know that was a thing.'

**f** The action verb 'sweating' is an economical way of telling us that the writer was in a panic.

**g** These adjectives provide the writer with a way of commenting upon the events, which adds to the tone of the text. The humorous effect is compounded by this highly descriptive language so that we can picture the scene.

7 afternoon, freezing cold, thin, standard issue, blue, grey, stiff, white

8 Answers will be individual.

## UNIT 6: INFORMATIVE TEXT—NOVEL

NARRATIVE TEXT
## Comprehension Work
page 53

1 raft
This is a **literal** question. All we need to do is locate a fact in the text. We read that he had brought rafts ashore *(line 3)*.

2 sugar cane, melons, grape vines, cocoa trees, orange trees, lemon trees and lime trees
This is a **literal** question. All we have to do is scan through the text to find the names of food sources. The word 'tobacco' and 'aloes' are also mentioned in the text but they do not produce foods so they must be excluded from the list. This leaves seven food sources.

3 **c** This is a **literal** question. We need to locate words that convey feelings—or emotive language—in the text. Crusoe says, 'This was a surprising discovery, and I was exceeding glad of them' *(line 14)*. The answer cannot be Answer **a** because he was not at all confused or disappointed; and it cannot be Answer **b** because although he would certainly have felt homesick and possibly frightened on the island at some point, the question specifically asks about his feelings as a reaction to his discoveries at the brook and meadows.

4 **c** This is an **interpretive** question. We need to use logic to put multiple facts together to arrive at the answer. Crusoe is stranded on an island where he has few supplies, so logic tells us that any food he gathers must be preserved for as long as possible in case he is not rescued for some time. We also read that he intended to 'keep them as dried grapes or raisins are kept' *(line 16)*. Answer **a** is not correct because a personal dislike of a particular food wouldn't stop a hungry castaway from eating it if there was no other food available. We know that Answer **b** can't be correct because Crusoe wouldn't have had an oven, flour or other ingredients to make raisin cakes on the island.

5 **b** This is an **interpretive** question. You need to look at the word in the context of Crusoe's statement 'I came to an opening, where the country seemed to descend to the west' *(line 21)*. Crusoe is describing the countryside so the answer must be a gap between hills. Answer **a** cannot be correct because nothing is being unwrapped, and Answer **c** can't be right because no buildings or structures that could have a doorway are mentioned.

6 **a** This is an **interpretive** question. We need to read carefully to determine which were just food sources he discovered and which actually had ripe fruit on them that were edible at the time. This leads us to exclude Answer **c** because he notes that there were very few fruit on those trees, and we can exclude Answer **b** because apples aren't mentioned at all. We know that he ate grapes because we read that they were 'very ripe and rich' *(line 14)*, and we know he ate limes because he describes them as 'pleasant to eat' *(line 33)*.

**7** **b** This is an **interpretive** question. We need to note the detail which tells us that Crusoe is on an island *(line 3)*. Then we need to pay attention to the date of the novel's publication, 1719, which tells us that the author intended the setting to be around or before that date. We also know the approximate era of the setting because of the old-fashioned language in the passage. We know the text is set in the past so the answer cannot be **a**. There are features of British life mentioned in the text, such as 'any lord of a manor in England', so the time period must be after the Celtic tribes of Britain had developed the social hierarchy that included lords, which occurred more recently than the last ice age, so Answer **c** cannot be correct.

**8** because he calls his first campsite 'home' twice
This is an **interpretive** question. To find the answer, we need to read the text carefully for clues about his thoughts and feelings. One way to gain insight into a character's thoughts is to pay attention to what they say, the expressions they use that contain shades of meaning. The word 'home' *(lines 19 and 36)* tells us that he must've spent quite a few nights at that campsite for him to consider it his home.

**9** He means that they may bear fruit in a coming season or at a different time.
This is an **interpretive** question. We need to locate the phrase in the text and then look at its context to make an interpretation. He notes that they were 'all wild, and very few bearing any fruit, at least not then' *(lines 31–32)*, which tells us that he thought they had potential to bear fruit at another time.

**10** Because it was watered by a spring.
This is an **interpretive** question. We need to look at a related fact about the valley that explains its condition. We read that there was 'a little spring of fresh water' *(line 22)*. Applying logic, we know that gardens flourish when they are well watered, so we can arrive at the answer.

**11** **c** This is an **applied** question. To work this out, we need to notice the first date given in the passage, the 15th of July, then realise that Crusoe spent that night away from his usual camp. He discovered the lime trees the following day, which was the 16th. We know Answer **a** cannot be correct because of the extra night, and we know it is not Answer **b** because this date is not mentioned at all in the text.

**12** No, he doesn't.
This is an **applied** question. We need to consider the implications of Crusoe's behaviour. We read that he is preparing to gather and store food for the coming wet season *(line 38)*, which tells us that he must realise he is unlikely to be rescued in the next few weeks.

NARRATIVE TEXT
## Spelling Work
page 54

**1** **a** cultivation **b** flourishing **c** delicious **d** descended **e** surveying **f** refreshing **g** approaching

**2** **a** cultivation **b** refreshing **c** proceeded **d** pleasant **e** approaching **f** abundance **g** flourishing **h** excellent

**3** **a** cul|ti|va|tion **b** sur|vey|ing **c** is|land **d** whole|some **e** ex|cel|lent **f** in|her|i|tance

**4** island

**5** wholesome

**6** flourishing and delicious

**7** After I'd eaten, I went up where I'd first brought my rafts on shore.

NARRATIVE TEXT
## Vocabulary Work
page 55

**1** Answers will vary. Suggested answers include:
- **a** One day, Crusoe discovered a pleasant valley inland.
- **b** I began to take more careful notice of the landscape.
- **c** I went exploring and found a little stream/creek.
- **d** I saw some sugar cane, but they weren't perfect because they were wild and needed proper cultivation.
- **e** I found a lot of melons on the ground.
- **f** There were many limes and I was very glad of them (OR I was very grateful for them).
- **g** I didn't sleep at home that night.
- **h** This was the first night I'd slept away from home.
- **i** There were green plants everywhere, with everything flourishing in the spring weather.
- **j** I decided to collect and store the foods.

**2** **a** alone **b** work **c** happens

NARRATIVE TEXT
## Grammar Work
page 56

**1**
- **a** had stepped, swung aside
- **b** was, had been shut up, wanted to see
- **c** put, began to pull and push
- **d** put, drew out, found, fitted
- **e** took, looked, see, was coming
- **f** did come, seemed, took, could not help
- **g** slipped through, shut

**2** **a** will not, won't **b** should not, shouldn't **c** are not, aren't **d** have not, haven't **e** is not, isn't **f** were not, weren't

# ANSWERS

CHECK YOUR ANSWERS

**g** did not, didn't **h** does not, doesn't
**i** might not, mightn't **j** cannot, can't

**3** **a** is **b** are **c** did **d** has or have **e** doing

NARRATIVE TEXT
## Punctuation Work
page 57

**1** The correct forms are:
**a** its **b** its **c** It's **d** It's **e** its **f** its **g** its

**2** **a** Plural **b** Plural **c** Plural
**d** Possessive **e** Possessive **f** Possessive

**3** **a** After the last letter **b** Before the last letter
**c** Before the last letter **d** After the last letter

**4** they are a title.

**5** in italics.

**6** They are not proper nouns.

NARRATIVE TEXT
## Writing Work
page 58

**1** the storyline; what happens in the story

**2** the place and time in which the events occur

**3** the main aim, message or idea the writer is trying to communicate

**4** chapters

**5** **a** 'pleasant', 'surprising', 'glad'
**b** '15th July'
**c** 'had spread indeed over the trees, and the clusters of grapes were just now in their prime, very ripe and rich'
**d** 'Crusoe discovers a pleasant vale inland'
**e** 'to furnish myself for the wet season, which I knew was approaching'

**6** **a** The plot can be summarised as follows: Crusoe is stranded on an uninhabited island and as he explores his surroundings, finds fresh water and a green valley that contains various sources of food.
**b** The setting is an uninhabited island that is remote from Crusoe's homeland. The story is set in the 1700s.
**c** The protagonist is Robinson Crusoe.

**7** Plot features: introduction, climax, conclusion, conflict
Setting features: place, mood, time, imagery
Character features: minor, antagonist, protagonist, dialogue
Theme features: aim, message, tone, moral

# UNIT 7: INFORMATIVE TEXT—BALLAD

NARRATIVE TEXT
## Comprehension Work
page 63

**1** **c** This is a **literal** question. All we need to do is locate the answer in the text. We read that Andy 'went a-droving' *(line 9)* and the word 'drover' appears again (*(line 21)*. We know that Answer **a** is not correct because the squatter is mentioned in the ballad as visiting while Andy is absent. We know that Answer **b** is not correct because he works with cattle, not horses, and although he may ride horses to move cattle, the poem is clearly about a farming enterprise, not horseracing.

**2** **c** This is a **literal** question requiring us to locate a simple fact. We read that Andy's gone to battle with drought *(line 4)*—a shortage of rainfall. There is no mention of a bushfire so we know that Answer **a** is not correct. We know that the word 'draft' means a breeze, which is not a weather-related disaster, so Answer **b** can't be correct.

**3** A squatter is a livestock grazier who operated on a large scale and controlled the activities of smaller farmers.
This is a **literal** question. All you need to do is read the fact that is included as a footnote *(line 27)* which defines the term 'squatter' for us.

**4** sandy
This is an **interpretive** question. First, we need to think about the rhyme scheme of the poem, which is ABAB. Then we need to look at line 23 to find a word that rhymes with 'Andy'. Because the word 'Andy' is positioned at the end of line 25, we know that the word 'sandy' must be the answer because it rhymes according to the rhyme scheme.

**5** The poem is set in the Australian outback in the 1800s.
This is an **interpretive** question that relies on some assumed knowledge. During this era, livestock was driven overland for thousands of kilometres each winter in search of better grazing land. We read that Andy went 'across the Queensland border' and that he 'crossed the Darling' river. We also read the term 'squatter', which refers to the system of land use in force in the early 1800s to 1860 in Australia's past.

**6** Answers will vary but should make note of the necessity for someone undertaking droving work to be physically fit, tough and used to surviving alone in the bush environment. This is an **interpretive** question that requires us to put details together to reach a conclusion. We read that he has a 'cheerful face' so perhaps he has physically attractive facial features. We do not read any details that suggest he has a family, so Andy is probably a young man.

# ANSWERS

CHECK YOUR ANSWERS

**7** **a** This is an **interpretive** question. The general mood of the speaker is 'dejection' when Andy is away, suggesting that he brings life to the homestead. In line 8 we also read that life is 'dull' since Andy went away. A contrast is drawn between the usual cheer and the current dullness by the rhetorical question in lines 10 and 11. We know that Answer **b** is not correct because of the occurrence of the phrase 'our hearts are out of order'. We know that Answer **c** is not correct because there is no element of surprise mentioned at all in the first half of the poem.

**8** Lawson is implying that drovers were viewed as heroic figures in their local areas.
This is an **interpretive** question. You need to consider multiple concepts drawn from the poem and draw conclusions about their combined meaning. We read that Andy is described as 'our Andy', giving the impression that he has cemented his place in the family and community through years of faithful and capable work. There is a sense of optimism that he will return safely, attesting to the community's strong belief in his abilities. 'Angels' are invoked to provide protection for Andy because he is well loved.

**9** **a** This is an **interpretive** question. The speaker is clearly one of Andy's relatives who lives on the farm, as they refer to him as 'our Andy', which indicates a close relationship. It is possibly Andy's mother or father, considering the hopeful mention of angels that are associated with protection of loved ones. Answer **b** is not correct because the only mention of angels is in relation to sending rain and Answer **c** is not correct because Andy' absence is the subject of the poem.

**10** **b** This is an **interpretive** question. It requires you first to identify the sorrowful mood at the beginning of the poem. We read that 'our hearts are out of order', 'he's left us in dejection' and life is 'dull' when Andy is gone. To detect the change of focus, we need to move beyond the series of rhetorical questions that signal feelings of loss and look for the first expression of a positive desire, which comes at line 18 in the form of a hope for showers of rain. Answer **a** is not correct because line 4 occurs immediately before the emotive word 'dejection' and Answer **c** is not correct because the hopeful tone shifts quite a few lines before the end of the poem.

**11** **a** This is an **applied** question. When we consider the connotations of the text (deduced by considering the combined effects of multiple facts), we realise that Andy went droving to find water and feed for the livestock, which implies that these are the most important needs. We also read about the importance of water for life on the land and the prayers for rain later in the poem. Although Andy's cheerfulness and cheek toward the squatter are mentioned, they are not of primary importance. This means that Answer **b** is not correct. The family also need money but they wouldn't have seen holidays as essential to life, making Answer **c** incorrect.

**12** It implies that livestock farming is difficult, risky and dangerous.
This is an **applied** question, where you need to consider the implications beyond the words. The inclusion of good wishes and prayers reveals that the drover's enterprise is plagued with difficulties. Success relies on certain weather conditions in certain seasons in order to keep the stock alive, well and able to reproduce.

NARRATIVE TEXT
## Spelling Work
page 64

**1** **a** ballads **b** rhythm **c** rhyme **d** imagery **e** emotive **f** colloquial

**2** **a** symbolism **b** emotive **c** image **d** repeat **e** poems **f** rhythms **g** emotions

**3** **a** metaphorical **b** rhythmical **c** structural **d** emotional

**4** imagery ballad repetition rhetorical stanza poetry

NARRATIVE TEXT
## Vocabulary Work
page 65

**1** **a** cows **b** period of no rainfall **c** wandering **d** happy **e** large volume of rainfall **f** a livestock grazier who operated on a large scale and controlled the activities of smaller farmers

**2** **a** drought **b** whistle **c** slackest **d** frowns **e** angels **f** roving **g** cheerful **h** snarling **i** dejection **j** battle

**3** **a** hearts **b** rain **c** border **d** desert **e** shall **f** now

**4** **a** c **b** f **c** b **d** e **e** d **f** a

NARRATIVE TEXT
## Grammar Work
page 66

**1** **a** cheerfully **b** thoughtfully **c** brightly **d** quietly **e** wildly **f** mildly **g** apparently **h** stubbornly **i** properly **j** hopelessly **k** really **l** clearly **m** excitedly **n** obviously

**2** **a** fiercely **b** definitely **c** nicely **d** bravely **e** largely **f** precisely

**3** **a** brutally **b** dismally **c** gradually **d** occasionally **e** eventually **f** hopefully

4 **a** **Although** there's been very little rain, we'll **still** get a reasonable harvest this season.
**b** My cows, **unlike** my neighbour's, are very fit and healthy.
**c** Our water tanks are full this summer **but** last summer they were bone dry for months on end.
**d** **Despite** the struggles involved in making a living from the land, we're making it work somehow.
**e** Beef cattle farmers raise livestock for meat, **whereas** dairy farmers raise them for milk.

NARRATIVE TEXT
## Punctuation Work
page 67

1 **a** In past times, drovers took herds of cattle on long journeys to find better grass for grazing.
**b** Why do Australian farmers stay working the land when there is so little rainfall?
**c** Henry Lawson was a bush poet and journalist who wrote a number of poems about drovers.
**d** We never heard whether or not Andy came home safely from his travels.
**e** The Darling is the river mentioned in the poem 'Andy's gone with cattle'.

2 italics or quotation marks

3 Andy's, Queensland, Darling

4 **a** — dash **b** . full stop **c** , comma
**d** ; semicolon **e** ? question mark **f** * asterisk
**g** D capital letter **h** ' apostrophe

NARRATIVE TEXT
## Writing Work
page 68

1 narrator, setting, plot, characters, themes, climax, a sense of the passage of time

2 A regular pattern simplifies the poem. It unifies the ideas and makes it sound like it might be being spoken aloud.

3 The poet intends to tell a story through poetry.

4 the hardships of life on the land

5 **a** 'Fortune frowns', 'grass grow green', 'stretches sandy'
**b** 'Oh, who shall cheek the squatter now' / 'When he comes round us snarling?'
**c** 'When Fortune frowns her blackest?'
**d** ABAB
**e** 'dejection', 'cheerful'
**f** 'selection', 'squatter', 'drover'
**g** 'a-droving', ''twill'
**h** 'the rain'/'desert', 'dull'/'cheerful'

# UNIT 8: INFORMATIVE TEXT—BIOGRAPHY AND AUTOBIOGRAPHY

NARRATIVE TEXT
## Comprehension Work
page 73

1 Uppsala
This is a **literal** question. All you need to do is locate the fact in the text.

2 a geologist
This is a **literal** question. It requires you to simply find a detail in the text that answers the question. We read that his reason for moving was to give lectures and that he was posted to Sweden by the Union of Geological Sciences.

3 three
This is a **literal** question. We simply look for a specific number fact from the text. In lines 3–4 we read that there were two brothers and the author herself, making three children in all.

4 Lines 11–13: 'He told us he was nervous and needed a bit of moral support, which surprised Mum as he'd spoken in front of large audiences many times at home.'
This is an **interpretive** question. You need to put facts and details together to arrive at the answer. We can tell from the author's words, including the cause and effect structure indicated by the word 'as', that she had associated her father's nervousness with his expectation of a large audience.

5 11.59 am
This is an **interpretive** question. You need to note certain details relating to time then use logic to synthesise them. We read that the author and her family were seated in the auditorium by eleven *(line 14)*. We know that the lecture was scheduled for the morning, and the phrase 'god morgon' means 'good morning', so the latest time possible for the lecture to begin was the last minute of the morning.

6 because in lines 3–4 she says the family consisted of 'two boys, myself and our mother'
This is an **interpretive** question that requires you to combine more than one detail and synthesise the meaning. The fact that she separates the description of herself from her two brothers implies that she is a girl. Another clue is the statement that she and her mother had their 'hair done nicely for the occasion' *(lines 13–14)*.

7 **b** This is an **interpretive** question. It requires you to put facts and details together and interpret their meaning. We know that Answer **a** can't be correct because it is illogical to generalise about a whole nation of people being 'bad'. Answer **c** cannot be

correct because we're told in the introduction that none of the family had been to Sweden before *(line 6)*, so it is unlikely that the author's father was from Sweden.

**8** **c** This is an **interpretive** question. You need to look at the details of the text in relation to each other and synthesise their meaning. We know that Answer **a** can't be correct because the words 'good morning' are specifically mentioned as part of the greeting. We know that Answer **b** can't be correct because the language mix-up occurred over the Swedish words for 'ladies and gentlemen'. Had the author's father used those words correctly in his lecture, the audience would not have been laughing.

**9** **a** This is an **interpretive** question. It requires you to read each answer option and work out which of them is making a prediction about an event yet to happen. The answer cannot be Answer **b** because it is written in direct speech and doesn't foreshadow or predict anything. Answer **c** can't be the answer because the timing of the lecture is not related to the embarrassing mistake.

**10** **a** This is an **interpretive** question. You can use the process of elimination to answer this question. The words 'laughter', 'boos' and 'tittering' describe different reactions. Some people thought it was funny and laughed, others were offended and booed, and some thought it was so amusing that they couldn't control their tittering. We are not told that the audience applauded so Answer **b** can't be correct. We know that the speaker said 'God morgon' but there is no information about any replies from the audience, so Answer **c** can't be correct.

**11** It implies that he was embarrassed and realised the foolishness of trying to pretend to know a language he didn't know in reality.
This is an **applied** question. It requires you to infer meaning from the details given in the text. In this case, we arrive at the answer by considering another part of the text *(including line 26)*, where the author mentions that her father blushed deeply. This implies that he was embarrassed by his mistake.

**12** **b** This is an **applied** question. It requires you to draw on your vocabulary knowledge to infer meaning from the text. We read that the café was 'on campus' *(line 27)*. The word 'campus' refers to an academic setting, such as a school, college or university. We can use logic to determine that an international lecturer in geology is unlikely to be posted to a primary or secondary school so the word 'campus' must indicate a university. Answer **a** is not correct because the incident occurred in an auditorium during a lecture and Answer **c** cannot be correct because this is a misinterpretation of the term 'campus', which has nothing to do with camping.

NARRATIVE TEXT
## Spelling Work
page 74

**1** pronunciation, audience, optimism, occasion

**2** **a** geological **b** memorised **c** audience **d** auditorium **e** unwarranted **f** sheepishly

**3** **a** listen **b** adventure **c** dignity **d** sheep **e** warrant **f** memory

**4** **a** pronunciation
**b** The second syllable changes from an 'ou' sound to a short 'u' sound.
**c** critique **d** The second 'c' is changed to a 'qu'.

NARRATIVE TEXT
## Vocabulary Work
page 75

**1** **a** auditorium, campus **b** adventures **c** memorised **d** sheepishly, audience

**2** **a** geology, geologists, geologically
**b** composure, composing, composition
**c** criticise, critical, critically
**d** occasions, occasional, occasionally

**3** not justified

**4** shamefacedly

**5** **a** knew not to make the same mistake again
**b** memorised it perfectly, without needing prompts or notes
**c** easily and with good marks
**d** imitates everything someone else does
**e** still learning how everything works; the rules
**f** does everything rigidly, strictly legitimately and without bending or breaking rules
**g** improvise; do it in an unplanned manner, relying on luck and quick thinking

NARRATIVE TEXT
## Grammar Work
page 76

**1** **a** into **b** between **c** to **d** out **e** at **f** after

**2** **a** in **b** on **c** to, from or from, to
**d** beside, behind or near **e** inside, around or in
**f** before or after

# ANSWERS

CHECK YOUR ANSWERS

**3** Solution to the puzzle grid

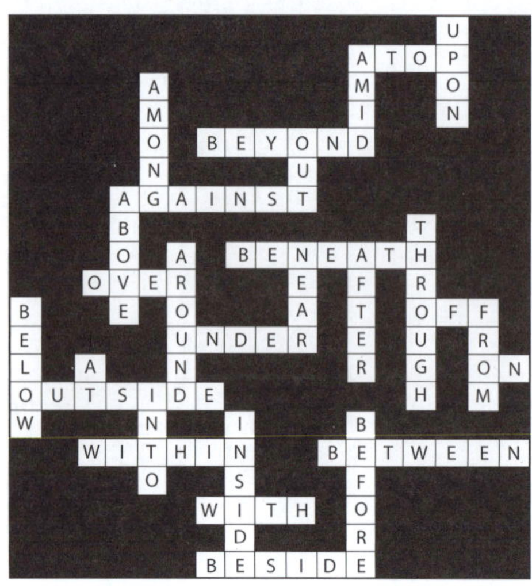

**4** **a** atop **b** on **c** inside **d** under **e** before

NARRATIVE TEXT
## Punctuation Work
page 77

**1** **a** The university campus has great facilities: modern lecture theatres, a large auditorium, a library and a café.
**b** I know two Swedish phrases: 'God morgon' and 'God natt'.
**c** When we flew to Sweden, we had three stopovers: Perth, Singapore and London.

**2** **a** We came from Australia to Sweden; from a hot summer to a cold winter.
**b** Dad's skills as a geologist are great; his skills as a linguist are not so great.

**3** **a** There are three children in our family: Kai, Brynn and Morgan.
**b** Five countries make up the region of Scandinavia: Denmark, Norway, Sweden, Finland, and Iceland.
**c** Dad's lecture tour took him to three other cities that year: Stockholm, Gothenburg and Malmö.
**d** On arriving in Sweden, I bought winter gear: a pair of mittens, a warm woolly hat and waterproof snowboots.

**4** Dad began his lecture by saying (*delete comma*) a few words of greeting in (*add capital S*) Swedish (*add full stop*). Some people could still be heard (*replace capital T*) tittering as the lecture went on. (*add capital W*) When (*add capital D*) Dad sat down I saw (*remove semicolon*) the host lean over (*remove full stop*) and whisper something to him (*replace question mark with full stop*). Until that day, (*change position of apostrophe*) I'd never seen my father blush so deeply.

NARRATIVE TEXT
## Writing Work
page 78

**1** life writing

**2** autobiographies

**3** Suggestions: photographs, maps, illustrations, reproductions of supporting documents

**4** first person past tense mode

**5** indirect speech

**6** **a** I'd sheepishly told them that I was trying to impress the audience with my language skills.
**b** I'd asked them to attend and give me a critique on my performance.

**7** **a** As Dad takes to the stage, I am feeling rather proud of him.
**b** When Dad sits down I see the host lean over and whisper something to him.

**8** 'I'd simply memorised the words from the signs on the restroom doors to complete my prepared greeting.'

**9** **a** Objective **b** Emotive **c** Objective
**d** Emotive **e** Emotive **f** Emotive

## UNIT 9: PERSUASIVE TEXT—BLOG

PERSUASIVE TEXT
## Comprehension Work
page 83

**1** **c** This is a **literal** question. All you need to do is look for a detail in the text. The username appears under each thread heading and in the copyright message at the base of the page. We know that the answer cannot be Answer **a** because LewChu9 posts a question to the site's owner, so they cannot be the same person. We know the answer can't be Answer **b** because Endermen are characters in the game not a username on this blog.

**2** **b** This is a **literal** question. You need to notice the message conveyed by the disclaimer. We read that the content on the blog is not officially endorsed by Minecraft or its owners. We know the answer can't be Answer **a** because if we read the disclaimer carefully we see that the blog is not official. The answer can't be Answer **c** because this text is the title of the blog and the word 'disclaimer' does not mean 'title'.

**3** **a** This is a **literal** question. Blacklisting is the removal and banning of the player from the server. It requires you to find the detail in the text. You can do this by skim reading the text for the word 'griefing' and reading it in its context. We know the answer can't be Answer **b** because this word is not used in the context of griefing. The answer can't

be Answer **c** because this would not logically be described as a punishment but rather a reward.

**4** Harvestfest, Tinker's Creations and Botanica
This is a **literal** question. All you need to do is locate these names and their descriptions as 'mods' in the text. We read about the mods *(line 38–39)* and their names are listed.

**5** Suggestions: ice-skating rink, theatre, garden maze, zoo, ocelots and Endermen enclosures
This is a **literal** question. We read in the text a list of features of the Magnificent Palace *(lines 24–25)* which includes each of these.

**6** None. It was built in 'vanilla', which means the unmodified version of Minecraft.
This is an **interpretive** question. You need to consider multiple aspects of the text at once. We read the phrase 'unmodded vanilla' *(line 23)* and we know the meaning of 'mods' because they are defined in line 20, where we read 'Many of you guys have abandoned vanilla (unmodified) Minecraft.' The post about the Albatross House clearly states that it was 'made using vanilla Minecraft'.

**7** Big Bird (from Sesame Street)
This is an **interpretive** question. It requires you to interpret the meaning of facts and details. The meaning of this detail, which appears in a comment, is clear from a straightforward reading of LewChu9's comment. The additional details that Big Bird is 'supposed to be yellow' tells us which character the poster had in mind.

**8** Yes. The blogger seems very willing to share.
This is an **interpretive** question. It requires you to consider facts and details in combination in order to arrive at a logical conclusion. We read an invitation to join the server *(line 41)* with the statement 'the more, the merrier' and we read of a communal garden and an invitation to let the blogger know what users think of the featured builds. All of these facts and details when considered together tell us that the blogger is willing to share their knowledge.

**9** **a** This is an **interpretive** question. We need to consider multiple aspects of the text at once. We read that mods 'transform the Overworld pretty nicely' *(line 21)* but there is still lots of potential for detailed builds. The conjunction 'but' signals to us that there is a contrasting statement coming next so Answer **b** cannot be correct. The potential for blacklisting is mentioned in another thread so Answer **c** cannot be correct.

**10** **b** This is an **interpretive** question. It requires us to think about connotations of a word, based on the context in which the word appears. The keywords 'new' and 'explore' *(line 37)* give us the clues. The word 'biome' includes the prefix *bio* which means 'life' in Greek. We know that the 'biosphere' is the environment so we can conclude that Answer **b** is the correct definition. Answer **c** cannot be correct because we know that new players are 'newbies' and are not 'explored' by other players. The word 'server' refers to the hardware and software used to play the game so Answer **a** cannot be correct either.

**11** **c** This is an **applied** question. We need to consider implications, reading beyond the lines to reach a conclusion. The words 'And yes' carry the connotation that the blogger is anticipating a question that has been asked before. We can see from the screenshot that the beak can't be larger than one storey high so Answer **a** is not correct. We know that the house is not real because the image tells us this design would be impossible to build in reality on a single pedestal so Answer **b** cannot be correct.

**12** because of the site link to Gardens and the screenshot image
This is an **applied** question. We need to apply thinking skills to develop insights. We know that there is advice about building gardens because of the site link to an archive tagged 'Gardens' under the second screenshot. We can also surmise that this advice exists because of the visible maze and garden in the screenshot.

## PERSUASIVE TEXT
## Spelling Work

page 84

**1** **a** technically **b** possibilities **c** policy **d** newbies **e** communal **f** theatre

**2** **a** five **b** three **c** three **d** three **e** two **f** one

**3** **a** gaming **b** goal **c** varieties **d** participate

**4** **a** Plural **b** Plural **c** Apostrophe **d** Plural **e** Apostrophe **f** Apostrophe **g** Plural **h** Apostrophe

**5** Our new **server** is up and running and we're waiting for new players to join us. There are new **functions** to explore and our **selection** of **frightening** enemies should keep you busy for **hours**. If you are **new** to the game, don't worry. There are plenty of **tips** and hints that will **enable** you to enjoy **yourself** as you learn. There are so many cool new **possibilities** for **building** large **structures**, either **individually** or as a team.

## PERSUASIVE TEXT
## Vocabulary Work

page 85

**1** Words and phrases selected may vary, but could include:
**a** a picture, photo, image
**b** really big, committed, super, enthusiastic

c floor, level
d awesome, massive, big, large, huge, vast, large-scale, impressive
e modifications
f errors, problems, weaknesses, faults, flaws, operating issues
g new to a game, inexperienced, still learning
h player

2 sorrow or misery; being upset by the loss of something or someone important to you

3 a hardcore b mods c noob d veteran e spawn f boss mob g want to buy h buff i nerf

PERSUASIVE TEXT
## Grammar Work
page 86

1 a speck b sip c smear d thread e sprig f kernel g flake h scrap i splinter j grain k blade l ray m puff n whiff

2 a dose b sheet c bolt d coat e wisp f wedge g length h slice i shard j lump k scoop l cake m spoonful n sprinkling

3 a violence b choices c selection d gaming

PERSUASIVE TEXT
## Punctuation Work
page 87

1 'but they're massive wings' and 'Read more …'

2 because it is the title of a product (a modpack)

3 in the square brackets, after 'Read more'

4 copyright

5 It doesn't follow the usual rules of punctuation. There is a combination of capital letters, lower-case letters and numbers so that the username is unique.

6 a In Minecraft, my sister built a house that's shaped like a bird.
b The best thing about playing Minecraft is the freedom players have to do whatever they want.
c I've been playing games on our private server all afternoon.
d Players will be blacklisted if they destroy anyone else's property in the game.
e The unmodified version of Minecraft is known as 'vanilla' among gamers.

PERSUASIVE TEXT
## Writing Work
page 88

1 web log

2 personal diary pages

3 They host links on their site to other sites. When users click to the advertiser's site, payment is made to the blogger.

4 advertisers

5 art, videos or music (answers will vary and may provide more specifically defined topics)

6 Tumblr and WordPress

7 An ordinary blog usually has just a single author, whereas a MAB has multiple authors.

8 a Suggestions: Hi; Thanks; Well, we're here!; this guy; To be fair; which is awesome for us; Champion sales assistant; Loving my comfy, fur-lined boots; That snoring you can hear is my feet; They've gone to bed.
Note: These expressions are both informal and colloquial: blog faithful!; the mighty U.S. of A.; squillions of people; coz we really wanted to see some snow; touched down; At last, we've hit Washington; packed in a lot of fine dining; (and walking it off!).
b Suggestions: hot apple cider with cinnamon—really unusual; There are squillions of people here in New York.; My feet have been freezing since we touched down in Buffalo; We've had some fine days in DC (there may be other answers that fall into this category based on personal opinion)
c Suggestions: me, we, our, your, us, he, my, I; also contractions incorporating personal pronouns: we're, I'm, they've, we've
d Suggestions: blog faithful!; the mighty U.S. of A.; squillions of people; coz we really wanted to see some snow; touched down; At last, we've hit Washington; packed in a lot of fine dining (and walking it off!)
e Suggestions: we're here!; great; demanded; How rude!; hoping; awesome; really wanted; loving; meekly

# UNIT 10: INFORMATIVE TEXT—MAGAZINE COVER

PERSUASIVE TEXT
## Comprehension Work
page 93

1 **b** This is a **literal** question. We need to recognise synonyms that are used for particular details. We read in the subtitle of the article 'Fireflies' that they are 'nature's candles'. There is no mention of stars in the magazine cover so Answer **a** is not correct. There is a mention of candle making in the text but not in relation to beeswax so Answer **c** cannot be correct.

2 **b** This is a **literal** question. All you need to do is use your comprehension to recount a detail from

the text. We read in the subtitle of the feature article that Houdini made a historic visit to the region in 1913 which is the subject of the article. We know that Answers **a** and **c** are not correct because the subtitle tells us he visited the area in 1913 and is long dead. The subtitle tells us he was a famous escape artist, so in order to be famous he would need to have been an adult when he visited the area. Born in 1874, if Houdini was alive he would be nearly 150 years old!

**3** **c** This is a **literal** question. All we need to do is locate a fact in the text. We read in the subheading of the magazine that it serves the people of the Violet Lakes region in Southern Victoria. Another, more obscure clue, is the mention of lyrebirds, which are a bird species endemic to Australia. Because lyrebirds are mentioned, neither Answer **a** nor Answer **b** can be correct. There is a Victoria in British Columbia, Canada, but it is a city, not a state. The Lake Victoria in Tanzania is a body of water.

**4** a powdered hot chocolate drink
This is an **interpretive** question. We need to apply our logic to find meaning beyond the words. The word 'taste' gives us a clue, as does the season of autumn that is featured in the text. The imagery all speaks of cooler weather. The word 'sachet' tells us the product's form of packaging. All of these facts lead us to the logical conclusion that the product is probably a powder sachet to make a hot chocolate drink.

**5** because the article title calls them 'antique tableware'
This is an **interpretive** question. We need to consider multiple aspects of the text at once, in this case the title and image together. The word 'antique' implies that they have been dried and decorated as part of a handcraft process. The word 'treasures' implies that they can be kept for a long time, which rules out any freshly picked produce.

**6** 'Homewares for autumn', 'Candle making', 'Antique tableware'
This is an **implied** question. We need to synthesise meaning by putting various facts together to reach a conclusion. The subtitle 'Handwoven fabrics to make yourself' implies that the reader will be shown how to do some form of craft. We can infer that the other articles about decorating and candle making probably have a craft focus as well.

**7** that it is a mountainous region with more than one lake
This is an **interpretive** question. You need to synthesise meaning by putting various facts together to reach a conclusion. We see the mountain and lake scene in the letter *O* of the masthead, the hills and mountains in the landscape of the main image, the title 'Mountain Magic Festival' and the inclusion of a featured local crop, peaches, which are a cool-climate fruit. All of these clues lead us to conclude that the Violet Lakes area is in the mountains. The word 'lakes' reveals the presence of more than one lake in the region.

**8** 'Peachy' means 'ideal', 'positive' or 'in good order', and it also means 'made from peaches' or 'tasting of peaches'.
This is an **interpretive** question. It requires you to consider the connotations of words rather than just their denotation (literal meaning).

**9** **c** This is an **interpretive** question. We need to look at language-related matters to find specific techniques in the text. Expressions that are alliterative feature repeated consonant sounds. In the examples 'The Mountain Magic Festival' and 'Wonders in Wax' we see the consonant sounds 'm' and 'w' repeated. There is no onomatopoeia in these examples so the answer cannot be Answer **a**. There is no assonance in the examples so the answer cannot be Answer **b**.

**10** **a** This is an **interpretive** question. There is no issue number shown on the cover, nor is there a specific date. Instead the issue is just described as 'autumn'. As there are three months in autumn, more specific information such as the month would be given if there was more than one issue each autumn. If it was only published once a year, the year date alone would be given. We can therefore assume that there are only four issues per year—one for each season. Our knowledge outside the text also tells us that a regional publication like this one would be unlikely to find enough new content to publish more frequently. Answer **b** cannot be correct because there are four seasons in a year, not three, and the issue is labelled 'autumn', implying that the magazine takes its theme from each of the seasons. Answer **c** cannot be correct because the month of the issue would appear on the cover if it was a monthly publication and the season's name would not appear because it would be the same for three months of the year.

**11** **a** This is an **applied** question. It requires you to think beyond the literal facts and details, and to apply the connotations of words, such as 'handwoven fabrics to make yourself', which imply that a printed pattern would be provided in the magazine from which people could make items by knitting, crocheting, sewing or weaving. We know the answer cannot be Answer **b** because jams are not 'printed resources'. We know the answer cannot be Answer **c** because they are in the magazine, so they wouldn't be described as resources separate from the magazine.

**12** The target audience is people interested in their local region, nature, food, arts and crafts, history and antiques.
This is an **applied** question. It requires you to make an informed judgement based on evidence from the text.

# ANSWERS

CHECK YOUR ANSWERS

## PERSUASIVE TEXT
### Spelling Work page 94

1 **a** articles **b** distilling **c** antique **d** publication

2 **a** autumn, unifying **b** magazine, aromatic **c** fruitful, festival

3 **a** publish **b** distil **c** decorate **d** fruit **e** collaborate **f** aroma

4 autumn, sachet, entrepreneur

5 sachet, mocha

6 homewares, handwoven, ecotourism, tableware

## PERSUASIVE TEXT
### Vocabulary Work page 95

1 **a** True **b** True **c** True **d** False

2 autumn, mountain, candle making, aromatic, fruity, fabrics, nature's candles, Mocha, peachy, fruitful

3 Mountain Magic Festival, mystery, the great Houdini, escape artist, wonders, treasures, mist, peachy magic

4 Tas. (Tasmania), Qld (Queensland)

5 NSW (New South Wales), WA (Western Australia), ACT (Australian Capital Territory), NT (Northern Territory)

6 **a** WA **b** Qld **c** Vic. **d** Tas. **e** NSW **f** NT **g** SA **h** ACT

## PERSUASIVE TEXT
### Grammar Work page 96

1 **a** autumn **b** magical **c** historical **d** fiery **e** nature **f** aromatic **g** treasured/treasurable **h** peachy **i** mysterious

2 Nouns: fabrics, community, mountain, destinations, entrepreneur, festivals
Verbs: making, make, visiting, tasting, distilling
Adjectives: violet, new, historical, aromatic, free, fruitful

3 **a** hand **b** sand **c** fire

4 **a** fruit **b** light

## PERSUASIVE TEXT
### Punctuation Work page 97

1 **a** full stop **b** full stop **c** exclamation mark **d** question mark **e** question mark

2 **a** The background image is a mountain scene that reminds us of autumn.
**b** Do the typefaces you've selected make the headings simple and easy to read?
**c** We've chosen images of fresh peaches to feature on the cover of *Violet Life's* autumn edition.
**d** We are offering a free product to encourage people to buy our magazine.

3 **a** semicolon **b** apostrophe **c** comma **d** ellipsis **e** parentheses or round brackets **f** speech or quotation marks **g** colon **h** slash or solidus

4 This weekend, we're going to Violet Lakes for the Mountain Magic Festival.

5 Violet Life, Southern Victoria's Violet Lakes, iTunes, Cocoa Mist Mocha, Mountain Magic Festival, Houdini (or The Great Houdini).

## PERSUASIVE TEXT
### Writing Work page 98

1 $14.95

2 Twice—once in a title 'The Mountain Magic Festival' and once in a subtitle 'Distilling peachy magic'.

3 new and free

4 Try new Cocoa Mist Mocha

5 Ecotourism is a kind of tourism where people try to get close to nature and ensure that their holiday activities benefit or support the natural world in some way. The content of the magazine suggested by the cover probably lists a number of new destinations in the Violet Lakes region where people can practice ecotourism.

6 Answers will vary. For sight, students should note the visually attractive landscape, trees, sunrise, fruit and text; for hearing, the reference to lyrebird song; for smell, aromatic wonders in wax, fruity treasures and the peaches; for touch, the handwoven fabrics and the peach flesh; and for taste, the peaches and fruit.

7 Colours should be warm in tone to reflect the autumn season. Explanations will vary.
**a** The sky could show a sunrise with a hint of orange.
**b** We might see orange foliage on the trees.
**c** The peach flesh should be yellow and the skin yellow or red, to reflect the natural colours of the fruit.
**d** Warm brown or amber would be the correct tone for the peach syrup bottle.
**e** Orange, brown or red table decorations would suggest autumn decorating.
**f** The masthead and footer, as pointed out in the annotations, should be violet.

8 Answers will be individual. Students should use the inspiration of the spring season to include bright

colours including greens, yellows and blue skies, light and bright fabrics, flowers, baby animals, fruit flavours and outdoor activities.

9 **a** a night time scene showing some fire flies glowing
**b** an old picture or painting of Harry Houdini
**c** shots of the crowd, stalls and activities from the Mountain Magic Festival.

## UNIT 11: INFORMATIVE TEXT—FORMAL LETTER

PERSUASIVE TEXT
### Comprehension Work
page 103

1 When James's tooth fell out, the Tooth Fairy failed to arrive to collect the tooth and bring James's Tooth Money.
This is a **literal** question. All you do is look for simple facts in the text. We read that they are writing to apologise 'for the Tooth Fairy's failure to arrive at your house on Wednesday night to do her duty' *(lines 18–19)*.

2 She was dismissed from her position.
This is a **literal** question. It simply requires you to find a fact in the text. We read that 'the Tooth Fairy has been dismissed from this office because of her forgetfulness' *(line 23)*.

3 Their policy requires that lost teeth should be wrapped in a tissue and placed under the child's pillow.
This is a **literal** question. All you need to do is closely read the text to find the correct details. In the three steps, we read '1 Please wrap the tooth in a tissue for safe-keeping. 2 Please remember to place the wrapped tooth under your pillow' *(lines 32–33)*.

4 the upper lateral front teeth
This is a **literal** question. To answer it, you need to find a basic fact in the text *(line 37)*.

5 regular brushing every night.
This is a **literal** question. To answer it, you need to find a basic fact in the text. You may need to look for slightly different wording. James is asked to remember to brush his teeth at the end of the letter, to ensure that his teeth are kept in 'top notch' condition *(lines 41–42)*.

6 The name is meant to be humorous.
This is an **interpretive** question. It requires us to use our vocabulary to interpret the meaning of the name. 'Paul Molar', when said aloud, is a reference to 'pulling teeth'. The name 'Paul' sounds like the word 'pull' and the word 'molar' is a term for the large permanent teeth that are sometimes pulled out by dentists. It is fitting that the Chief Minister of Teeth has a toothy-sounding name.

7 **a** This is an **interpretive** question. It requires you to notice that the text is written in the style of an informative text and it has the features of a letter to make the Tooth Fairy seem to come from an official government department, which creates humour. Because the Tooth Fairy is not real, we know that Answer **b** cannot be correct. We know Answer **c** is not correct because someone is pretending to be an official called 'Paul Molar'.

8 **c** This is an **interpretive** question. It requires you to find a detail in the text and then interpret the reason for its presence in the text. We read in the text before the information about the policy that James is not to 'wobble or wiggle any loose teeth in an effort to speed up the process' *(lines 39–40)*. We can use logic to interpret the reason for this advice—which is that pain and bleeding occur when loosening teeth are forced to come out early. The answer cannot be Answer **b** because this advice encourages him to look after his teeth and the answer cannot be Answer **a** because earlier we read that they pay 'the same fixed sum for every tooth lost, regardless of size, to ensure fairness to all children' *(lines 28–29)*. Even if two teeth are lost at once, the amount paid per tooth remains the same.

9 **b** This is an **interpretive** question. It requires you to note the language style of the text and determine whether those features follow the conventions of a formal letter. The place of origin of the letter is not relevant to this question so the answer cannot be Answer **a**. Nor is the recipient's age relevant so the answer cannot be Answer **c**.

10 **a** This is an **interpretive** question. You need to understand the implications of the phrase 'distress caused on Thursday morning' *(line 25)* and consider why such distress might have been experienced. We can use our logic and wider experience to reach some conclusions about what happened to prompt someone to write the letter. It seems that when James went to bed on Wednesday night after placing his lost tooth under his pillow, he was looking forward to receiving his Tooth Money when he woke up the next morning. Because the tooth had not been collected, he was disappointed. The answer cannot be Answer **b** as the letter states that the tooth will be collected the same night so it can't have been rejected through damage. The writer also states that the Tooth Fairy forgot to collect the tooth. The answer cannot be Answer **c** because there is no mention of pain in the text.

11 **b** This is an **applied** question. We need to consider the fact that the Tooth Fairy is made up and that the Tooth Money must be delivered by James's family. When we consider this, it becomes obvious that they do not want James awake when they exchange the tooth for the money. The answer cannot be Answer

**a** because the Tooth Fairy isn't real. It cannot be Answer **c** because Paul Molar is a made-up character too, and would not do the exchange himself in any case. We can also arrive at this answer by using logic to eliminate the other possible answers.

12 **a** This is an **applied** question. We need to consider the fairytale content of the letter mixed with the official-sounding language used. Logically we know that the Tooth Fairy is a figure made up to help children deal with the loss of their baby teeth. And the letter is addressed to the specific bedroom and bed of the recipient, James, which is a fact that only a close family member would know. We can consider all of these facts together and apply reasoning to conclude that the answer must be Answer **a**. Answer **b** cannot be correct because we read that the letter is from 'the Department of Dental Affairs' *(line X)*, which isn't a real government department. Answer **c** cannot be correct because James is clearly a child of around six to eight years, and would not be capable of using such formal and official-sounding language and ideas in his writing.

## PERSUASIVE TEXT
## Spelling Work

page 104

1 **a** schedule **b** forgetfulness **c** inconvenienced **d** sincerely **e** eligible **f** inferior

2 **a** condition **b** damage **c** simultaneously **d** dismissed **e** inferior **f** unreliable

3 **a** ap–o–lo–gies **b** or–gan–ised **c** con–di–tion **d** loose– **e** el–i–gi–ble **f** de–part–ment **g** sim–ul–tan–e–ous–ly

4 **a** have not **b** will not **c** he is **d** cannot **e** should not **f** might have

5 **a** they'll **b** I've **c** she'd **d** we'd **e** could've **f** you're

6 **a** suffix (in the word 'department')
**b** prefix (in the word 'unreliable')
**c** suffix (in the words 'organised', 'inconvenienced' and 'dismissed')
**d** suffix (in the word 'simultaneously')

## PERSUASIVE TEXT
## Vocabulary Work

page 105

1 **a** a division of an organisation
**b** allowed or asked to leave
**c** suffered disadvantage or delay
**d** not tight or firm **e** state of repair
**f** expressions of regret **g** pre-organised plan

2 **a** unreliable **b** department **c** loose **d** forgetfulness

3 **a** inferior **b** damage **c** loose **d** organised **e** dismissed **f** schedule **g** unreliable **h** sincerely

4 eligible, condition

5 apologies, forgetfulness

6 loose, damage, inferior

7 apologies, responsibilities, children

8 **a** Suggestions: dental, Molar, teeth, tooth, lower front, upper front lateral teeth
**b** Suggestions: Chief Minister, Department of Dental Affairs, Government, records, office, we are pleased to advise, schedule, position, dismissed, fixed sum, eligible, according to Department policy, it is our policy

## PERSUASIVE TEXT
## Grammar Work

page 106

1 her, she

2 personal

3 its

4 her, theirs, we, yours, he

5 **a** your, you, your **b** our, our **c** its **d** I, my, whom, I **e** his, their

6 **a** who **b** relative

7 The correct forms are:
**a** their **b** me **c** my **d** its **e** that **f** who

## INFORMATIVE TEXT
## Punctuation Work

page 107

1 **a** Regular brushing, flossing and rinsing are important aspects of good dental hygiene.
**b** I loved getting my Tooth Money as a child, although it was usually only twenty cents back then.
**c** Four children lost their front teeth this week—Brad, Amy, Chris and Kate.
**d** The Tooth Fairy, a made-up character, comforts children who are anxious about losing their teeth.

2 **a** 'It's coming out,' said Mia, wobbling her loose tooth.
**b** 'If the Tooth Fairy doesn't come tonight,' James announced, 'I'm going to write a letter of complaint.'

3 **a** The Chief Minister of Teeth, Mr Paul Molar, told us he couldn't accept damaged teeth.
**b** An eight-year old boy, James Lewis, lost a tooth on Wednesday evening.

4 James Lewis was disappointed on Thursday morning after failing to receive his Tooth Money.

The Tooth Fairy forgot to collect and pay for the lost tooth. James, who had placed the tooth under his pillow with great anticipation, awoke to find that the tooth was still there, much to his annoyance. Upon checking the post, James was pleased to find a letter waiting for him from the Department of Dental Affairs, an organisation of which he'd never heard. He was delighted to read that the replacement Tooth Fairy would be visiting him that very evening with his Tooth Money.

PERSUASIVE TEXT
## Writing Work
page 108

1 Suggestions: an introduction, a body of paragraphs and a closing section; the sender's address; the date the letter will be posted; the recipient's address; a brief and polite greeting (called the 'salutation'); a summary that clearly presents the main reason you are writing; a clear description of what the recipient needs to know or do; a sign-off phrase, such as 'Yours faithfully' or 'Yours sincerely', finishing with a comma; your first and last name, your position or official role, and the organisation or business you represent.

2 Suggestions: Formal letters follow the structure of introduction, body paragraphs and conclusion. They include many of the structural features already listed. Formal letters also contain specific language features that distinguish them from informal writing, including uncontracted expressions, connectives and jargon. There are no colloquialisms, idioms, slang or abbreviations.

3 Answers may include receiving information from government departments or agencies, or exchanging correspondence with professional organisations, registered businesses, authorities, hospitals and schools.

4 The sender's address is shown at the top of a formal letter to provide a return address for the sender to use.

5 Numbers should be in the following order:
**a** h **b** d **c** j **d** g **e** c **f** a **g** b **h** i **i** f **j** e

6 **a** 'simultaneously' (rather than 'at the same time'): The use of language in an economical way helps to convey an impression of efficiency to the reader. By not using unnecessary words, the writer is being considerate of the reader in a formal letter.
**b** 'Please remember to …': This polite expression helps to soften the strong effect of imperative commands created by the use of high modality verbs.
**c** 'Consequently …': The use of connective words and phrases helps to join the letter together logically. Connectives signal that there is more information to come about the topic of the previous sentence. They act as signposts for readers to use to navigate the text, and they often express a cause-and-effect relationship to help make meaning clearer.
**d** 'do not' rather than 'don't': Avoiding contractions helps to retain the formality of the tone, rather than making it sound too conversational.
**e** 'You must try to go to sleep immediately …': The high modality verb, 'must', conveys a sense of importance and urgency to the reader, making them feel compelled to take the requested action.
**f** 'Mr Lewis': The use of this expression to identify the recipient makes the greeting seem polite and not too personal, emphasising the formal nature of the letter.
**g** 'Wednesday, 16 October' (instead of 'last night'): The precise detail makes the meaning unmistakeably clear so there is no room for misinterpretation.
**h** 'your upper front lateral teeth …': The effect of the jargon is to lend the writer an air of authority and knowledgeability about the issue, indicating that they can be trusted to provide proper advice and reliable information.

# UNIT 12: INFORMATIVE TEXT—ADVERTISING SCRIPT

PERSUASIVE TEXT
## Comprehension Work
page 113

1 A slow zoom.
This is a **literal** question. All we need to do is locate a fact in the text to answer the question. We read the instruction to do a slow zoom on the ocean's surface *(line 11)*.

2 four
This is a **literal** question. All we need to do is identify the number of places named. Skim read the text to identify the place names, then count them. They are Venice, Athens, Corfu and Barcelona.

3 **c** This is a **literal** question. We simply need to use our comprehension to read the reference information at the top of the script and realise that it provides the number of drafts. The answer cannot be Answer **a** or Answer **b** because we read on the top of the script *(line 4)* that the version is 'Draft 3', not one or two.

4 **c** This is a **literal** question. To find the answer, we simply need to use our comprehension to find

facts and details. If you scan the text, you'll find no mention of skydiving. Logic would also tell us that this is an unlikely sport to host on a cruise ship. We see both ice-skating and rock climbing mentioned *(lines 21–23)* so Answers **a** and **b** cannot be correct.

**5** because the vox pops name destinations around Europe
This is an **interpretive** question. We need to use logic to find additional meaning behind the words. We read the lines spoken in the vox pops *(lines 25–30)* and realise that Venice is in Italy, Athens and Corfu are in Greece and Barcelona is in Spain, which means the cruise must operate in Europe.

**6** an adjective
This is an **interpretive** question. It requires us to look at language-related matters to find meanings conveyed by certain words and phrases. We need to look at the context in which the expression appears to find the answer. We read that guests are invited to 'discover our award-winning onboard service' *(lines 35–36)*. The word 'service' is the noun that tells us the expressions used before it in the sentence describe it, so they must be adjectives.

**7** **a** This is an **interpretive** question. We need to do a simple calculation to find the answer. To calculate the answer, we simply need to add the number of seconds in scenes 004 and 006 together, then subtract them from the total length of the commercial. The addition sum equals 11 seconds and the subtraction sum gives us 19 seconds running time. We know that Answer **b** is not correct because 30 minus 11 doesn't equal 22 and Answer **c** is not correct because it only gives us the first part of the answer (the total time of the two scenes).

**8** **b** This is an **interpretive** question. We need to use logic to find additional meaning behind the words. We see that the word 'grab' appears in the Vision column *(line 32)* so we know that it must be composed of visual images. The answer cannot be Answer **a** because there is nothing about theft mentioned in the text. The answer is not Answer **c** because there is no specific shot or camera movement mentioned in scene 005.

**9** Suggested answers: the impressive size of the ship in the first zoom shot; the medium close-up of the relaxing woman; the montage of exciting activities; the vox pops; the footage of the smiling staff member and customer; the onscreen text showing that the cruise company has won awards
This is an **interpretive** question. It requires us to consider multiple facts and details, in particular the descriptions of visual features in the visual column of the text.

**10** **a** This is an **interpretive** question. It requires us to synthesise meaning by putting various facts together to reach a conclusion. We can examine our own emotional reaction to the ad and test the effect of the vox pops on ourselves. Clearly the intention is to make us feel invited to visit these destinations. We know that Answer **b** cannot be correct because the placenames are well known and most viewers would know how to pronounce them. We know that Answer **c** is not correct because the text states that the vox pops are done by locals not crew members.

**11** **c** This is an **applied** question. It requires us to consider connotations that convey additional meaning beyond the words. Although the voice over doesn't specifically mention the stage show, the footage appears during the mention of the cruise ships being 'destinations in themselves' *(lines 33–34)*. This implies that there are various activities to entertain guests, including a stage show on-board. The answer cannot be Answer **b** because there is no mention of American destinations, and the answer cannot be Answer **a** because there were other activities that involve exercise before we see this footage. Logic would tell us that guests would not take part in a professional show onboard.

**12** that the viewer isn't currently happy in their lives because of stress and overwork that can only be alleviated by a relaxing cruise, which will help them rediscover who they really are
This is an **applied** question. It asks you to read beyond the lines to understand the implications of the statement. When we notice the word 'rediscover' is used *(line 15)*, we realise that the message is implying that the viewer has the potential to be 'better' already but just needs a cruise to help them 'rediscover' it.

PERSUASIVE TEXT
## Spelling Work
page 114

**1** surface horizon version exciting destinations discovery dreamt memories experiences

**2** **a** False **b** True **c** True **d** False **e** False **f** True **g** False

**3** **a** True **b** False **c** False **d** False **e** False **f** True **g** True

PERSUASIVE TEXT
## Vocabulary Work
page 115

**1** **a** VO **b** secs **c** dissolve **d** zoom **e** grab **f** vox pops **g** track **h** scene **i** onscreen text **j** montage

# ANSWERS

CHECK YOUR ANSWERS

**2** **a** Italy **b** Greece **c** Spain

**3** **a** idiom **b** idiom **c** abbreviation **d** abbreviation **e** abbreviation **f** idiom

**4** **a** the Tasman Sea between the two countries **b** tropical **c** because it has air pollution

PERSUASIVE TEXT
## Grammar Work
page 116

**1** **a** might or may **b** will **c** may be **d** won't **e** may have to

**2** **a** can **b** could **c** shouldn't **d** won't be **e** must **f** won't have to

**3** **a** necessarily **b** messily **c** daily **d** happily **e** busily **f** hungrily **g** noisily **h** tidily **i** steadily **j** lazily

**4** **a** hourly **b** daily **c** yearly **d** monthly

**5** **a** must, should **b** will **c** won't

PERSUASIVE TEXT
## Punctuation Work
page 117

**1** **a** mustn't **b** should've **c** can't **d** doesn't **e** haven't **f** needn't **g** didn't **h** weren't

**2** **a** Discovery Cruises use persuasive techniques to encourage people to book a holiday with their company.
**b** There are numerous destination cities to explore, including Athens and Barcelona.
**c** Kids of all ages have access to a whole range of activities designed just for them.
**d** Sunbathing is one way in which people relax and enjoy themselves on a cruise.

**3** Taking a cruise is a great way to see some of Europe's greatest cities. The city of Athens is one of the Mediterranean Sea's most popular ports. Athens is the gateway to the Greek Islands. Athens's remarkable history draws thousands of tourists each year. The capital of the ancient Greeks, the city's landmarks include the Parthenon, which sits high on the hill called the Acropolis. The columns of the Parthenon are one of the ancient world's great marvels. They demonstrate the genius of mathematicians and engineers who lived and worked thousands of years ago. Each column's shape helps us perceive the building as perfectly square, although in reality the pillars have slightly curved lines. A tourist's experience of Athens would not be complete without a brisk walk up to the Parthenon, one of the Greek civilisation's most enduring icons.

**4** seconds (secs)

**5** a colon (:)

**6** Voted Best Family Cruise Operator in 2016.

PERSUASIVE TEXT
## Writing Work
page 118

**1** It is laid out in two columns showing the visual and audio components.

**2** dialogue and voice over.

**3** shots, angles and movements

**4** voice over

**5** music and sound effects

**6** the way scenes change from one into another

**7** 30 seconds long

**8** seven scenes

**9** The base word 'discover' is present in every scene. It effectively reinforces the brand name, Discovery Cruises.

**10** To discover it all for yourself. Another indirect call to action can be seen in the on-screen text: 'To book, go to www.discoverycruises.com'.

**11** Scene 003 features a montage of activities showing families enjoying themselves and scene 007 presents on-screen text advising viewers that the cruise company was voted 'Best Family Cruise Operator' in 2016.

**12** The desire to escape everyday life; the desire to spend time with family; the desire for adventure and to see new places; the desire for fun and action.

**13** Answers will vary but should express ideas similar to these: they should be relaxing, fun and full of activities, and they should take place in exotic locations.

**14** Answers will vary, but should express ideas similar to these: laughter, live music, water splashing.

**15** Answers will vary.

## SAMPLE TEST 1

SAMPLE TESTS
## Part A Reading and Comprehension
page 126

**1** Pepo the parrot

**2** Nothing. They don't exist.

**3** She opened her owner's stitches with her claws.

4 iron and wood

5 She will be able to spend time alone in the garden and play alone.

6 The lock and the key are old and rusty.

7 to tell her that he hit her dog with his car, and to explain what happened

8 The girl's appendix had ruptured.

9 He stopped the car, he looked for the dog, he knocked on Ms Roberts' door, he left the scene.

SAMPLE TESTS
### Part B Language Conventions page 127

1 Suggested answer: The catchy subheadings (e.g. 'Cat the Ripper') and sarcastic tone (e.g. 'WOW, right?') lighten the mood and show that bad or dangerous situations like these can also be funny.

2 Possible answers include the wind (that 'rushed') and the ivy (that 'crept'). Ideas about the effect of personification will vary. Sample answer: The effect of personifying the ivy and saying that it 'crept' gives the impression that it is being sneaky and secretive, like Mary. The author is also suggesting that the ivy is keeping the garden a secret by hiding the door. These uses of personification create a magical and mysterious mood.

3 Mr Drake probably also wants to persuade Ms Roberts to understand what happened and to allow him to explain, apologise and help out.

SAMPLE TESTS
### Part C Comparing texts page 127

1 Sample answer: The main difference in structure is the use of subheadings in Text 1. Text 2 is a single story so it doesn't need them. Another difference is the use of introductory and concluding statements in Text 1.

2 Suggested answers: Text 2: This short sentence builds suspense and makes the reader want to know what happens when she opens the door. Text 3: This short sentence makes it clear why Mr Drake had to leave the scene of the accident. Also, by placing it on its own line the writer has given it extra importance.

3 Sample answer: The three texts all tell stories. This is the main thing they have in common. Text 1 is a group of three separate stories with the same theme, Text 2 is an excerpt from a longer story and Text 3 recounts a true story and explains how and why it happened. Also, the three stories all tell about unusual situations. Odd animal cases, the discovery of a secret garden and having two medical emergencies at once (human and animal) are all extraordinary situations.

SAMPLE TESTS
### Part D Themes and meaning page 128

1 Sample answer: Text 3 suggests two main messages. The first message is that, when something is our fault, we must take responsibility for it and tell the truth about the situation. Mr Drake does this by writing the letter to Ms Roberts about hitting her dog with his car. He risks her anger and possibly revenge by doing this, but he tells her anyway, because it is the right thing to do. The second message is that sometimes accidents just happen. Mr Drake didn't do anything terribly wrong or unsafe, yet he still hit the dog with his car. The circumstances involving the sick girl made an accident more likely but it's possible that the dog would have been hit by his car or another one despite these circumstances.

## SAMPLE TEST 2

SAMPLE TESTS
### Part A Reading and Comprehension page 132

1 They were worried about tree limbs falling on their caravan.

2 They would probably have been crushed, because 'the bed area was the only space in the van that was spared.'

3 Rosewood Street

4 a simile: 'like a mermaid drest in long green weed and barnacles'

5 sixty years ago

6 Everyone is terrified of the 'ghost ship', which seems to have returned from the bottom of the sea.

7 $4.50

8 'Guinea pig games' and 'Learn how to speak my language'

9 It suggests that people reading the magazine have at least heard of alfalfa hay, so it also suggests that the readers own pet guinea pigs.

SAMPLE TESTS
### Part B Language conventions page 133

1 Suggested answer: Readers are told about various other things, including the impact of the storm on

other local properties, information about the Koala Hospital and what to do if they come across injured wildlife after storms.

2 Sample answer: A sound technique used by Robert Graves in the poem is alliteration. For example, 'by and by the breeze', 'sprang to a storm' and 'foundered in frothy seas'. The effect of these sounds is the creation of an image of the rough seas that sink the ship for a second time.

3 Suggested answer: The photo competition, with prize money of $1000, is the most persuasive feature of the magazine cover. It encourages people to buy the magazine.

SAMPLE TESTS

## Part C Comparing texts

page 133

1 Suggested answer: A specific purpose of Text 1 is to encourage people to report injured animals if they come across them. A specific purpose of Text 2 is to frighten and intrigue readers with a tale of mystery.

2 In both texts readers are encouraged to care for animals. In Text 1 readers are asked to 'keep an eye out for wildlife that may have been injured in the storms' and in Text 3 readers are encouraged to care for and gain a better understanding of guinea pigs.

3 **a** Suggested answer: The reader is likely to be an adult or a young adult with good reading skills. This person is interested in a range of texts, including local news and poetry.

**b** Suggested answer: Text 3 is likely to be read by older children and teenagers, as the simple, colourful design would appeal to this audience. These readers are also likely to be interested in keeping guinea pigs as pets.

SAMPLE TESTS

## Part D Themes and meaning

page 134

1 Sample answer: Two themes presented in Text 2 are death and mystery. The theme of death is shown from the beginning when the word 'ghost' is used. This theme runs through the poem and is also seen when the 'old woman' states that her husband died when the ship sank. The theme of mystery is created by the basic plot: a ship that sank sixty years ago has suddenly returned. The visual imagery of the ghostly ship adds to the sense of mystery.

# NOTES